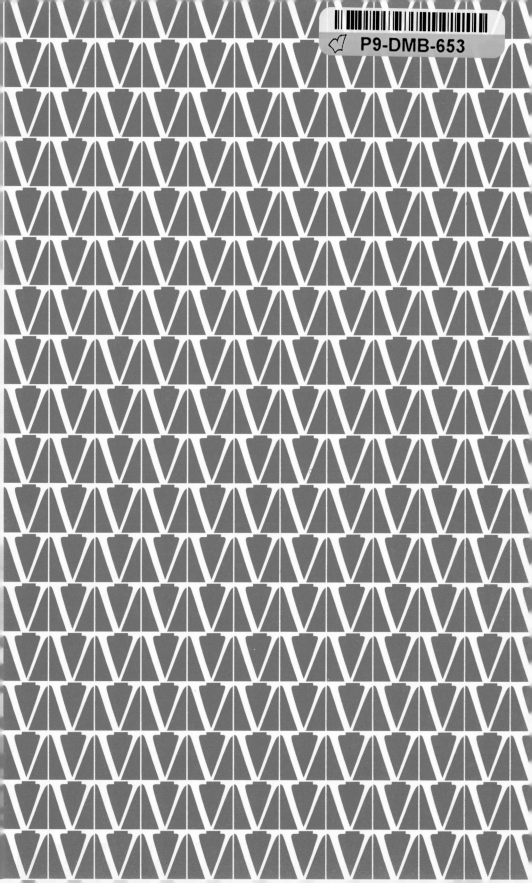

# THE

# FEMININE

# MISTAKE

# THE

# FEMININE

# MISTAKE

ARE WE GIVING UP
TOO MUCH?

LESLIE BENNETTS

VOICE

*Hyperion • New York*

Library of Congress Cataloging-in-Publication Data

Bennetts, Leslie
    The feminine mistake : are we giving up too much? / Leslie Bennetts. — 1st ed.
        p. cm.
    Includes bibliographical references and index.
    ISBN-13: 978-1-4013-0306-8
    ISBN-10: 1-4013-0306-4
    1. Women—Employment.    2. Sex role—Economic aspects.    3.    Feminism. I. Title.
    HD6053.B42 2007
    331.4—dc22                                                                      2006052273

Hyperion books are available for special promotions and premiums. For details contact
Michael Rentas, Assistant Director, Inventory Operations, Hyperion, 77 West 66th
Street, 12th floor, New York, New York 10023, or call 212-456-0133.

*Design by Chris Welch*

FIRST EDITION

10 9 8 7 6 5 4 3 2 1

*This book is dedicated with my love to four extraordinary women:*

To my mother, Chaucy Bennetts, who worked and raised her
children with such strength and competence that I never
questioned whether it was possible to combine a
career and a happy family;

To my baby-sitter, Norma Mohabir Ingram, who cared for my
children with unfailing love and contributed so much to the
wonderful people they have become;

To Emily Gerard, my strong, brilliant daughter, in hopes that she
will realize all her dreams and challenge any barriers
that stand in her way;

And in memory of Betty Friedan, the visionary
who first opened my eyes.

# ACKNOWLEDGMENTS

*The Feminine Mistake* was originally inspired by my exasperation at the public glorification of stay-at-home motherhood and the failure of the media and other analysts to warn women about the risks of sacrificing their financial independence. But a point of view, no matter how passionately held, is not a book, and I would like to thank my agent, Amanda Urban at ICM, for her invaluable contributions in developing this idea. Since we spent nearly a year arguing vigorously about what to do with it, her patience was as noteworthy as her suggestions were helpful.

During the early stages of this process, I also appreciated the enthusiasm of Hilary Black, Andrea Miller, and Elise O'Shaughnessy, whose support led to the initial *Tango* magazine essay that became the starting point for the book.

When I began to interview women about marriage, motherhood, and work, I was astounded by the willingness of complete strangers as well as friends and acquaintances to talk about the most painful feelings and difficult issues in their lives. This book would not exist without the riveting testimony of countless women as well as more than a few men, and I owe an immeasurable debt to them all for their candor in opening their hearts to a reporter. Their insights gave me a great deal of help in developing my understanding of these issues, and I am most grateful for the cooperation of everyone who consented to an interview, both those who are named and those who asked me to protect their identities.

Many of the sociologists, economists, legal scholars, and other experts I interviewed were also kind enough to share their own experience as wives and mothers. I appreciated their time and generosity, and I found these personal histories from such accomplished women to be tremendously inspiring. I would also like to express a special thanks to Ann Lewis, Dorothy Weaver, and Mary Alice Williams for their input, and to Carrie Carmichael, Amanda Butterbaugh, and Laura Shapiro for introducing me to relatives and other women in the heartland.

Throughout this process, I felt fortunate that *The Feminine Mistake* would be published by Pamela Dorman, the editorial director of Voice at Hyperion, and Ellen Archer, the publisher. From the outset, they understood the importance of the information I wanted to present, and their excitement about my message was very encouraging. I appreciate the efforts of all the hardworking professionals at Hyperion/ Voice who contributed to this project.

But long before *The Feminine Mistake*, I was a working mother struggling to be a good parent as well as a productive journalist. I am forever grateful to Graydon Carter for my wonderful job at *Vanity Fair* magazine, which has permitted me to work at home, make dinner, and hear my kids' after-school reports while meeting my deadlines all these years. I am also deeply indebted to Tina Brown, Graydon's predecessor as editor of *Vanity Fair*, for hiring me while I was pregnant with my first child.

Many thanks as well to Judy DeYoung and to Kathryn Belgiorno for their painstaking work in fact-checking this book. Julia Simon provided research assistance that helped me to meet a ridiculously tight deadline.

Finally, and most importantly, I would like to thank my husband, Jeremy Gerard, for his crucial insights as my in-house editor, and my beloved children, Emily and Nick Gerard, for their patience, cooperation, and good humor about becoming part of this book. I love you more than I could ever put into words.

Leslie Bennetts
New York City
October 2006

# CONTENTS

# PROLOGUE

My grandmother made the world's best rhubarb pies and sewed extraordinary silk garments with exquisite craftsmanship worthy of a French couturier. Raised to devote her all to marriage and family, she worshipped her talented husband, doted on her children, and baked homemade bread whose enticing aroma drew everyone to the kitchen. Although she lived for nearly eighty years, she never worked outside the home or held a paying job.

Such latter-day paragons of traditional femininity often make people nostalgic for bygone times, but even then, the truth was frequently a lot darker than the champions of conventional gender roles like to admit. Although my grandmother's life adhered faithfully to the old-fashioned stereotypes so often held up as a modern ideal, the result was a disaster, not only for her but also for her children and relatives.

In 1932, when my mother was nine years old, her father left the family for his mistress, a stylish black-haired beauty unencumbered by the mundane burdens of domesticity. For my grandmother, who came from a well-to-do family, the emotional devastation of losing her husband was exacerbated by the dizzying plunge into poverty that accompanied it. My grandfather was an architect who had done pioneering work with men like Philip Johnson and R. Buckminster Fuller, but employment was hard to come by during the worst years of the Depression, and he soon defaulted on his financial obligations to his wife and children.

Left with no means of support, my grandmother considered getting a job, but her straitlaced sisters pressured her not to do so. Firmly in thrall to the Victorian concept of "separate spheres" that divided the world according to gender, they believed that men should be the breadwinners and that women—or at least ladies—should not work outside the home. If my grandmother began supporting herself, her sisters warned, that would absolve her husband of his familial responsibilities, and then he would never return to his wife and children. Best to wait until he got tired of "that trollop," as my grandmother and her sisters referred to the Other Woman (who may have been an adulteress but was also a hardworking schoolteacher with considerably more modern ideas about women's place in the world).

The loss of her husband left my grandmother virtually paralyzed with grief; according to family lore, she simply went to bed for two years. My mother's older brother was soon out of the house, so my mother was left on her own to care for my deeply depressed grandmother. In addition to the emotional toll that entailed, the rest of my mother's childhood was blighted by one financial crisis after another as she and my grandmother were evicted from a series of increasingly shabby apartments, unable to keep up with the rent.

My grandmother's family owned a great deal of land out west, but as a woman she was deemed unable to manage her own affairs, so her only brother assumed control of her share of the family assets. Over time, he apparently "managed" my grandmother's property out of her name and into his own. As a result, she was forced to depend on the charity of her four sisters—or, to be more precise, their wealthy husbands—for support.

My grandfather's abdication of financial responsibility also torpedoed my mother's dream of attending Vassar. She was elated at being accepted, and my grandfather had promised to pay the tuition. But the day before my mother left for college, she learned that her father hadn't paid for her enrollment—and wouldn't be doing so. By then my great-uncles were all tired of being saddled with financial responsibility for their sister-in-law, so my mother went to work and supported them both while putting herself through school, eventually graduating from Barnard College.

My grandmother spent the next forty years mourning the loss of her marriage and waiting for her ex-husband to come back to her, even though he had long since wed his mistress. Until the day she died, my grandmother clung to the illusion that her husband would eventually return to her. In all those years, she never looked at another man, politely but firmly turning away all suitors. Nor did she ever question the strictly segregated gender roles that prevented her from exploring her own potential. As far as she was concerned, marriage was "for time and all eternity," just as her wedding ceremony had promised, and her role in life was as a wife, even when there was no husband around.

In the meantime, my mother had met and married my father, giving up her budding career as an actress in order to stay home and have her own family. But when she asked him to take over the financial support of my grandmother, my father declined, unwilling to shoulder that long-term responsibility.

So when I was five and my brother was four, my mother took a job at a publishing company where she worked her way up from secretary to copy editor to children's-book editor. From her own earnings, she paid her mother to take care of my brother and me after school. This was fine with us; our grandma made up wonderful stories and sewed elaborate costumes for the plays we wrote and staged in our basement.

My mother never had to worry about whether we were well cared for, and I don't think she ever had a guilty conscience about going to the office every day, because we adored being with our grandma.

Our mother left the house every morning with a briefcase and commuted into the city with all the men in their gray flannel suits. In an era when such choices were rare, I was the only one of my friends whose mother was a professional woman. But in other respects, she functioned like a typical 1950s housewife. Every night she came home and made an elaborate meal for our family—no TV dinners for us!—along with baking cookies for the next day's Girl Scout meeting, cleaning the house, washing and ironing our clothes for school, and helping us with our homework while my father dozed in front of the television set.

Although she undoubtedly didn't get enough sleep, my mother never complained. To the contrary; she told us all the time how lucky she felt. After the insecurity and humiliation of her childhood, she was thrilled to have a comfortable home and a stable family. She loved being a mother, but she also enjoyed her work, which she talked about with enthusiasm. As a result, it never occurred to me that a woman couldn't have both.

My mother supported my grandmother until she died, shortly before her eightieth birthday, still waiting for her husband to come back. He died soon afterward, leaving the "trollop," by then a sweet white-haired little old lady who had been his wife for more than four decades, as his widow.

Although I understood that my grandmother had spent most of her life quietly nursing a broken heart, the larger significance of this family history was lost on me until my mother heard about *The Feminine Mystique* and gave it to me. "Read this," she said, so I did.

That book had such a profound effect on American culture that Betty Friedan used the most frequent comment she heard from her readers as the title of a subsequent book: *It Changed My Life*. It certainly changed mine; I was thirteen when *The Feminine Mystique* was published, and it helped to guide my views and choices from then on. By the time I was a teenager, my parents had moved from Manhattan's Upper East Side to a Westchester suburb, and I was beginning to notice how much truth there was in Friedan's observations about affluent women trapped in unsatisfying domestic lives. Palpably unhappy, many of my friends' stay-at-home mothers were doubly wounded when their marriages broke up as soon as their kids left for college. My parents were among the few couples we knew who stayed together.

In retrospect, it's hard to parse the varied influences that shaped my life. How much of a role did one revolutionary book play in determining my future? How much did I learn from my own family history? Since my coming-of-age coincided with the blossoming of modern feminism, how many of my choices were simply a product of the exhilarating times I grew up in during the 1960s and '70s, when the very air seemed electric with the promise of exciting new possibilities?

Back then, even as conservatives railed against the changes being wrought by the women's movement, it was clear to me that the conventional social roles hadn't necessarily worked out very well for the women who actually lived them. When my grandmother was abandoned by her husband and swindled out of her share of the family fortune by her brother, the prescribed gender roles of her day rendered her powerless to deal effectively with either calamity. Because those roles were so confining, she never replaced her identity as a wife and mother with an independent life that might have consoled and sustained her during the decades she spent alone.

I certainly knew that my mother had been forced to go to work by my grandmother's lifelong economic dependency, which burdened so many other family members over the years. I knew that my father had refused to assume the financial support of my grandmother—but I also knew that this abdication of patriarchal responsibility had galvanized my mother into forging a career that proved to be enormously gratifying.

In the end, it became far more than that. The summer before I graduated from the University of Pennsylvania, my mother and I went to Europe for three weeks. My father had worked for the same company since he was a young man, and his life savings were invested in its stock. That company had just been taken over by a conglomerate whose stock price suddenly plummeted while my mother and I were away. By the time we got home, the stock was worth next to nothing. Our family's substantial net worth had simply vanished.

My mother couldn't believe that my father had just watched this catastrophe unfold, doing nothing to salvage our assets. How could he have been so passive when confronted by a colossal disaster that would forever alter our lives? When the stock price began its nosedive, why hadn't he sold our shares? My father, who assumed that it would eventually recover, had no answer. Nor did he have an income; nearly two decades older than my mother, he had recently retired and was no longer earning the handsome salary that had paid for my expensive riding camp and Ivy League education. But my mother was still working, so she became the breadwinner, as she had been for her own mother. Her income kept our family afloat when all else failed.

As a child, I didn't really focus on the destructive role that women's economic dependency had played in this linked chain of family dramas—but I surely got the message that you couldn't depend on men to take care of you. I also understood that when you asserted control over your own life, it made you strong and free.

As a professional woman during the 1950s and '60s, my mother was ahead of her time in many ways. But she was also a mother, and so—conforming obediently to the classic models for female behavior—she adjusted her work schedule according to what she thought was best for her husband and children at a given moment, as so many women continue to do today. The end result was that despite a long career, she suffered a significant financial penalty, having sacrificed her own economic interests to those of her family.

When I entered seventh grade at the age of ten, she left her job to become a full-time mom again, because she had heard from other mothers that junior high school was a difficult transition for many kids. Having started school early and then skipped a grade, I was at least two years younger than most of my classmates, so my mother was particularly concerned about how I would adapt to an adolescent environment.

As it turned out, I was fine, and after a year as a stay-at-home mother in an empty house, she went back to work. A decade later, when I got engaged to my first husband, she left that job as well—"to plan your wedding," she said. Six months of intensive planning ensued; the wedding was beautiful, and when it was over, my mother got another job.

Even after her children were grown, however, she continued to subordinate her career to what she perceived as her family's needs. After my father retired, my mother felt that she should be more available to spend time with her increasingly elderly husband. Although she had been a children's-book editor for many years, she decided to return to the job of copy editor, which paid less but had predictable hours that enabled her to leave the office promptly at 5:00 P.M. and hurry home. She spent the final phase of her working life in the same job she had held during the 1950s.

But my mother paid a high price for these interruptions to her professional life. During a career in book publishing that spanned more than thirty-five years, she worked for three major companies, spending at least a decade at each. As a result, she received three different pensions when she retired. One is for $161.82 a month; one earns her $183.45 a month; and the third brings in $236.75 a month. The grand total of my mother's pension income is $582.02 a month. My father died in 1985, so my mother subsists on her pensions, which add up to

$6,984.24 a year, plus her meager Social Security payments. Needless to say, this does not provide a lavish lifestyle.

My own professional history has been very different. Like my mother, I first went to work at the age of sixteen; I held down a full-time job during my senior year in college and began my career at the age of twenty. But I've never taken more than a weekend off between jobs since then. Because there have been no interruptions to my labor-force participation since I came of age, my work history looks much more like that of a man in terms of continuous employment, steadily increasing compensation, and the resulting investment and retirement-planning opportunities. Over the years, my career has become a significant ongoing asset, rather than a temporary source of income that I dip into and drop out of in response to personal considerations. I'm not rich, and you never know what the future might bring, but I am far better prepared to withstand its economic challenges than either my mother or my grandmother ever was.

These days, as I listen to younger women talk about their choices, the echoes of the past reverberate like a Greek chorus in the background—one that many of them seem unable to hear. Occasionally a powerful voice will break through, trying urgently to communicate the dangers that can lie ahead like jagged rocks underneath calm waters, waiting silently to sink an unwary ship.

On New Year's Day 2006, *The New York Times* published an essay by Terry Martin Hekker, a mother of five who had once crusaded as a self-appointed spokesperson for the joys of being a full-time homemaker. More than a quarter of a century ago, Hekker wrote a book called *Ever Since Adam and Eve* and made a national tour: "I spoke to rapt audiences about the importance of being there for your children as they grew up, of the satisfactions of 'making a home,' preparing family meals and supporting your hard-working husband," she recalled. "So I was predictably stunned and devastated when, on our 40th wedding anniversary, my husband presented me with a divorce."

While her husband took his girlfriend to Cancún, Hekker sold her engagement ring to pay for repairs to the roof of her house. "When I filed my first nonjoint tax return, it triggered the shocking notification that I had become eligible for food stamps," she reported.

Hekker was able to parlay her involvement with the local village board into a stint as mayor of her community—"a challenging, full-time job that paid a whopping annual salary of $8,000," she noted dryly. How many of today's affluent wives would welcome the prospect of spending their later years trying to live on eight thousand dollars a year?

Looking back on her life, Hekker—the grandmother of twelve—said she doesn't regret marrying her husband, because the result was the family she cherishes. What she regrets is having sacrificed her ability to support herself adequately.

Will younger generations learn to heed such cautionary tales? Not unless more women speak out to tell them why and show them how.

The prize, in the end, is incalculable: the chance to live the fullest possible life, to become our own most complete and authentic selves as well as to protect ourselves from the vicissitudes of fortune. In the history of the world, no females have ever enjoyed a greater range of opportunities than do American women today. Most of the barriers to realizing those possibilities are self-imposed—the products of an anachronistic myth that encourages female dependency while obscuring its price.

Fortified by a strong sense of their options and entitlements, many of today's young mothers see their decision to give up paid work and stay home with their families as a positive choice that reflects their values—one that should therefore be respected. But the real issues involved here can no longer be assessed in terms of such familiar catchwords as "choice" or "values" or "respect."

It has become inescapably clear that choosing economic dependency as a lifestyle is the classic feminine mistake. No matter what the reasons, justifications, or circumstances, it's simply too risky to count on anyone else to support you over the long haul. In an era of disappearing pensions, threats to Social Security, high divorce rates, a volatile labor market, and attenuating life spans, the social safety net continues to erode even as the needs grow—particularly for women, who are twice as likely as men to slide below the poverty line in their later years.

Choosing dependency can therefore jeopardize any woman's future—and that of her children. No matter what one's politics, this much is indisputable. But the ultimate toll of this willfully retrograde choice is even greater than the financial vulnerability it entails. Just as the Victorians sent men out into the public realm to earn a living while confining women to the private domain of the home, today's culture continues to promulgate a modern version of the female "cult of domesticity." Women are still presumed to find true fulfillment by limiting themselves to the care of their families rather than exploring their own intellectual, creative, financial, and political potential in the larger world.

But in striving to become a fully mature, fully realized human being, there is no substitute for taking complete responsibility for your own life. In making such a statement, I want also to make it clear that this book is not intended as a contribution to the Mommy Wars, an overdone subject most mothers got sick of a long time ago. I am not criticizing stay-at-home moms for placing the needs of their children ahead of other considerations; I did so myself, and I personally think every member of our society should give top priority to the care and education of our children. Nor am I disparaging the domestic arts; far be it from me to underestimate the satisfactions to be found in practicing such skills or to devalue the solace that one can provide a family with a good meal and a comfortable, well-ordered home. I have the utmost respect for the art of homemaking, in which I am an enthusiastic participant. I love to cook; I spend inordinate amounts of time arranging flowers and tending my plants; I am utterly absorbed by such tasks as the selection of sheets and towels, not to mention the ever-engrossing comparison of different paint colors and wallpaper. I would rather plan dinner than work any day.

I would also like to stress that this is not a book about the virtues or failings of feminism. It does, however, constitute a sharp rebuttal to those foes of feminism who—whether through ignorance, negligence, or deliberate, politically motivated dishonesty—encourage women to adopt a high-risk lifestyle that no longer serves their best interests, if indeed it ever did.

What I want to do is sound a warning to women who forgo income-producing work in favor of a domestic role predicated on economic dependency. My first goal is to document the long-term dangers of that choice in hopes of persuading these women to reevaluate its costs. My second goal is to reaffirm the immense value of income-producing work that gives women financial autonomy along with innumerable other rewards. In the endless acrimony of the culture wars, those key factors seem to have been largely overlooked, at least in the media and the standard public debate.

But unless they've got their eyes tightly closed so they won't have to see it, most women—certainly those past the early years of adulthood—secretly know the truth. When I finished writing this book, I gave it to a friend to read. A classic suburban soccer mom, she is struggling valiantly to support her children after downscaling her career to stay home, only to find that she couldn't get a decent job when she needed to resume full-time work after her husband ended their marriage and defaulted on his child-support payments.

Her reaction to reading the stories contained in this book was intense. "I just can't believe the way women get screwed," she said bitterly. "I finished your manuscript at the soccer field, where I was watching the game with three other women. Two of us are divorced;

our husbands left us for younger women. One is widowed; her husband suddenly dropped dead last year. Only one of the four is still married. Then I went home and ran into my next-door neighbor, who told me her husband just announced that he's in love with someone else and he's moving out. She's a lawyer, but she hasn't worked in eighteen years and has no idea how to get a job. I tell you, it's carnage out here."

Still wearing the impressive diamonds her ex-husband gave her during their marriage, this particular friend always looks like the picture of affluence; but the truth is that she can barely pay her monthly bills. In coping with such an unwanted challenge, she has a dismaying amount of company. I've been a reporter for more than three decades, and I couldn't possibly count the number of women I've interviewed who thought they could depend on a husband to support them but who ultimately found themselves alone and unprepared to take care of themselves—and their children. With heartbreaking frequency, I've sat in so many lovely living rooms over the years, listening to women wearing beautiful clothes and expensive jewelry tell me they are broke and have no idea how they'll earn a living on their own, now that their breadwinner is gone.

"The feminine mistake" has cost women far too much over the last century, but we can escape it only by recognizing economic dependency for the dangerously anachronistic trap that it is. It's high time to confront reality, to protect ourselves and our children, and to embrace the happier, more secure lives we can earn by taking full responsibility for our own futures.

But in order to do so, women must reevaluate their assumptions and consider their long-term interests as well as their family's short-term needs before making major life choices. My hope is that this book will help them do that more effectively. Knowledge is power, but all too often, women make critical decisions that will circumscribe their futures without fully understanding the facts—and then get blindsided by the consequences.

Far better to arm ourselves with adequate information, prepare for reasonable risks, and march forward with strength and confidence to enjoy the intellectual, emotional, and material benefits of an independent life. That's a lot more fun than cheating ourselves out of all those rewards and resigning ourselves to living with insecurity and fear—because dependency inevitably breeds fear. Anyone who is not in control of her own circumstances must, unless she's got her head firmly buried in the sand, at times feel anxious about what could happen to her if something happened to her spouse.

What a contrast with taking control of your own destiny, which is both exhilarating and profoundly empowering. Women rarely talk about what it feels like to have power; many don't even think they have any, and those who do typically observe the social taboos that inhibit females from talking about it. In this culture, power is seen as a male attribute; the very word seems unfeminine. And yet having power over our own lives is a vital component of happiness. Enjoying a broad range of options, and knowing that we can exercise them to change whatever we don't like about our circumstances, is tremendously liberating, not to mention the best possible hedge against depression.

Although my children are growing up and I am well into my fifties, I have never felt more excited and energized about my future as an individual. My daughter is preparing to leave for college, and I will miss her tremendously, but there's so much I want to do in my own life that I feel as if my personal universe is expanding rather than contracting. When the road ahead is full of enticing opportunities and unexpected possibilities, every new day is an adventure. The only thing I regret, as a working mother who has spent the last eighteen years raising children, is all the time and energy I wasted on feeling guilty about dumb things.

And yet women continue to buy into a mythology that puts them at risk and consigns them to living what amounts to half a life, because nobody is telling them the truth about the feminine mistake. Wouldn't you rather focus on all the astonishing pleasures you can reap from making a different choice?

What I offer you in the pages that follow is the bad news and the good news. The bad news is a lot worse than you've been led to believe.

But the good news is infinitely better than you ever imagined.

# AUTHOR'S NOTE

The names marked with an asterisk in this book have been changed, at the subject's request, to protect the privacy of the families involved. All other names are real, including those in which the subjects asked to be identified by their first name and last initial. No other facts have been altered in any way.

# THE

# FEMININE

# MISTAKE

## CHAPTER ONE

# BACK TO THE FUTURE

## "IT'S A 1950S LIFE!"

The homemade cranberry scones are sublime—flaky and moist, a difficult combination to achieve, but one that Margaret Hein has clearly mastered. As she serves me an excellent cup of coffee to go with them, her living room is so immaculate it's hard to believe that she has three kids; the inevitable detritus of life with children must be stashed somewhere else in this tidy four-bedroom house, which sits on two-thirds of an acre in Rye, New York, only a block from Long Island Sound. But on this weekday morning, the kids are in school, the coffee table is clutter-free, and the comfortable suburban home is silent and empty.

If she didn't have a visitor, Hein would be running errands or doing housework right now; with an eleven-year-old son and daughters who are seven and nine, her days are busy indeed. Her husband commutes to Pennsylvania for his job as a financial consultant at a money-management firm, and Hein is in charge of the child-rearing and domestic chores.

"I do everything," she says. "I do all the grocery shopping, I do the cooking, I take care of all the minutiae of our lives. He takes out the garbage."

At forty-four, Hein has been a stay-at-home mother ever since her first child was born. "I saw my sister going off to work and leaving her nanny with fifteen pages of instructions and coming back and saying, 'Ahhhh—she didn't tell me how much formula she gave him!'" Hein recalls. "I loved being a mom to a baby, and I didn't want to leave him."

The arrival of two more children only strengthened her conviction that she was doing the right thing. "I felt like they were going to grow up so fast," she says. "I wanted to be home with my kids, and I always felt incredibly lucky that I had the choice. After I had children, the women I knew who were working were doing it because they felt like they had to. I got to do what I wanted to do."

Hein is certain that her decision has worked well for the family, and her husband is very supportive. "Rick loves that I stay home; he loves that I'm raising the kids," she says. "He really appreciates what I do. It gives us so much more freedom. On the weekends, we can say, 'What do you want to do today?'—whereas with friends who work, on the weekends it's 'You go to the grocery store, I'll go to the cleaners!' The rhythm of our lives is so much less stressed."

Dressed in a pretty sweater and slacks, Hein looks every inch the contemporary suburban mother, appropriately attired for her active life. But while she may not be wearing the crisp shirtwaist dress, sensible pumps, and single strand of pearls that characterized Donna Reed or June Cleaver, Hein's lifestyle resembles that latter-day ideal more closely than not—as she is the first to point out, with considerable pride in her role as the indispensable mom. "It's a 1950s life," she says.

For several decades, it seemed as if that archetypal maternal role was becoming an endangered species. The conventional nuclear family built on traditional gender stereotypes—the breadwinner husband, the stay-at-home wife, and children who receive round-the-clock attention from a mother who runs the entire domestic operation—went out of fashion as the burgeoning feminist movement of the 1960s and '70s broke down workplace barriers and generated new opportunities for women's employment.

To the Baby Boomers just reaching adulthood in those heady times, the new ideal was "having it all." Emboldened by the radical idea that they could combine work and family rather than being forced to choose one or the other, women embraced it with enthusiasm, pursuing challenging careers even as they married and raised their children.

Since then, several successive generations of American women have built richly rewarding, if harried, lives by combining work and family. Today's labor force is full of mothers who are working outside the home, at every socioeconomic level and in virtually every field. Over the last three decades, such multifaceted lives have represented the ultimate achievement for countless women who believed that personal and professional fulfillment are neither mutually exclusive nor a male prerogative.

During much of that time, the "feminine mystique" of the 1950s seemed as passé as the domestic tracts that used to counsel women to have a delicious dinner ready when their husbands came home from work, to apply fresh lipstick and don a frilly apron, to greet The Man at the door with a cold martini, and to let him do all the talking, since his topics of conversation were far more important.

Once considered ancient history, such retrograde advice is enjoying a comeback these days, abetted by mainstream media grown inexplicably hostile to women's achievement and by an antifeminist punditocracy bent on rolling back the clock. Last year, Caitlin Flanagan, an essayist who made her name writing inflammatory diatribes for the *Atlantic Monthly* and the *New Yorker*, published a collection called *To Hell with All That: Loving and Loathing Our Inner Housewife*. Its targets included those slatternly wives who fail to "plan a gentle reentry into home life" and to have a hot dinner on the table for their husbands every night, not to mention the slackers who neglect to plot a "thrilling seduction" duly inspired by wifely gratitude to the manly bread-winner.

Even when a woman is the family's major income producer, she gets no sympathy from Flanagan, who reserves special fury for working mothers who hire baby-sitters to help care for their children. The hard-working heroine of Allison Pearson's bestselling novel *I Don't Know How She Does It* earns far more money than her husband, but Flanagan dismisses her as a "ballbreaker" because she's angry that he doesn't per-form his fair share of domestic tasks. In discussing women who work outside the home, Flanagan's tone is invariably excoriating, her judg-ments lethal: "Children crave their mothers," she proclaims. "When a mother works, something is lost." No mention that some things might also be gained, no mention of an economy that forces millions of women to work to support their families, no mention of what children lose by having absent fathers working inhuman hours to sustain the burden of being the sole breadwinner. Such practical realities don't intrude upon Flanagan's universe, in which there is never any discussion of the finan-cial vulnerability that nice women who wear frilly aprons may incur by giving up their economic self-sufficiency to spend 24/7 servicing the needs of their children and husbands.

Flanagan's take-no-prisoners attitude might seem, to some, like a stunning throwback to an earlier era—but a startling number of today's young mothers have eagerly adopted its basic premises, re-creating the 1950s lifestyle with renewed enthusiasm. That era effectively ended in 1963 with the publication of *The Feminine Mystique*, Betty Friedan's groundbreaking book about the idealized images of femininity that led women to forsake educational and professional opportunities in favor of confining themselves to the roles of housewife and mother.

Although many women of that era subsequently regretted their choice, this fact seems to have been lost on the new generation of stay-at-home moms. A recent poll cited by *Psychology Today* found that 40 percent of today's women would actually prefer a return to the gender roles of the 1950s. Once seen as a quaint relic of bygone times, the stay-at-home mother who depends on a husband for economic support while taking care of their home and children has come back into vogue with a vengeance, as newly stylish as a vintage alligator purse.

According to the U.S. Census Bureau, the workforce participation of married mothers with a child less than one year old dropped from nearly 59 percent in 1998 to 55 percent in 2004, reversing a twenty-two-year increase. Among married mothers, the workforce-participation rate fell to 68.2 percent in 2004, down by nearly three percentage points from 1997, the peak year. The father was the sole breadwinner in 31.2 percent of married families with children under the age of eighteen, a 3 percent increase since 1997, and in 40.2 percent of married couples with children under the age of six.

The Census Bureau also reported that an estimated 5.6 million mothers stayed home with their children in 2005—about 1.2 million more than did so a decade ago. Contrasting the Baby Boomers born in the postwar years with Generation X, people who were raised in the 1970s and '80s, another survey found that "twice as many Gen-X mothers as boomer mothers spent more than 12 hours a day 'attending to child-rearing and household responsibilities,'" according to *The New York Times*. Startling numbers of women are now devoting their lives to their children's schooling: "More than 1.1 million . . . children are being home-schooled, most often by their mothers," reported conservative polling expert Kellyanne Conway and political strategist Celinda Lake in their book *What Women Really Want*.

The stay-at-home ideal now exerts such a potent lure that many more women would apparently quit their jobs were it not for financial considerations. "Seven in 10 working women tell pollsters they would stay home with their kids if they could," according to *What Women Really Want*. "The difference is less family *values* than family *income*.

Among many affluent younger moms, staying home with the kids has become the new status symbol."

When mothers are fortunate enough to have that choice, a notable proportion of them seem to find it an appealing one. "Half the wealthiest, most privileged, best-educated women in the country stay home with their babies rather than work in the market economy," wrote Linda Hirshman, an emeritus professor of philosophy and women's studies at Brandeis University, in an essay for the *American Prospect.*

In her subsequent book, *Get to Work,* Hirshman reported her findings when she tracked down a group of the brides who had been featured in *New York Times* wedding announcements in 1996 to see what choices they made in the ensuing years. Although all were college graduates with budding careers, 85 percent had stopped working full-time within eight years. Half the mothers were not working at all.

Many other surveys have demonstrated a similar pattern. A 2004 survey by the Center for Work-Life Policy showed that among women with children, 43 percent of those who had earned graduate degrees or high-honor bachelor's degrees had dropped out of the workforce. A study by Catalyst found that one in three white women who had earned MBA degrees was not working full-time, compared with only one in twenty of the male degree-holders. A survey of the Stanford University class of 1981 found that "fifty-seven percent of mothers spent at least a year at home caring for their infant children in the first decade after graduation," according to *The New York Times.* And in 2001, when Harvard Business School professor Myra Hart surveyed female Harvard MBAs from the classes of 1981, 1986, and 1991, she found that only 38 percent of those with children were working full-time.

Like Margaret Hein, most of these women cite the needs of their families as the reason for giving up their careers. But this explanation reveals only part of the truth. Hirshman discovered that half the *Times* brides stopped working before they even had children, and half of that group said they hoped never to work again. Such data make it obvious that these choices reflect more than a rejection of the logistical difficulties of juggling jobs and family life. When women voluntarily relinquish their economic independence the moment they get married, other factors are clearly influencing that decision.

So far, such women represent a minority of the population as a whole, and some feminists have challenged the very existence of a back-to-the-home trend on the grounds that more than two-thirds of all American mothers still participate in the labor force. Other analysts simply filter the data through a different lens. Heather Boushey, a senior economist at the Center for Economic and Policy Research in Washington, D.C., contends that any falloff in women's employment is the result of the recession of the early 2000s, not of a back-to-the-home movement. "There is no trend of mothers dropping out of the work force," Boushey told *The New York Times.* "It just looks like they are because the economy has been so hard on working moms."

With characteristic acerbity, Hirshman refers to these rebuttals as the "it's not happening" argument. Whether or not you buy such denials, however, they overlook a larger point: Even if the majority of women with children work outside the home, many out of financial necessity, millions of other women do not engage in income-producing activity at all. Moreover, even among working women, patterns of female employment are notoriously inconsistent; women interrupt their labor-force participation by dropping out, coming back in, working full-time, scaling back to part-time, and making every adjustment they can think of to accommodate the needs of their families.

And yet the inevitable corollary is rarely even mentioned, let alone examined. If a growing proportion of American women is opting out of the labor force, increasing numbers of American women apparently believe that depending on a husband for support remains a viable long-term way of life. Given the economic, social, and actuarial realities of twenty-first-century America, this alone is a stunning fact, albeit one whose significance is almost universally ignored.

Other analysts have challenged the idea that we're witnessing a resurgence of stay-at-home motherhood by attacking the news stories describing this phenomenon. Individual articles have often been based on shoddy reporting, and some bellwether stories were admittedly biased or incomplete. But anyone who spends time with today's young mothers must recognize that such coverage contains a great deal of truth. Despite the record numbers of women enrolled in law schools, medical schools, and business schools around the country, a lot of the best and the brightest seem more interested in becoming soccer moms than doctors or lawyers or CEOs. Even those who feel ambivalent appear to accept the idea that giving up their careers may be the most sensible solution to the inevitable conflicts between work and family.

"Among women my age, it's all everyone talks about," says a thirtyish Ivy League graduate who asks me not to use her name because she doesn't want her employer to know she's thinking about quitting her job. "Everyone wants to have it all, but with people who are hard-charging and well educated, you don't necessarily pick the easy jobs. I'm not in a situation where you can work part-time; there's a lot of work and a lot of pressure, and you're at the beck and call of the people you work for. All my friends are in different fields, but they're in the same situation. I want to do the best I can at work, and with a kid I know I would do less than that. My husband's making more and more money, and I would feel pressure if I were running myself ragged and having a nanny raise the kid. So the question becomes, 'What am I doing it for, if my family would be okay if I didn't work?' People say, 'You'll just be working to pay for the baby-sitter.' How you balance it all is a constant topic of conversation among my friends, and it keeps me up at night. I don't know if I can continue to work as hard as I do and still have a family. I have to look for another choice."

Unwilling to accept the compromises they might have to make in order to achieve a reasonable balance, many young women simply decide to withdraw from the fray. Morphing from hard-driving career women into what some sociologists have called the "new traditionalists," they embrace the practice of "intensive mothering" and elevate the domestic arts to levels of refinement that would have seemed unimaginable to the average 1950s housewife. Convinced that focusing all their energy on their families will help them raise the best possible children, they micromanage their kids' lives and create homes worthy of a Martha Stewart photo shoot. Having forgone the competing claims of the workplace, they put all their energy into the home, in the belief that this choice will protect them from divorce and disillusionment in years to come.

Accompanying this dedication to domesticity is a pervasive rejection of the rewards of the labor force. Many stay-at-home wives dismiss work as highly overrated. To them, "having it all" has become a discredited goal. It's too hard—too stressful, too exhausting, too frenetic, according to what sociologist Susan Shapiro Barash has called "the new breed of wife." Having earned their Ivy League diplomas and advanced degrees, they want to be done with the arduous frustrations of the workplace. They prefer to stay home and enjoy "a pleasurable, struggle-free life," as Barash puts it—conveniently supported by their husbands. They take it for granted that those husbands will continue to pay for their comfortable lifestyles forever. And they feel no obligation to fight for the social and political changes that would help make the workforce more hospitable to mothers—or fathers.

Although Barash's observations were based on the extensive interviews she conducted for her book *The New Wife: The Evolving Role of the American Wife*, such assertions tend to enrage stay-at-home mothers, something I discovered when I first wrote about this subject. *The Feminine Mistake* originated as an essay about the risks of economic dependency that was published in *Tango* magazine in 2005. Some readers understood my point about the financial vulnerability of women who give up their careers. "I think [the] article touches on a hard cold reality for some women," one reader e-mailed after the piece was published on *Tango's* Web site. "I saw it happen many times while growing up in a wealthy community. But also, my sister's husband just passed away, totally unexpectedly. She was a stay-at-home mother and now finds herself scrambling to pay bills, while also saving for college tuition for two children. If a woman decides to quit her job to raise children, I think this article sheds light on possible important ramifications for loss of years gaining job skills. It could be a very sad reality, especially if the woman did not consider the possibility."

But most of the women who wrote to *Tango* were incensed by my reference to Barash's suggestion that they chose easier lives than they'd have had if they were juggling jobs and families. "Today's women put a priority on spending time with their children during these formative years. That is the motivation behind career choices, not living a 'Cushy Life,'" one irate reader retorted.

A middle-class mother who does all the family housework while taking care of four young children might well resent any suggestion that she has chosen a cushy life. But in wealthy communities, even the most dedicated stay-at-home mothers usually admit that many of their peers employ housekeepers and nannies in order to escape some of the domestic drudge work—and some of the child care. These women may not be working for pay, but their tennis lessons, hair and manicure appointments, shopping dates, volunteer commitments, and social engagements frequently keep them out of the house for longer hours than many of the working mothers I know. "I don't know why they call them stay-at-home mothers; they're never at home," one teenage boy commented to his mother, a working woman, about his friends' nonworking moms.

But when a husband makes more than enough money to support his family, a wife's job can seem like an inconvenience that gets in the way of their lifestyle instead of an asset. "I wanted to be able to travel

# CIBC
## Wood Gundy

MARIE-FRANCE DELISLE
418-659-8785

DIANE CARON
418-659-8766

To: _Michelle de Freitas_

Date: _April 13, 2007_

☑ As promised

☑ Thought you might be interested

☐ Per your request

☐ Please sign where indicated and return in envelope provided

☐ Please fill out, sign and return in envelope provided

☐ Please call when received

COMMENTS:

Have good time reading
This book
            Best regards
                    M.F.
                    Denise

with my husband and share some of the experiences his career afforded us," says one Washington wife who gave up her own formidable career to do so.

And in some privileged enclaves, this choice has become the norm. At a program on "opting out" of the labor force sponsored by the National Council for Research on Women, a high-powered financial executive talked about attending a social event in New Canaan, Connecticut, where the other wives—all well educated and well-to-do—were astonished to learn that a woman in their midst actually had a job. "No one in New Canaan works!" one exclaimed.

Such women enjoy the lavish approval of conservatives who applaud old-fashioned gender roles and believe that women's place remains in the home. "Power is in the kitchen," wrote *New York Times* op-ed columnist David Brooks in an essay attacking Hirshman's *American Prospect* article.

Some women readers were not convinced. "No group can hope to secure and protect its social and political rights without economic power, whose source is money and property of one's own," responded Corina Linden in a letter to the editor. "Women must be an ambitious, tenacious presence in the wage-earning work force, if only out of self-preservation." And yet even Linden, a Seattle woman with a Ph.D. in political science, confessed that she had retreated to the home after having children.

Despite the widespread cultural support for full-time motherhood in recent years, some analysts nonetheless discern a double standard that discriminates between the haves and the have-nots. Right-wingers have long railed against welfare mothers who stay home with children while living on public assistance, and conservatives applauded the welfare reforms requiring low-income mothers to work as a condition of receiving benefits, which resulted in sharp declines in welfare caseloads. But those very same conservatives are among the most impassioned advocates of full-time motherhood for the privileged.

"We seem to be saying, 'It's very good for middle-class women to stay home, but it's very good for poor women to go to work, because we don't want them to be dependent on welfare,'" observes Heidi Hartmann, an economist and president of the Institute for Women's Policy Research in Washington, D.C.

Women with high-earning husbands obviously have more options than those who are struggling merely to survive, but Hartmann believes that the stay-at-home ideal is affecting women across the social spectrum. "I don't think it is an elite phenomenon," she says. "It's my sense that it's pretty much across the board, in terms of socioeconomic levels and age groups."

The latest data from the Bureau of Labor Statistics confirms that analysis, demonstrating that the back-to-the-home trend "has been broader than previously believed, with women at all income levels taking job breaks, not just the highly educated, prosperous moms examined in many recent studies," the *Wall Street Journal* reported last November.

For middle-class couples, the decision to make do on a single income often entails considerable sacrifice. Margaret Hein's family enjoys the many services she provides as a stay-at-home wife, but the costs have included cutbacks in their standard of living as well as increased stress for her breadwinner husband, who feels his financial responsibilities keenly.

The Heins originally moved to Rye because it offered a better school system than their former home in Port Chester, but buying into the new community strained their household budget and necessitated significant changes in their lifestyle. "I think many people here have a lot more money than we do," Margaret admits. "It's definitely harder for us to live here, financially. After we bought this house, things were really tight."

As a result, the Heins have been forced to defer their dream of renovating the original 1948 bathrooms and kitchen, which have leaky plumbing and ancient appliances. "Fixing up the house is probably the biggest thing we can't do," Margaret says. "If I was working, we probably could at least start the process of doing some of this stuff, but we're not anywhere near that."

The Heins have also curtailed their discretionary spending. "If someone invites us to a party, we'll get a baby-sitter, but we don't say, 'Let's go out to dinner Saturday night,'" Margaret reports. "I know people who go to the manicurist and the personal trainer and get their hair highlighted, but I don't do that."

Their vacations have been limited as well. "The last time Rick and I went away together was five years ago," says Margaret, whose parents and in-laws have been responsible for most of their family vacations, inviting them to rented houses at the Jersey shore or in the Catskills.

In making such choices, the Heins have consciously decided to exchange certain material rewards for the benefits provided by Margaret as a full-time homemaker. The result is a noticeable gap between their own habits and those of many neighbors. "We're not keeping up with the Joneses," Margaret acknowledges cheerfully.

Although the Westchester suburbs are teeming with Mercedes-Benzes and Lexuses, Margaret drives a 1997 Ford Taurus station wagon whose rear window won't close. Rick drives a hand-me-down from his mother, a dented 1990 Honda Accord, two of whose four door handles don't work and have to be opened from the outside. So far the Heins are putting up with those inconveniences in hopes of avoiding the additional burden of car payments for new vehicles.

Such trade-offs multiply as a family's income dwindles. Lisa T., a forty-two-year-old mother of two who lives in upstate New York, has been a full-time homemaker since her first child was born ten years ago. "I never really thought about having a career," says Lisa, a former office manager who doesn't miss working and has no desire to return. "I had always hoped to stay home with my kids."

But recently her husband, an engineer, went back to school to earn an M.B.A., and he is pressing Lisa to get a job. "Financially it's been rough," she admits. "We are being tighter with money, but he does not handle the stress very well; he has a very difficult time with it. He'll take things out on me. One day, he just snapped. He made this comment, 'You haven't had to pay for anything!' I'm not very materialistic, but he seems to feel he cannot survive without certain things, and he doesn't want to do the sacrificing. He's got to have high-speed Internet access and computer games or whatever. It's appealing to him to have a little more money coming in, but I don't feel it's necessary for me to go back to work. I will cut corners where I have to."

In the meantime, however, her husband's eagerness for her to rejoin the workforce has made Lisa feel that her contributions at home are not fully appreciated. "He doesn't see that the mom job is a lot of work," she complains. "He's never had to do the laundry or look for clean clothing. He's always got a nice meal—nothing out of boxes or the freezer. You take care of all the tough issues at home with the kids, and you do everything for them in the house, and they just don't see it. I do resent it."

Another source of conflict is the family's health insurance. "He's having to pay a lot more money for health care, and the plans are not as good these days," Lisa says. "Having to deal with all those bills gets to be crazy, and he would like me to find a place where the benefits would be better than his benefits package."

Although lower-income families typically face an even greater struggle to maintain such amenities as health insurance, some nonetheless view a stay-at-home wife as a status symbol. Particularly among minority communities, a family's ability to manage on one income is often seen as testimony to the husband's success.

"For many black women, it becomes an aspirational model: If the man is doing okay, the woman doesn't work," says Vicki Gault, who used to be an executive at a high-tech telecommunications company before becoming a full-time mother of three in Montclair, New Jersey.

"Very few black women have that chance. Very few of my friends are staying home; they're working to pay the bills. Statistically, it's more likely for black women to make more money than their husbands. From an African-American perspective, we've worked since the days of slavery; everyone we knew worked, so being able not to work is part of what defines success."

And in affluent white communities, this definition is affecting the way females envision their lives at ever-younger ages. "My friends' mothers are all telling them to marry a rich guy so they'll never have to work," reports a Houston teenager who goes to public school. At an exclusive private school in New York City, the senior girl with the highest grade-point average has just been accepted at Harvard—but she is quite forthright about her intention to forgo a career and become a homemaker. These aspirations have become so prevalent that they are already being satirized in popular fiction; when Wendy Wasserstein's novel, *Elements of Style,* was published last year, *The New York Times* noted that "one character's thirteen-year-old daughter is in a women's studies class in which half the students plan to grow up, have children, stop working and exploit a lot of household help."

AT A DINNER party in Waccabuc, New York, a leafy enclave of manicured lawns and faux-Provençal mansions, a successful businesswoman shares her dismay about the views of her own daughters. "They are eighteen and twenty-two, and neither of them wants to have the kind of career I've had," she tells me. "They saw the sacrifices I made, and they think it's just too hard to juggle work and family the way I did. Both of them say they're going to stay home after they have kids."

Even women who begin adulthood with a different attitude often change their minds after grappling with the harsh realities of the workplace. Some have a difficult time matching their abilities to meaningful work. "I've always felt like I have this really great contribution to make somewhere, and I don't know exactly what it is," says Katie Hof-stadter, a twenty-four-year-old from Macon, Georgia. "I need to find a place for myself. Getting married scares me; I feel like if I did give up a career, and I didn't have the pressure to make a living, I would lose that scrappy, resourceful side of myself. It's a scary fantasy of being rudderless and uninspired."

After a few years in the workplace, however, that determination to find and steer your own course can easily be replaced by different goals. Karen Eames* is a twenty-nine-year-old chemical engineer who is currently working as an asset trader for an oil-energy company in Chicago. She has always been ambitious and driven to succeed. "When I was in high school, I swore I was never having children," she says. "I left college with an 'I'm going to take over the world!' attitude. I was going to be vice president of some company."

Although her career has soared, her feelings have changed consider-ably in the years since then. "It was a gradual progression," says Eames. "I don't know if it's this particular career that I've realized I don't want or if it's the corporate environment, with all the red tape, being on call twenty-four hours a day, solving problems because people can't get along—you burn out. I've enjoyed my time here; I think it was something I needed to do, to prove that I could compete with the best of them. But I'm worn out with the rat race, and I want to change directions."

Eames is getting married in a few months, and her expectation of starting a family has intensified her desire to escape the demands of her job. "I've been giving a hundred and ten percent to my career, and I'd give at least that to my family, so something has to give," she says. "The kind of balance I want, where you have a good family life, is something I couldn't attain if I was going to be high up in a company like the one where I'm working now—and that balance is really im-portant to me."

So Eames has decided to quit her career. She asked me to use a pseudonym in quoting her, because she hasn't told her employer yet, but she and her new husband are planning to move to Colorado, where he has landed a new job. "It's the perfect time for me to make that shift," she says. "I'm looking at nonprofit work or teaching high-school chemistry. A big part of the reason is anticipation about having a family."

But even if she finds less taxing work, Eames is prepared to give that up, too. "I don't really want someone else raising my kids," she explains. "I feel like it's my responsibility as a parent to guide my children and teach them things; I want to feel responsible for how they turn out. I don't want them to have an attachment to some other person who could just quit the job and walk away. I don't want to run myself ragged to get the kids to day care or get a call that my child is sick when I have to have a meeting. I don't want that pace. I would anticipate stretching myself thin, and it's not worth the gratification of having a career to stress myself out like that."

For the immediate future, the major impact of Eames's decision to give up her job will be the loss of income. Up until now, she has been the high earner, while her fiancé, a doctoral student, was finishing his Ph.D. "When we go out to dinner, it's my dime," she says.

His new teaching position will be substantially less remunerative than her own job has been, but Eames is not concerned about the financial sacrifice. Although she recognizes that becoming financially dependent on her husband may entail some risks, she sees no compelling reason to make contingency plans in case her husband someday loses his job or gets sick. "You never know what life's going to throw at you," she acknowledges, "but to me, to prepare for something that may not happen would be kind of irrational. Should something happen, you do what you need to do."

That attitude is common among younger women, for whom many of life's potential challenges still seem largely theoretical; older women who have experienced the loss or incapacitation of a husband have a much more acute sense of their own vulnerability. Young women leaving the workforce also tend to be very optimistic about their ability to return at a later date. "I do believe I could come back, even if it's five or ten years from now," Eames says. "I'm realistic enough to know that I'm not necessarily going to be able to jump back in where I left off, but I've got a skill set to offer, and I'm a very determined person."

Eames also believes she is prepared for what will surely be a major shift in her sense of identity. "I do think it will be an adjustment, but my definition of success was very different when I was younger," she says. "It definitely was going out and being a strong, powerful woman in the workforce, but that view has been changing. I look at my mother, who has raised four children who turned out okay, and I think that's something to be as proud of as running a company."

Eames's decision to downsize her career in favor of family priorities constitutes a striking example of women's willingness to sacrifice their professional advancement, even when their own prospects are far brighter than those of their partners. Although Eames's husband-to-be will earn only a fraction of what she's been earning, neither of them questions the assumption that her career is the one to be jettisoned.

Pamela Stone, a Hunter College sociology professor, studied this phenomenon in a report called "Fast-Track Women and the 'Choice' to Stay Home." "Despite the high-powered nature of their own careers . . . they seemed to implicitly accept that their career was secondary," Stone wrote. Among the women she interviewed, who ranged in age from thirty-three to fifty-six, such views were reinforced by their husbands—even when the wives were the main breadwinners. "Significantly, about one-third of the women who described their husbands' implicit or explicit preference for a stay-at-home wife as a factor in their quitting were earning comparable incomes or outearning their husbands at the time of their job departure," Stone reported. "Thus, economics was not the only factor at play in these couples' perceptions that the wife's career was secondary."

More often than not, however, a couple decides in favor of the husband's career because his long-term earnings potential is perceived to be greater than hers. "I'm in a marriage where one person makes more money, so I'm going to be the one who figures out something that's more doable," says Kathy Tanning,* a thirty-two-year-old television producer whose husband works on Wall Street. "I don't know if I can continue to work as hard as I do and still have a family; I have to look for another choice. I'm facing the fact that I don't know if both people can go for it, pedal to the metal. If you have two people pushing themselves in jobs where you have to work long hours in order to be successful, something has to give if you also want to have a family and be happy, and a lot of the time that becomes the wife's job. Where I am now, I think it could be tough to continue what I'm doing. I feel frantic here, and I don't know if I want to feel frantic. I just don't know that you can have it all. Just because you *can* work sixty hours a week and have a kid, do I want to? Having one person who's already earning more money than the other, by a long shot, makes it harder to say that one person isn't going to have to give up something. Most likely, because I make less money, it's going to be me. You say to yourself, 'I'm in a good marriage, and I have this choice.' "

And yet few women making that choice stop to consider its financial implications. In an era when parents scrupulously outfit their windows with child guards and their cars with baby seats, when they babyproof every square inch of their homes and scour *Consumer Reports* to research the safest strollers, it's hard to understand why so many women are willing to turn over their very ability to feed their children to another person who—if history is any guide—may not always live up to that responsibility. No matter how lovely their homes are, economic dependency is the proverbial elephant in the living room—the enormous issue that is almost universally ignored despite its power to destroy everything in its path.

One reason for this potentially disastrous oversight is the extent to which women identify their own interests with those of their husbands and children. In choosing the stay-at-home lifestyle, they often don't differentiate between what they believe will benefit the family and what is best for themselves as individuals. Although the consequences can be horrendous, it's hardly surprising that women continue to fall into the same trap. A steady flow of cultural propaganda encourages wives and mothers to think about their situations in precisely those terms—and to overlook their own unique vulnerability. Even when media coverage focuses on the financial consequences of staying home, it almost never considers the woman as an individual whose needs may someday diverge from those of her partner; she is seen only as part of a larger economic unit.

In October 2006, *USA Today* offered a typical example with a story that purported to examine the pros and cons of giving up one job and relying on a single breadwinner. "If you're willing to cut your budget, staying home with your child might not be as financially painful as you think," enthused the writer, John Waggoner.

Waggoner conceded that the partner who leaves the workforce will "stop accruing credits toward Social Security benefits . . . forgo several years' work experience . . . and . . . lose pension benefits, as well as the opportunity to contribute to a corporate 401(k) savings plan." But, he added brightly, "the impact of losing one income might not be as huge as you imagine . . . There are also downsides to dual incomes," including higher tax brackets, commuting costs, day care, and—yes, he really said this—"a daily coffee at Starbucks."

Although Waggoner carefully avoided specifying the gender of the partner who leaves a job to become a full-time caregiver, he ended his story with a carefully selected anecdote that made it all too clear where a woman's duty lies. He described a Cincinnati woman who left her job teaching high school when her son was born, a decision that deprived the family of about 20 percent of its income. But, her husband said, "It's worth it. You have to be cognizant of the things that matter to you." And what mattered to him was having his wife at home with his child.

The *USA Today* story also reinforced the conventional way of assessing child-care costs. "If you continue to work, you'll have to pay for day care," it stated (as if women need to be alerted to such startling news). "The average cost of infant care is 10.6 percent of household income, according to the National Association of Child Care Resource and Referral agencies, a trade group. For low-income families, that can soar to nearly a quarter of household income."

Discouraged by such warnings, women often decide to give up their careers, rationalizing that choice with the thought that they would be working only to pay for child care, and that their work would therefore be pointless. But this argument completely fails to take into account the long-term development of any worker's earnings potential. Your own career is an investment you make in yourself, one that—unless it is interrupted or derailed—will pay dividends throughout your life. Some benefits are financial, some are intellectual or creative, and others involve different kinds of personal growth. If you devote your life to supporting your husband's career, all those dividends belong to him—as does the career itself. Ultimately it's his asset, not yours. This basic fact may not become apparent unless you lose your breadwinner, whether through divorce, illness, or death—but the harsh truth is that a dependent wife spends her life enhancing an asset that, in the end, may not even belong to her. This makes about as much sense as putting millions of dollars' worth of renovations into a house you don't even own. Few intelligent people would sink a lot of money into refurbishing a rental, but stay-at-home wives think nothing of subordinating their own financial interests to those of their husbands, blithely assuming that those interests will never diverge.

"If a woman is earning less than her husband, and if someone has to stay home, it makes sense that it's the lower-wage earner who does it— but what makes sense for the family unit is not what makes sense for the woman," says Martha Fineman, a professor at Emory School of Law in Atlanta. "In the event of divorce, men tend to benefit, because what women typically get in custody and child support is inadequate to compensate for the sacrifices they have to make in order to take care of children."

But women don't think about the possibility of divorce when they're making these sacrifices, which often begin as soon as they become part of a couple. Like Karen Eames and the *New York Times* brides in Linda Hirshman's study, Margaret Hein started to wean herself away from professional rewards as soon as she married.

While Hein was single, she worked as the publications manager for an educational consulting firm in the Washington, D.C., area. "I loved my job, and I loved the people I worked with," she says. "I worked really hard, stayed late, and went in on weekends when I had to." Back then, her husband-to-be was working in Connecticut, and they had a commuter relationship. But when they got married, Rick took a job in New York City, and Margaret decided to give up her own position in order to be with him. "I felt like I had to quit my job," she says. "He was making more money than I was, and I couldn't support him on my salary."

Finding alternative work in New York took longer than Hein expected. "I didn't know anybody," she explains. She finally landed a new position as a financial editor at First Boston, and by the time she became pregnant, her career was flourishing again. "I was getting all these job offers while I was pregnant," she says wistfully.

Even then, however, she doubted whether she would continue to work after her son was born—"just for financial reasons, because of how much it was going to cost me to go back to work and have somebody take care of my baby," she says.

Like most young mothers, Hein thought only in terms of her salary at that moment, rather than factoring in the likely growth of her income over time. The emotional impact of becoming a new mother only reinforced her inclination to give up her career. "People say, 'Are you going back to work after the baby comes?'" she says, "but nobody knows, even the hardest-driving professional. I didn't know how I was going to feel, but once I had William, I wanted to be home with him."

Hein's career, which had occupied a central place in her life, suddenly seemed like a youthful indulgence it was time to outgrow. "I worked for such a long time, but to me it felt like a phase," she says. "I had a great time working; I felt I'd had all that, and I felt I could get it back."

That belief typically plays a crucial role when women decide to drop out of the labor force. Confident that they can return at will, many new mothers quit their jobs, convinced that they'll have no problem resurrecting their abandoned careers or beginning new ones when their children are older. Indeed, the majority fully intend to do so: According to the Center for Work-Life Policy in New York, a poll of nearly five hundred well-educated women who left their jobs primarily to stay home with their families found that 66 percent wanted to return to the workplace eventually. Secure in the knowledge that they are smart and accomplished, these women assume that their past credentials will enable them to opt back into the workforce after a prolonged hiatus—and they do not believe they will be penalized for a lengthy time-out.

"Some of these women are ideologically committed, but most see it as a temporary break in their labor-force participation that might last five or six years," says Barbara Risman, the head of the sociology department at the University of Illinois at Chicago and co-chair of the Council on Contemporary Families. "They expect this to be a break until their children are older, but I think they underestimate the toll this will take on their lifetime earnings and their ability to keep up in a field. They overestimate their chances of getting back in the game."

When you are young and hopeful, however, such depressing subjects seem to have little relevance. Twenty-nine-year-old Jennifer Fry

is working for an advertising agency in Chicago and planning her up-
coming wedding to an investment banker. The potential conflict between career and family is very much on her mind. "I think about it
every day," she says. "I work for a big agency where we're responsible
to our clients, who can call at 4:30 P.M. and say, 'I need something by tomorrow morning.' This lifestyle was fine when I was single and didn't
have anyone waiting for me to get home. But we would like to have
kids in a couple of years, and I'd like to stay at home, at least while the
children are young—maybe ten to fifteen years. It's more important to
me to be available to my children when they need me than it is to
achieve something in my career. I don't see it as a sacrifice."

When I ask Fry about the risks of financial dependency, she is non-
plussed. "I've never thought about it as being dependent," she says. "I
don't think I have any hesitation about that. It would be a mutual
agreement. My husband would be earning the money, but we'd both
be working; I'd be taking on roles and responsibilities that may not
earn money but that we have identified as being important to us. If I
end up in a situation where I need to go back to work for financial reasons, I feel as if I've proven that I can do it, so I don't worry that I
would be stuck with no options."

Nor is Fry concerned about the difficulty of reentering the labor
market after a substantial hiatus. "I don't think I've ever spent a whole
lot of time thinking about it," she says. "I don't think of myself as an
older woman yet."

But time passes with stealthy speed, and one day you wake up and
realize that your options have dwindled in direct proportion to the
years that have crept up on you.

AT FORTY-FOUR, SUSAN YARDLEY* might seem to have the ideal
life. Her husband, a partner at a leading New York law firm, earns a
seven-figure income that pays for their children's expensive private

school education as well as the family's luxury co-op apartment and
their weekend house in the Hamptons. Like her spouse, Yardley is a
graduate of Harvard Law School, but she has been a full-time mother
for twelve years, ever since she got pregnant with the second of her
three daughters.

Sipping a skim latte at a Starbucks near her Central Park West
apartment in the middle of a weekday, Yardley seems the quintessen-
tial chic Manhattan wife—whippet thin and sinewy, her auburn hair
artfully colored and fashionably tousled. In fact, however, she grew up
in a small Kansas town where her mother's life choices instilled some
mixed messages about parenting and work. "My mother was a schoolteacher who quit and stayed home when I was born," says Yardley,
who has three siblings. "She loved having kids, and all of her friends
were in the same situation. But she went back to work when I was in
high school and my youngest brother was six or seven. Within the last
year or two, she said to me, 'That was the best thing I ever did, going
back to work. I always felt so stupid going to things with your dad
and his colleagues. I felt like I didn't have anything to talk about, and
going back to work did so much to build up my confidence.' "

For Yardley, being admitted to Harvard Law School was the magic
ticket out of Kansas and into a world where such an illustrious creden-
tial would always win respect. She began adulthood determined to
build a professional career. "I fully intended to be a lawyer," she says.

She met her future husband at Harvard, and after Yardley earned
her degree, they got married. Both joined big New York law firms, but
Yardley, a litigator, soon grew discouraged by the absence of viable female role models. "In the litigation department, there were two
women partners out of thirty or so," she says. "It was very rare for a
woman to make it all the way through as a litigator. It involves travel,
and you have crazy hours, and the fun cases are often the most demanding."

The women who did persevere seemed extremely stressed by the conflicting demands upon them. "The partner I worked with most closely had two children, and her family situation was always in turmoil," Yardley says. "She was very nervous, her husband was not emotionally available, and her kids weren't doing so great."

So when Yardley's first child was born, she cut back her work schedule to four days a week—a move that did nothing to enhance her career prospects in the highly competitive world of major Manhattan law firms. "On a four-day week, I felt like I wasn't really part of things," she says. "I concluded that to do what I was doing and stay on that track wasn't going to work. I thought it was highly unlikely that I would make partner. Nobody explicitly said to me, 'You can't be considered for partner while you're working part-time,' but no one had ever been made partner while working part-time."

And Yardley's attention was already turning elsewhere. "I did a little bit of interviewing to be a staff lawyer for a corporation, because that's supposed to have better hours, but nothing particularly grabbed me," she says. "By this time I was pregnant with my second child, my husband's hours were getting worse and worse, and we decided it would be a good idea for me to stay home. We would put our effort into making him partner. At the time, I didn't feel any regret, and I didn't feel like I was sacrificing my job for his. I wanted to stay home. I really wanted to enjoy my children while they were little, and I thought, 'I can always go back.'"

Besides, many of Yardley's peers were doing the same thing. "I had so many friends who hated their jobs at law firms, and the minute they got pregnant, they quit. My best friend from law school quit as soon as she got pregnant, so we had play dates and went to play groups together."

As her children grew older, Yardley found that she had more free time, which she has tried to fill with volunteer work. "The focus of my life now is being involved with my kids' school," she says. "I want to know what's going on, and it gives me something to do."

Yardley prides herself on being in charge of the annual used-book fair at her children's school, but at times she is conscious of unfulfilled yearnings. "My biggest complaint is lack of intellectual challenge. Your brain can get rusty, and I haven't been involved in anything that is in any way intellectual for years," she acknowledges. "If I go to a cocktail party with my husband and hear about a case somebody is working on, I think, 'I remember that—that was so exciting!' I do miss that. I have free time to read books, but that's not the same as having a job that really taxes you and challenges you mentally. I miss having colleagues, and I miss having my own life. But I don't think about it unless I'm in a situation where I'm listening to what somebody else is doing, and then I think, 'Wow—that sounds like fun!' "

So Yardley fills her time with domestic tasks, structuring her day around driving her children to school and picking them up—a service that is not strictly necessary, since most of their classmates travel to and from school on a private bus. "My kids could ride the bus, but this is part of our routine," says Yardley, whose oldest child is now fourteen. "They're all very dependent on me. When you've stayed at home as long as I have, you do so much stuff that no one else knows how to do."

When I ask what sort of irreplaceable things she's talking about, she replies earnestly, "Grocery shopping and cooking—my family really likes my food, and my kids are so used to having a homemade dinner every night."

Yardley feels sure that no one else could buy groceries or cook dinner for her family and that she herself couldn't accomplish such tasks if she worked outside the home. This kind of assertion—which I encountered frequently while interviewing stay-at-home wives—leaves many working women scratching their heads in disbelief. Many of us also make dinner for our families every night; a couple of my friends like to cook during the weekends, freezing individual dishes for each night's dinner, but the rest of us cope with this chore on a day-by-day basis. While the job of feeding a family requires some elementary organizational skills and a willingness to plan a few days ahead, it is hardly impossible, as any number of working women can attest. But stay-at-home mothers typically describe their domestic contributions as if there were no conceivable way a woman could manage to work and also to put nutritious food on the table at night. Many have an enormous emotional investment in the idea that the services they provide couldn't be obtained in any other way.

Ruth F., a fifty-seven-year-old stay-at-home wife who lives in Michigan, never left her two children while they were growing up. "I do remember feelings of being sort of confined," she admits. "If I wanted to go off for a weekend with the girls, sometimes I'd think, 'Oh, should I do that?' My husband probably would have encouraged it, but I felt, 'Am I indispensable? Can I be away?' "

Convinced that her family wouldn't be able to cope with her absence, Ruth didn't take a break until many years later, when her father got sick and she went to visit him. To her astonishment, her family managed just fine while she was away. "I came to find I was not indispensable," Ruth marvels, still amazed.

Susan Yardley has not yet arrived at this juncture, and she continues to feel that her domestic responsibilities preclude any other opportunities. "I will go back to work someday, but I don't know when," she says. "I do feel confused about that question; five to ten years from now would be when I would like to get a job. I'm a little concerned about that, because I've been out for so long. But I always have my degree, and I don't feel like I've made a choice I can't recover from."

By the time she starts looking for work, however, Yardley will probably be in her fifties, and she will have been out of the job market for twenty years or more. Asked whether she is worried about age discrimination, she looks surprised. "I guess I hadn't thought about that," she says.

She also hasn't considered the possibility that her comfortable life might be threatened by divorce. "I just don't see it ever happening to us," she says, shaking her head decisively. "We're both very committed to each other and our family. I know that my husband is with young women all day long; he travels, and he tells me about partners at his firm who leave their wives and end up marrying an associate—but I just can't see one of us upending our lives that way."

Even when such traumas afflict her peers, Yardley's sense of security remains undisturbed. "I have a friend in Texas whose son found a used condom in their car," she confides. "Her husband had been saying he was going to the gym every night, but obviously he wasn't. He ended up marrying his girlfriend." But in Yardley's mind, upheavals like that occur only to other people. "I just don't worry about that happening to us," she says firmly.

Despite her own financial dependency, neither does she fret about what she would do if her husband ever got sick, or even died. "If he got run over by a bus, I'd worry about the lifestyle we have, with three kids in private school," she says. "I guess I'd sell the house and get a job. I could always move back to Kansas. But I don't worry that much about economic vulnerability—maybe two on a scale of ten."

Nor is Yardley concerned about what her daughters may learn, consciously or unconsciously, from a mother who has devoted her life to performing unpaid domestic services. "When I left my job, one of the male partners said, 'Why don't you stay at work and be a good role model for your daughter?'" she recalls. "I do think about being a role model, but there are many great things about our situation. My husband makes plenty of money, but he has a very demanding job. He comes to the parent-teacher conferences, but I'm the one who does everything else. My kids probably do think that's what the mom does. My husband's job is extremely stressful, and there are times when I'm complaining about a problem with the kids and he says, 'Don't bother me with that; I cannot deal with this. You don't know what I had to deal with today!' And there are times when I feel angry about that, but the reality is that I have a lot more time than he does."

In the fall of 2005, when *The New York Times* ran a front-page article about Ivy League women giving up their careers to stay home, Yardley experienced a brief twinge about her choice. "I had a moment of guilt," she admits. "I really enjoyed my legal education, and maybe I did squander it."

But she quickly dismissed such doubts. "What's wrong with education for the sake of education?" she says. "It's made me who I am today."

Although Yardley insists she feels good about who she is, she was nonetheless adamant that I change her name in writing about her, which I have done. She was hardly alone in making this request; in general, I found that stay-at-home moms reacted very differently from working women to the interview process. With few exceptions, the working mothers were willing to talk on the record about their lives, hectic and messy though they might be. The full-time mothers presented a striking contrast: Although virtually all claimed to be at peace with having sacrificed their careers, a disproportionate number insisted that I not use their real names. Our conversations usually involved nothing more scandalous than making cupcakes and picking up the dry cleaning—but their embarrassment about discussing their lives publicly was often acute. Although they couldn't explain why they felt the need to hide their identity, their discomfort was so visible that their protestations of domestic bliss began to seem puzzling.

This held true no matter what their other circumstances. The women I interviewed for this book ranged in age from seventeen to eighty. They were urban and suburban, black and white, immigrant and born in the U.S.A., married, single, divorced, and widowed. Their circumstances spanned the entire socioeconomic spectrum, from the wife of a high-flying multimillionaire to an impoverished cleaning lady. They lived in regions around the country, blue states and red.

But whether they had dropped out of high school or had earned advanced degrees from Ivy League universities, the stay-at-home wives were united by having shared the belief that it's safe to depend on a man for support.

During our initial conversations, almost all maintained that they were happy with their decision to stop working, that their families had benefited immeasurably, and that they were not concerned about suffering from adverse consequences in the future. But as the conversations became more intimate, darker undercurrents emerged and unexpected secrets often popped out. Lurking behind the cheerful facades these mothers presented to the world were stories of disappointment and disillusion, grief and anger—or simply a growing fear that something might have gone wrong with their lives, something they didn't even fully understand.

Days or weeks later, I would often hear from them again, and their tone was very different. My questions about the risks of dependency had made them reconsider, and they were feeling uneasy about their heretofore-unexamined assumptions.

After my first interview with Margaret Hein, she e-mailed me, "I don't think I totally realized the ramifications to my career of staying home, and I was probably too confident that I could go back any time, on my terms. . . . I felt like I knew that I could take care of myself and make my way in the world, so that gave me the confidence to give it up.

"Now, in retrospect, maybe I was kidding myself," she concluded.

# CHAPTER TWO

# OPTING OUT

## "IT'S LIKE THE SLAUGHTER OF THE LAMBS."

Looking back on her decision to stop working, Diane Miller sometimes wonders what she was thinking—or if she was thinking at all. An experienced social worker who loved her job, she underwent a strange transformation when she became a mother, almost as if some internal program she didn't recognize had been activated and had taken control of her faculties. "It's very mysterious," says Miller, who lives in Easton, Pennsylvania, with her husband, a teacher, and their two young daughters.

When she delivered her first child seven years ago, she hadn't even planned to quit her job. "It wasn't a well-thought-out decision," she admits. "While I was on maternity leave, a friend who was a child psychiatrist asked me what I was going to do. She said, 'If you don't have to work, you should take advantage of the opportunity to stay home.' Women always seem to talk about not 'having to work,' as if there's no reason to do so if your husband earns enough money. It's like a status thing that you don't 'have to' work. No one ever mentions that there might actually be rewards you get from working, other than money.

When my friend told me to stay home, I didn't say, 'Why would this be a good idea?' "

Without Miller's income, the family finances would have been very tight—but when her mother died a few weeks after the baby was born, she received a modest inheritance. "That gave me the option of staying home," she explains. "I was kind of torn, but I guess my concept of motherhood, based on my childhood experience, was that the mom stays at home."

So Miller quit her job. "What was I thinking? I wasn't thinking," she says. "But I definitely had a very negative association with day care. I think it's because of the way it's portrayed in the media. You read so many horror stories—'Those poor kids have to spend so much time in day care, away from their mothers!' I was very critical of people who put their kids in day care, and I was really frightened at the thought of the logistics I'd have to deal with if I was working."

When she was single, Miller had lived in big cities where there were many high-powered professional women. That environment was very different from the smaller town where she now lives, and Miller found a lot of support for staying at home from the full-time mothers who dominate the social environment in her community. "I think that women are programmed or led to believe that we'll be taken care of," Miller says. "You read the books, you watch the movies, you see the TV shows, and women's goal still tends to be finding that knight in shining armor—the prince who's going to take care of them. When I talk to friends who are working women, they say, 'You're so lucky you don't have to work!' "

That view has received an extraordinary amount of support in recent years. In October 2003, a *New York Times Magazine* cover announced the new trend in a controversial story titled "The Opt-Out Revolution." Written by Lisa Belkin, herself a working mother, the story featured a group of Belkin's fellow Princeton graduates, all of whom had given up their careers to become stay-at-home mothers.

For the most part, the article accepted at face value the blithe assertions of its privileged subjects that they could always go back to work
if and when they wanted to. Belkin gave short shrift to the potential
barriers to reentry and the economic vulnerability of women who depend on husbands to support them, let alone the long-term implications of that choice.

The mainstream media have embraced this trend with enthusiasm,
promoting the alleged peace and comfort offered by a return to the home
while contrasting this domestic bliss to the ostensibly unbearable stress
of juggling work and family. In March 2004, *Time* magazine featured a
cover story headlined "The Case for Staying Home: Why More Young
Moms Are Opting Out of the Rat Race." In September 2005, *The Times*
gave front-page play to a story reporting that 60 percent of the young
women interviewed for a study of Yale University students were planning to cut back on work or stop entirely once they had children. Many
believed that work and family presented an either/or choice for women.
"My mother's always told me you can't be the best career woman and
the best mother at the same time," said Cynthia Liu, a sophomore with a
4.0 grade-point average. "You always have to choose one over the other."

Like the Belkin piece, the page-one story also provoked a firestorm
of controversy; it was based on a questionnaire that a journalism student had sent to women in two of Yale's residential colleges, and the
story's detractors charged that its methodology was suspect and its
conclusions fatally flawed.

Once again, however, both the story and the resulting commentary
almost invariably failed to consider the economic implications of giving up one's career. The decision to become a full-time mother was
framed in terms of personal choice, with virtually no mention of its financial consequences. "Why shouldn't the raising of children be considered a career as well?" a Massachusetts man wrote in the Letters to
the Editor column of *The Times*. "Few would deny that being a stay-at-
home parent is a terrifically demanding job." He neglected to mention

that no one pays you to do it and that if your breadwinner changes his mind about picking up the tab, you're out of luck.

Whatever their individual weaknesses, however, news articles predicated on the idea that it's too hard for women to combine work and family have a powerful impact, particularly when they also promote an uncritical view of the stay-at-home option. "My daughter was in college when the Belkin piece came out, and when she called me about it, she was so upset, so despairing," says Kathleen Gerson, a professor of sociology at New York University and author of *The Time Divide: Work, Family and Gender Inequality*. "What she was seeing was, 'All my hard work, and this is what's going to happen to me?' I think the biggest effect is not on women who have already made their choices; I think the really pernicious effect is on the younger generation who are trying to figure things out and who are being given information that is not only inaccurate and misleading but extraordinarily discouraging. We don't write stories about men having to give up their aspirations in order to have a family; we don't ask men to choose, or even to agonize about it."

Many dissenters were also struck by *The Times'* apparent determination to champion the retreat-to-the-home story line without providing adequate social context, let alone any real factual information about the downside of economic dependency. "This line about how women have to pick between having a family and having real work is sexist," says Sylvia Law, the Elizabeth K. Dollard professor of Law, Medicine, and Psychiatry at New York University School of Law. "When you say to women, and only women, 'You have to pick,' it's a way of keeping women in their place by saying, 'This is the way it is.' *The Times* likes to tell the story as if the structures are immovable and you have to accept them. The idea that you can't be a successful professional unless you commit to it a hundred and ten percent for your whole life—that's just wrong. The idea that the women's movement sold women a bill of goods by saying that you can have family and have real work—well, you *can*. It's true; there are millions of women who do it every day. We all know that middle-class and lower-class women manage to have both wage labor and families. It's only the elite women who somehow lack that capacity. The best and the brightest are somehow incapable of doing this—I mean, hello? I just think it's such a myth."

Law herself constitutes a prime example, having raised an outstanding son while maintaining a stellar career that included her selection for a MacArthur Foundation "Genius" Award, even while running a SoHo apartment and a country house in upstate New York and hosting wonderful dinner parties with homemade cooking, all accomplished with a partner who shared the domestic work and child care. Like many women who succeeded in "having it all" and enjoyed it to the hilt, Law is appalled by the current glorification of stay-at-home motherhood and its implicit discouragement of women who might also yearn for something more.

"The truly depressing thing is that it influences my students," she says. "Some of them feel like they shouldn't aspire to have both a family and a high-powered work life; they hear this message that it's impossible. I think that's wrong. Both men and women can have both a family and a high-powered work life, and there are many ways to do it. The false message that's being put out there is that it's either/or, all or nothing—either you completely devote yourself to your career and you don't have a family or you have a family and end up working at Starbucks. That's wrong, but that's the message the mainstream media is projecting to students."

Many critics saw the privileged status of the women portrayed in these stories as the key factor in determining such coverage. "The men who are running the media institutions probably do see wives opting out," says sociologist Barbara Risman. "To the extent that there are women who are opting out, they are married to men earning over two hundred thousand dollars a year and working ninety hours a week. High-income men are married to their jobs, not their families, and that's who these women who are being written about are married to.

What journalists hear at dinner parties influences what their views of the trends are. I think those two things work in tandem to create a buzz around these stories."

Defenders of the stay-at-home lifestyle have taken to describing it as a manifestation of so-called choice feminism, which argues that being a full-time mother should simply be seen as another feminist option, on a par with work. These "new traditionalists" proclaim their right to "choose" domesticity over careers; after all, wasn't the women's movement about giving women the opportunity to determine their own destinies? "There's a sense of entitlement these young people have. I've interviewed young women who see it as refusing to live a male-model career choice: They don't have to do it like the boys," Risman says.

But what women want is a lot more complicated than many ideologues are willing to admit. As the Dutch tulip mania of the seventeenth century demonstrated, the question of why people want what they want when they want it is subject to a host of outside forces. Whether or not women realize it, a momentous life choice like sacrificing a career to stay home with children tends to be multidetermined, as a psychiatrist might say—the product of different feelings and influences, some conscious and others subconscious.

Many women suspect that the seeds of that decision were sown decades ago by the archetypal myths that permeate the childhoods of virtually all American girls. Whether it's Prince Charming rescuing Cinderella or such pop-culture equivalents as the billionaire businessman rescuing the beautiful hooker in *Pretty Woman,* such stories always revolve around the damsel in distress whose future is secured when the white knight rides up on his horse, or in his Bentley, to alter her fortunes. In their never-ending quest to sell more goods, the engines of capitalism are only too happy to support those fairy tales. When Disney introduced its Cinderella line of products, which recast the orphan in rags as a latter-day Material Girl lavishly equipped with fancy possessions, a vice president of the company's consumer-products division was quoted as saying, "She has almost everything a girl needs: a fairy godmother, a royal ball, fabulous ball gowns, a royal coach." No mention of a girl needing an education, a career, an individual identity, or a way to earn her own living should Prince Charming ever get bored with her.

Like many mothers, New Jersey mom Vicki Gault worries about the impact of such propaganda on her three daughters. "All those myths still exist in the media, in the films they see, in the books they read," she says. "You go to the teen-lit shelf and the boy books are sci-fi and fantasy books; they're about boys who are out slaying the dragons. The girl books are about cliques and boyfriends. I don't think society grooms girls to be achievers the way it grooms boys to be achievers. There is still this myth that Mr. Right works on Wall Street and is either going to stay married to you forever or make so much money that the alimony will keep you going."

Some women instinctively understand that they cannot trust the old-fashioned fairy tales. "I was brought up in Texas at a time when there was something wrong with you if you didn't marry early," says Marna Tucker, a prominent matrimonial lawyer who was elected the first woman president of the District of Columbia bar. "From the time we were little girls, there was this Cinderella complex. I didn't stay in Texas, because it was embarrassing to be in law school and not be married."

Tucker went on to wed and raise two children with her husband, a judge, while building her illustrious career. But other women simply follow their cultural programming, failing to recognize the social context in which seemingly voluntary decisions are being made, let alone the psychological stresses that may contribute to them.

One reason is the widespread assumption that women will serve as the primary caregivers for children and providers of domestic services within the home. "There's a double standard in parenting," says Heidi Hartmann. "There's the feeling that a woman is not a good mother if she doesn't stay home with her kids. Nobody says a man isn't a good father if he doesn't stay home with his kids."

Such expecatations can generate tremendous pressures. "In upper-middle-class worlds where kids have to be chauffeured to after-school activities in order to be raised within the cultural norms of their communities, the mummies have to be there to drive and shuffle," says Risman. "We've constructed a sense of moral responsibility where it's the mothers who feel inadequate if the kids don't get these opportunities. The fathers don't feel inadequate; the social system makes the mothers feel inadequate. In this hothouse parenting, we've constructed both schooling and after-schooling, which presumes that mothers have nowhere else to be."

Many analysts see the escalation of such unrealistic expectations as part of a cultural backlash against women's autonomy. "Even as women have gone to work, we have raised the standards on mothering, and it's not an accident," says Kathleen Gerson. "The more women go to work, the more they're subjected to these pressures. I don't think it's a conscious conspiracy, but as women have gone to work, the women who stayed at home felt devalued, and this is a way of elevating the value of their work with these completely insatiable standards. As a result, parenting has become very anxious. In a world where the middle class can no longer ensure the future of their children, economically and socially, there's a lot of anxiety about giving your children that leg up, which feeds into these ridiculous notions of being the perfect parent."

The conservative political climate of recent years has helped to ratchet up the pressure with its vociferous support of the stay-at-home lifestyle. Dr. Laura Schlessinger, the national radio host and bestselling author, often admonishes women to be full-time mothers no matter what economic sacrifices this may require. In families who cannot manage on a single income, the result can be an overwhelming sense of maternal guilt at not being able to live up to the much-vaunted ideal.

But there is often a considerable chasm between the purported values of such public figures and their own personal choices. In that regard, Schlessinger and Caitlin Flanagan have followed the blueprint laid down by Phyllis Schlafly, who spearheaded the successful movement to defeat the Equal Rights Amendment during the 1970s. The ERA, a proposed amendment to the U.S. Constitution, was submitted to the states in 1972 with a seven-year deadline for ratification. Arguing that the amendment would lead to taxpayer-funded abortions, same-sex marriage, unisex bathrooms, and a military draft for women, Schlafly founded a grassroots organization called Stop ERA to defeat it. Although she had six children at home, Schlafly—who also founded the antifeminist group Eagle Forum—spent her time traveling around the country as a political organizer, running for Congress, and becoming a high-profile spokeswoman for traditional female roles—even as she blithely declined to confine herself to such domestic servitude.

Similarly, Schlessinger made her name with sanctimonious pronouncements like the daily tagline she used as her radio self-identification—"I am my kid's mom!"—even as she devoted her time to broadcasting a national show and churning out mercilessly disapproving self-help books about other people's lifestyle choices. But in Schlessinger's household, her husband was the one who actually put dinner on the table.

Flanagan is no more a fan of cooking and cleaning than is Schlessinger. "Ms. Flanagan confesses that she can't sew, doesn't dust, and is grievously stressed each night by the prospect of summoning yet another dinner to the table," reported the *Wall Street Journal* in its review of *To Hell with All That*. "If pressed, she could not tell us how much anything in her refrigerator cost. She has never applied for credit in her own name and does not scrub her own bathtub. When her twin boys were small, she staggered about the house and street in a helpless fog each morning until the nanny took over at nine. She requires the help of maids, gardeners, organizers, and shrinks to make her life run smoothly.... For Ms. Flanagan, being an 'at-home mother' doesn't require much actual mothering."

Despite such hypocrisies, self-appointed provocateurs like Flanagan, Schlessinger, and Schlafly have long helped to inflame the tensions between working mothers and stay-at-home moms, an ongoing stand-off that was recently explored in a collection called *Mommy Wars*. In one essay, writer and editor Sara Nelson took issue with the implicit bias reflected in the phrase "full-time mother."

At her son's school, Nelson wrote, "One morning one of the stay-at-home mothers referred to herself, quite pointedly, as a 'full-time mom.' Those three words made my blood boil. I've been a mother every second of every day for the last ten and a half years, whether I'm researching an article or pushing a swing. Would anyone dare to suggest that a woman who worked in a factory, or as a cop or a firefighter—a woman who worked at least partly so that her children could have food and shoes and the occasional trip to Toys 'R' Us—was any less a mother than my school acquaintance, who'd had the privilege to opt out of the workforce? Motherhood is a state of being, I felt like telling her. It's not a job description."

On one level, of course, Nelson is right: As any woman who has a child can attest, we're all full-time mothers. Whether my kids are at school or at sleepaway camp or in the next room, I am their mother, and that responsibility determines many of my choices and much of my emotional reality. The implication that I am a part-time mother because I work is obviously ludicrous; I don't cease to be my children's mother when I go downtown for a meeting.

But, after considerable thought, I decided that the phrase "full-time mother," while loaded and often used with snide intent, does reflect another, larger truth. I am a mother all the time, and being a mother constitutes a crucial part of my identity—but that fact does not define the entirety of who I am. For many full-time moms, however, motherhood has become far more than a facet of their lives. It describes their identities, in a way that it could never describe the totality of my own. But then, I am what sociologists call a nontraditionalist, as opposed to the new traditionalists who structure their lives around home and hearth.

Notwithstanding the widespread cultural support for full-time motherhood, some of these women feel awfully defensive about it, judging by the aggrieved tone of *Total 180!*, a new publication billed as "the magazine for the professional woman turned stay-at-home mom." Founded by three California women who abandoned their careers, *Total 180!* offers advice for the CHO—Chief Household Officer—along with such other measures of the current zeitgeist as one mom's angry blast about being asked, "What do you do all day?"

Even angrier were some of the responses posted on *Tango* magazine's Web site about my original essay on the economic risks of dependency. "I cannot imagine a mother wanting to miss out on any part of her children's lives, which SHOULD be her life!" one woman wrote. "If you choose to have kids, then you should choose to raise them. . . . Our kids need strong values, which they can NEVER get when they are 'thrown out' by the parents. . . . And shame on the women who will leave their kids with someone else just so they can 'have a life'—you're a bunch of cowbirds! Being a stay-at-home mom is the biggest job anyone can have . . . WHAT HAPPENED TO REAL WOMEN?"

Such indignant protestations are common among stay-at-home mothers, but despite their affirmative claims about what they want to do, social scientists have documented a very different take on the underlying reasons for the decision to drop out of the workforce. It turns out that what these women secretly *don't* want to do may be far more relevant than what they ostensibly *do* want to do.

Under questioning, many stay-at-home wives admit that they were bored or unhappy with their work before quitting their jobs. Like most full-time moms, Noreen Sullivan,* a forty-three-year-old mother of four, cites her family's needs as the major reason for her decision to abandon her career, but when pressed she acknowledges that she never found real happiness as a lawyer. After graduating from Harvard Law School, she spent eighteen months as a corporate attorney for a big firm before giving up.

"I hated it," says Sullivan, who lives in an affluent Connecticut suburb. "I worked very long hours and did a lot of white-collar-crime work; I couldn't believe how awful the people were. At the time, the money didn't mean anything to me; I had already met my future husband, and he said, 'Do whatever you want to do.'"

So she quit and took a far less remunerative job at a nonprofit environmental organization. But when she had her first child twelve years ago, Sullivan found that she loved being a full-time mother. "I thought, 'This is the best thing I've ever done!'" she recalls. "We had this great life. I thought, 'I really love this! This is what I want to do.'"

Since then, Sullivan has tried part-time work and consulting as well as one unsuccessful attempt to resume a full-time job. "My kids were really miserable, because I wasn't there," she says. "They were used to having me home."

But she still feels guilty about not contributing to the family's income. "My husband feels it's a huge burden to support all of us," she says. "He's definitely stressed out."

What Sullivan would really like to do is write fiction, but she has been unsuccessful at turning that into an income-producing enterprise. Although she continues to write, she has resigned herself to the idea of getting a job when her youngest child, who is now four, begins school full-time. But she is not looking forward to it. "I never really liked law that much," she admits. "If we won the lottery, I would be the happiest person. I would love not working. I would keep on writing and keep playing tennis and read all the time. I wouldn't be bored at all."

Like Sullivan, many stay-at-home mothers didn't like the work they were doing or felt ill-suited to its demands. "I was making eighty thousand dollars a year as a stockbroker and trader for Bear Stearns, but every morning I felt like, 'I can't handle this,' " says Lucy Peters,* who ultimately quit her job to become a stay-at-home mom in a New York suburb. "I was just waiting for the day when I was going to make a huge error and cost the firm a ton of money. I hated the job and would have done anything to get out of it."

Although some women lack the skills to advance in the careers they choose, others are emotionally unprepared for the harsh realities of the workplace. "The way that elite institutions in law, medicine, and banking are set up makes it more attractive to women to drop out," observes Miranda Blake,* a New York City defense lawyer specializing in white-collar crime. "Women aren't prepared for the ugly mind-set at these places, for the hours and the drudgery that goes along with the hours. If you're reviewing documents for eighteen hours a day, it's hard to believe you're doing God's work, and the lack-of-civility factor is huge. Those places treat people like shit. When I was a baby lawyer, people would hand back a brief and say, 'This is a piece of shit!' That's not criticism; that's humiliation. They think this is normal human discourse, but I don't think women are prepared for it. The guys are expecting it, but the girls are not. All their lives, they've been cosseted and encouraged; these are people from very elite environments, and they're not prepared for this very cold, impersonal world where some of the interaction is abusive. Even when it's not, the women don't feel valued or encouraged. A lot of them feel very keenly disappointed in these worlds, and they have a built-in excuse: 'I've got to take care of my children.' It's not such a great environment, so it's not like you miss all these people telling you what a fuck-off you were, no matter how hard you were trying."

Despite their vague talk of returning to the workplace in some nebulous future, a surprising proportion of these career dropouts also admit that they will probably be unable to resume their previous professions when their children are older—and wouldn't want to in any event. But in portraying such women, our culture typically promotes a story line that idealizes the virtues of stay-at-home motherhood while ignoring the more complex reasons behind that choice, as well as the risks it may entail. Little attention is given to an intransigent workplace that refuses to accommodate the parenting needs of men or women, and even less attention is paid to the unique nature of women's response to workplace frustrations.

But there are frustrations and obstacles in any career, and when men hit roadblocks, they figure out ways to get around them. For women, however, having children provides the perfect excuse to give up. When full-time mothers discuss their own work histories in greater depth, frustration and disillusionment emerge again and again. Instead of finding more meaningful work, or more flexible work, or figuring out new strategies to overcome barriers, they decided to exit the arena entirely.

In her study on women "opting out" of the workplace, "Fast-Track Women and the 'Choice' to Stay Home," Hunter College sociologist Pamela Stone challenged what she refers to as "choice rhetoric."

"Choice rhetoric assumes that the feminist revolution has been accomplished and that women have relatively wide discretion in what they're going to do with regard to work and family—and that their decisions therefore reflect true preferences," Stone explains.

She cites Lisa Belkin's magazine story on "The Opt-Out Revolution" as a prime example. "It asked, 'Why don't more women get to the top?' and answered, 'They choose not to,'" Stone wrote in "Fast-Track Women."

A suburban mother herself, Stone was inspired to conduct her own research by the stay-at-home moms she encountered in Larchmont, New York, where she lives with her husband and two children. "I ran into a lot of women who had had these big careers and were now at home, and it intrigued me," she says. "Anybody in a professional job can afford child care; professionals have the most flexibility, the most autonomy, and the most to lose by leaving their jobs. So why do women like this, who have all sorts of economic support, stop working? The first reason they give you is the socially acceptable response about staying home and taking care of their children. These are highly empowered women; they're not women who see themselves as buffeted by the currents of fate, so this is the narrative they use. They have been high-achieving women throughout their lives, many have graduate degrees, and they're professionally socialized about what it means to be a doctor or a lawyer or an executive. These women do frame their stories in terms of choices. But when you look deeper, you get a different understanding of what's going on."

Stone's study focused on "very capable, competent women with great credentials" whose ages ranged from thirty-three to fifty-six and who worked in professional and executive jobs. "The prevailing media take on this is that women have rediscovered motherhood and are throwing over their careers in some kind of return to the 1950s," she says. "In my research on why they are tending to quit, I found that, far from opting out, they are being pushed out. In terms of reasons for leaving, workplace pushes played a really profound role, and women's degree of freedom was much narrower than the 'choice' rhetoric would have us believe. What I found was that many women come to the decision to stop working as a last resort. It was a highly conflicted decision that reflected a complex decision-making process with many factors—and work was typically the precipitating factor. They asked for part-time work and couldn't get it; they asked for flextime and couldn't get it. They were stigmatized and marginalized. One woman said, 'The idea that you would work anything other than a fifty- to sixty-hour week just wasn't within the realm of possibility.' These weren't women who were buying into the supermother syndrome that they had to be with their kids all the time. I had a very small proportion of 'new traditionalists' who felt that was important, but the other women didn't. These women are making very difficult and conflicted decisions, but the media are really oblivious to this part of the picture."

Within unyielding institutions dominated by male values and a brutal corporate culture that demands excessive work hours, women find little support for dealing with parenting issues, according to Stone, who has expanded her research into a book entitled *Opting Out? Why Women Really Quit Careers and Head Home.* "Once women are even thinking about being mothers, they start to feel the hostility of the workplace, and it becomes a private problem," she explains. "I can't tell you the number of times women said to me, 'There were no role models.' They had no models of success they could emulate. The family is so cut off from the workplace that women feel that even talking about it is somehow illegitimate; you're supposed to keep it to yourself. There are tons of motherhood penalties, so they are not wrong in keeping it quiet. Seeing it as your own problem is part of the workplace culture."

Although such women left the labor force reluctantly, Stone was startled to discover that their reservations typically did not include the vulnerability that financial dependency would entail. "In asking them about the costs or the downside of their decision, surprisingly few mentioned the loss of their own independent income, and very few mentioned the prospect of economic dependency on their husbands," she reports. "It hadn't entered actively into their decision making."

Louise Roth, a sociologist at the University of Arizona who has also studied women departing the labor force, found similar results. "When male politicians leave a position and say they want to spend more time with their families, people know that's a cover-up," Roth says. "When the average woman does it, they think it's the real thing— but it's the same thing; it's a cover-up. Either the women are unhappy with some aspect of their position or they get forced out. People just don't recognize it for what it is. When a woman of child-bearing age is involved, they just think, 'Oh, yeah, she really needs to be with her kids.'"

The women Roth studied typically were married to men who made more than enough money to support their families, which gave their wives the option of quitting their jobs. But their departure was often precipitated by the hostility of the workplace. "There was a lot of discrimination against mothers, and sometimes even single women were discriminated against, because all women were viewed as potential mothers," Roth reports. "There was this attitude of, 'Oh, well—she might want to have a kid!' that was negative, whereas for men there were no negatives to having children; it was seen as positive. The perception was that mothers were not committed—and that single women were not committed because they might become mothers."

Contrary to the affirmative hype, the women who quit their jobs after having children generally did so for negative reasons. "The ones who left all felt they were dissatisfied with the jobs and/or their pay," Roth says. "One woman in academia hated her department, so having a baby was a good opportunity to quit. A teacher in New Jersey never had a job she liked, so when she had kids, it was a no-brainer. One woman made a lot of money but got fired during her second pregnancy. She was a highly ranked Wall Street research analyst, and she thought it was discrimination, but they paid her a lot of money not to say anything. She got a big severance package, so she said, 'Oh, well,' and decided to be a homemaker. It just seemed like it would be more fun to be with the kids."

The women who kept working were very different. "Most of the women who stayed in the workforce really loved what they did," Roth says. "They talked about the intellectual challenge; they found work intellectually stimulating. One investment banker told me that as time goes by, your hours get fewer, the work gets more interesting, and the pay goes up. She liked the social interaction of working with clients. She felt that working with smart people makes you smarter."

To this kind of woman, even the joy of a new baby doesn't necessarily compensate for losing the rewards of a thriving career. "For someone who's used to a very stimulating work environment with crises going on all the time, staying home with an infant can be kind of boring," says Jennifer Friedman, a thirty-four-year-old public-interest lawyer in New York City. "My happiest stay-at-home friends are people who didn't love their work to begin with. It almost works best for women who never found work they loved, who never found a niche where they flourished."

But even those who enjoy their work can be defeated by the intransigence of their employers. "One woman wanted to work out a job share that was supposed to be available at her company, but she came back from maternity leave and they had nothing for her," Roth reports. "She wanted to work, but she didn't want to work fifty-five hours a week, and the choice was fifty-five hours a week or nothing. Another woman, a trader, worked out a flexible time arrangement and reduced her hours by twenty percent, but they started treating her poorly. She said, 'You should just pay me for what I produce,' but she was penalized on her bonus; it was really unjust, given what she had produced. That was the last straw."

Such findings challenge the narrative that has become standard in most news coverage. "This opt-out thing is about false choices," says sociologist Barbara Risman. "If you've been raised thinking you can do everything, and your husband works eighty hours a week, and you work eighty hours a week, and he's not willing to budge an inch, and you never see your children, so you opt out—that's not really opting out; that's being pushed out."

"Women aren't opting out of the best jobs; they're driven out, just as they're driven out of the worst jobs when they have a sick child or parent or partner," wrote Ellen Bravo, former director of 9to5, National Association of Working Women, in a letter to *The New York Times* last year. "Enough about the glass ceiling. It's time to redesign the building so that women and men at all levels can be good employees and good family members."

In another letter to the editor about "choice feminism," Barbara Cohn Schlachet wrote, "The word 'choice' has been used, in the context of women working at home versus working outside the home, as a euphemism for unpaid labor, with no job security, no health or vacation benefits, and no retirement plan. No wonder men are not clamoring for this 'choice.' Many jobs in the workplace also involve drudgery, but do not leave one financially dependent on another person."

And yet those with an agenda continue to spin this story very differently. "The idea that it's women's preference to stay at home, and that what makes women happy is to be with their kids, is very appealing to conservative think tanks, and they get their press releases out," Roth observes. "The idea that this is what women want and children need plays into the stereotypes that people have, but the data doesn't fit as neatly into a box as this very stereotypical idea that children need their mothers and mothers need their children."

Seduced by the prevailing mythology, some working women are astonished to find they don't enjoy even the limited domestic immersion of a maternity leave. "Every good marriage is a partnership, but when I was home, it was as if my husband and I didn't speak the same language," says Jennifer Friedman. "You're not energized in the same way. I didn't really like the role of taking care of things—doing the laundry, making the dinner. I didn't like the feeling that my function was being supportive of the man. That really didn't work for me. I would much rather make money. To me, the marriage itself works better when there's more equity."

Those who quit their careers expecting domestic bliss are even more dismayed when their emotions don't fit the prescribed role. "I thought I would be really happy staying home, going to Mommy & Me classes, doing all the things women do—but I hated it," says Lucy Peters, who lived in Bedford, New York, when she left her job to stay home with her two children. "All those PTA power women drove me insane. They were happy homemakers, baking cookies; they liked having dinner on the table. But I was stuck in my home, and I felt trapped."

Those who remain at home often resign themselves to their own ambivalence. "I love being at home, but a lot of days I wish I was working," admits Molly Bazzani, a twenty-nine-year-old mother of two who lives in Chicago. "It's a Catch-22, because if I was working, I'd feel sad that I wasn't with my children, but I feel like I'm on duty twenty-four hours a day. I'm lucky if I get five minutes to myself, and I miss just being around adults. When I'm around adults now, it's other moms, and all everyone talks about is their kids. I miss using my brain in a different way. I feel like I've sort of lost myself."

Although Bazzani's life revolves around her children, she still doesn't feel confident that she's doing a good job. "There's so much pressure to be a supermom," she says. "Everything makes you feel guilty that you're not doing enough, that you're not doing it the right way, that you're going to ruin your kid. There's so much you 'should' and 'shouldn't' be doing. Even as an at-home parent, there's no way you can possibly do it all."

With a two-year-old and a two-month-old baby, Bazzani feels sufficiently overburdened that she has yet to formulate any plans for her own future. "To be honest, I haven't thought long and hard about that," she says. "At the moment, I'm so consumed by what I'm doing that I'm not thinking that far past now. I would probably like to go back to work, but I don't know in what capacity, or what industry. I used to work in health-care administration, and then I went back to school and got a master's degree in elementary education. But I have no real classroom teaching experience, so getting back to work has been a concern of mine. Is someone really going to hire me?"

At present, however, Bazzani doesn't waste much energy worrying about such things. "Having a family was always a huge priority for me, and I guess I never was overly ambitious," she says. "I think my identity has become my kids. My needs are definitely on the back burner; I don't have time for myself right now. Most of my friends just want this experience with their kids; they don't talk about the future. I don't think a lot of people do think long-term about these things. You get so caught up in what you're doing."

This mixture of wistfulness, ambivalence, and genuine enjoyment often characterizes even those who were committed professionals before giving up their careers. Patsy Wiggins,* a thirty-nine-year-old Manhattan mother of three, was a hard-driving attorney until her frustrations over her husband's unpredictable hours, constant travel, and unwillingness to share domestic responsibilities finally drove her to quit her job. "Some days I think it's fabulous being a stay-at-home mom," she says. "I volunteer on everything, I sit on every committee, I do all the school-board stuff, I'm in a book club, I go on field trips, I ran the nursery PTA—but I do so much because I crave the adult interaction I had at work. I put myself out there so I can feel important, feel like I'm doing something. As a full-time mother, I feel that people are looking at me and thinking, 'What a sellout! Who goes to law school and spends all that money and doesn't work? Who lets her husband pay for everything?' I am surrounded by stay-at-home mothers who have no problem with shopping and spending time at the gym. It's just amazing to me that they have no guilt, no doubts, no second thoughts. I feel guilt about not living up to my intellectual potential, and I feel some guilt about not bringing in money. But I think that identity has been the biggest issue for me. I always identified myself as a powerhouse, and when people talk about me as a stay-at-home mother, I feel like, 'Put "loser" in the box next to that.' I feel like it's not impressive. Servicing everybody is a thankless role. It's not so much fun."

Wiggins's candor is unusual among stay-at-home mothers, most of whom emphasize the socially acceptable cover story that they gave up their careers for their families and insist they're fulfilled by serving the needs of their husbands and children. "I don't think you can just blame society," says sociologist Kathleen Gerson. "Women are participating in creating this culture; the question is why. The difficult thing to untangle is what is cause and what is effect. If you hate your job, you're overwhelmed with work, the workplace is family-unfriendly, you want to have another child, and your husband won't share the workload, then do you begin to convince yourself that quitting your job is a reasonable choice because you can depend on your spouse? Once you get to the point where not working starts to seem appealing to you, there are a lot of messages you can give yourself to help make it seem like a palatable choice. They're perfectly reasonable messages, taken one at a time. But these women are not exploring other options, like 'Maybe I could find a job I would be happier in,' which is what a man would be more likely to say in that situation, or 'How can I get my husband to share more of the workload?' The short-term attractions of leaving the workforce can outweigh the long-term concerns, but it's a dangerous choice. We continue to clothe the economic arguments in the romantic notion that we make these choices based solely on love, and the market doesn't play a part. The reality is that both play a role in marriage, but we're living in a culture that does not talk about the dangers of dependency."

As a result, those dangers are rarely factored into the decision-making process of today's stay-at-home mothers. "Out here you are a mom first and foremost," says Michelle Young, a thirty-three-year-old high-school counselor in Wichita, Kansas. "I go to the Junior League, and there are twelve women on the committee, and I'm the only one who has a real job. I don't think most of my friends have a plan for what would happen if they got divorced or if their husband got really sick or whatever. It's easier to not think about it."

The result is a plague of silence across the land. Because denial is so prevalent, interviewing women who have dropped out of the labor force can be a very odd experience; even the intelligent and well-educated frequently respond to the most obvious questions with an uncertain look on their faces. "I never thought about that," they admit hesitantly. Many of these women wouldn't dream of raising their children without medical insurance, home insurance, and life insurance—and yet they claim they've never considered what they'd do if their husbands left them, got sick, became disabled, lost their jobs, or dropped dead. Trying to ascertain how they envision their own futures, one runs into a blank wall. It's as if they look into the future and see only a void.

In studying women who dropped out of the workforce to raise their children, Louise Roth found that unpleasant contingencies never even crossed their radar screens. "None of them talked about 'What if I end up divorced?'" Roth reports. "They never mentioned other risk factors like death or illness or unemployment."

But even if no worst-case scenarios come to pass, time goes by and toddlers become teenagers. As the years roll on, women with older children begin to respond differently to these issues. When you ask them about their prospects of returning to the workforce, or how they feel about not having any money of their own, or whether they've remained in unhappy marriages because they can't support themselves, these women often seem confused and disoriented, as if slowly reawakening from a dream. They sense that a different time is coming, one when the services they're now providing will become less relevant and that old question—what do you want to do with your life?—returns to haunt them once again.

Although Margaret Hein used to be quite content with her stay-at-home lifestyle, she has recently begun to question that choice. "I was fine with not earning money when the kids were younger, because I was so busy," she says. "I never had any help, so just getting the shopping done was a challenge. If you had interviewed me six months ago, I would have said, 'I'm never going to go back to work.' But then I started feeling, 'Gee, we could really use the money.' My youngest is in second grade now, and it's hard for me to justify being at home."

She is increasingly concerned about leaving her husband with the burden of being the sole breadwinner. "There are four people he's supporting; that's a lot of financial responsibility," Hein says, a troubled crease furrowing her brow. "There's no safety net."

She worries that her husband's job is the only protection the family has against financial ruin. She has also begun to think about the rewards of a life outside the home. "I got really involved in our church and in the PTA. I was feeling like, 'This is fun—this is what I used to do!' It kind of whetted my appetite," she admits. "I feel like I really might want to go back to work. But last week the kids were all sick. So what do I do? Do I say, 'I have to stay home for a week, because the kids are puking'?"

Any parent finds such circumstances excruciating; figuring out solutions is an ongoing process that requires flexibility, compromise, determination, and courage, as well as a reasonable amount of good luck. Confronted by such demands, many stay-at-home mothers respond by postponing the moment of reckoning. As their doubts multiply, they bury their concerns in the needs of the moment, dismissing the future with the airy "I'll think about it tomorrow" that Scarlett O'Hara always resorted to in *Gone With the Wind*.

For those who enjoy a secure dependency, the comforts to be found therein may seem so pleasant that they would prefer not to wake up at all. But reality has a nasty way of intruding on even the pleasantest dreams, and a rude shock can startle you into wide-eyed alarm when you least expect it.

"The year our son was born, my husband left me," says Lucy Peters, who was then a thirty-three-year-old suburban homemaker with a toddler daughter in addition to her baby boy. "When he said, 'This isn't really what I want,' I was blindsided. It was like a classic midlife crisis—he was earning close to a million dollars a year, he had just turned forty, he bought a sixty-thousand-dollar Porsche, and he left in it. I didn't see it coming; I was like, 'Are you kidding me?' I cried for three months; all I did was cry."

Although she had previously worked as a Wall Street stockbroker, Peters was alarmingly unprepared to support herself and her children. "If you've been out of the workforce even for a year or two, the realities of it just suck," she says. "I never considered the fact that I could be trapped; I thought I would always have choices. I had always figured everything out; why wouldn't I figure this out? But if you don't have financial self-sufficiency, you don't have choices. Going back to the beginning, I should have found a career I actually liked, rather than just taking a job that enabled me to have my own apartment. That was the goal, and I achieved the goal, but I was miserable. I should have found a career that was not only income-producing but that I enjoyed. But I was just kind of following the path, always figuring it would work out somehow. There's a part of me that feels like I'm an idiot for not having protected myself better."

Peters eventually opened her own gift shop, and at forty-four she is struggling to make ends meet. "How am I living? My dad helps me," she says sheepishly. "I'm in a scary spot if the store doesn't work out, but I'm happy, because I just feel free. Nobody else is making my choices, and nothing intimidates me anymore. I think working women are happiest, by far. They may feel stressed out and overwhelmed, but they're empowered and in control."

Watching the stay-at-home moms who flock to her upscale store, Peters now has a very different perspective than she did when she, too, was a full-time homemaker. "I used to be intimidated by them," she says. "They seemed very powerful. They were in charge of the school, and if they didn't say you could go on the field trip, you couldn't go on the field trip. But now I can see that there are hardly any of them that are happy. They're running as fast as they can so they don't have to see that they're unhappy. They say, 'I don't know if I can buy this; my husband says we can't spend money right now.' It's like they're little kids; they have no say. Who wants to live like that? Very few of the marriages I see are teams. For the most part, it's the women feeling intimidated and weak, being sneaky and hiding things. When you're home, you're being submissive and feeling like everybody has power but you. When you're out there doing what you want to do, making your own choices, you get more respect. The working women are tough like me. They don't take shit from anybody."

Peters has become a mentor to the young women who work in her store, and these days she has strong opinions to share with them. "Every woman should know she can't depend on a man," she says firmly. "You can't assume anyone is going to take care of you. You have to be responsible for yourself; that's the most important thing. There are too many what-ifs to be lulled into a sense of complacency like that; it's dangerous. It's like the slaughter of the lambs."

CHAPTER THREE

# BUT WHAT IF...

## "I NEVER THOUGHT ABOUT THAT!"

On the surface, Wendy Greenberg* seems like most of the other Manhattan mothers who play an active role at her children's exclusive private school: Their families are rich, their lives are extremely privileged, and when the women aren't doing volunteer work, they're often shopping for inordinately expensive handbags. An exuberant forty-three-year-old, Greenberg is the life of any party and a passionate defender of full-time motherhood.

Although she was a lawyer when she married, she gave up that career before she even had children, a fact that is usually glossed over in her recitation of her life history. "I really wanted to be home with my kids," she says. "I do not think it's possible to have a fabulous marriage, fabulous children, a fabulous life, and a fabulous career. And I can't imagine leaving my kids with some nanny while I go to the office."

A scathing critic of substitute caregivers, Greenberg loves to regale other mothers with dire stories about child-care workers run amok; to her, every nanny is a potential ax murderer, every baby-sitter a feckless moron unfit to hold a child's life in her hands, even for long enough to let his parents go to a movie together. Greenberg scoffs at the idea that caregivers can be competent and compassionate and that other women might actually have positive experiences with paid help.

Freed from income-producing activities and well schooled in Martha Stewart–worthy arcana, Greenberg has perfected the labor-intensive skills of the consummate modern homemaker. Her annual holiday party features a staggering array of baked goodies piled on fancy tiered trays and artfully heaped on expensive platters, a display so lavish it could easily be immortalized as a gorgeous magazine cover depicting holiday extravagance at its most impressive. But if you dig deeper than Greenberg's effervescent public persona and talent for hostessing, her story becomes far more complicated. It seems that the poster girl for stay-at-home motherhood is not a happy camper after all.

"When I graduated from college, my parents said, 'What are you going to do?' and I didn't know," Greenberg confesses. "I really wanted to be an actress, but I was totally petrified about rejection, so I was too much of a chicken to pursue what I wanted to do. I wanted to go to the Yale School of Drama, but my parents said, 'Are you out of your mind? We'll pay for law school!' So, for me, law school was the default position. But I hated law school, and I had absolutely no interest in being a lawyer. I really didn't know what I wanted to do with my life."

She laughs. "I still don't know what I want to do with my life," she says gaily. "I hate working."

Marriage seemed like the perfect excuse to avoid such annoying questions. "I was in my second year of law school when I met my husband, and I thought, 'He's really brilliant,'" Greenberg recalls. "I felt that by marrying someone like that, I would be able to pursue the things I enjoy without having to worry about financial issues or approval or acceptance. I felt very vulnerable out there on my own, and marriage was comforting. He said, 'You don't have to do anything you don't want to do.' It seemed like the ideal thing for me."

Greenberg maintains that she's enjoyed her life as a full-time mom; her older daughter is a serious ballet student, and much of Greenberg's life revolves around shepherding her to lessons and rehearsals. "Having children has been very fulfilling for me," she insists. "It's a wonderful thing. And I still don't feel like I want to get a job. I really don't like having to be in an office at nine in the morning and knowing I have to sit there for the next seven hours."

For a long time, her marital arrangement also seemed to work well, although she was irritated by her husband's refusal to discuss money. "When I would speak to him about our finances, he would dismiss me. He would say, 'Don't worry about it. I've got it all under control,' " Greenberg reports. "When I found out that he didn't, I was really angry."

Overwhelming rage might be a better description of Greenberg's reaction to the catastrophe that has befallen her in recent months. To her horror, the former financial whiz kid who once seemed destined to make a large fortune has let her down in the most egregious way. "He lost his job last year, and he lost all our money," she says. "I was screaming at him for months. I tortured him: 'You've disappointed me! We had this deal; you were going to be very successful, and I was going to take care of the children, and everything was going to be fabulous. But this is not what I bought in for. What good are you now to me?' "

Having hitched her wagon to her husband's star only to watch it fizzle, Greenberg finds herself consumed with bitterness and disappointment. Her comfortable lifestyle might seem enviable to most Americans, but it pales in comparison with those of friends whose husbands earn millions of dollars a year. Greenberg expected to own a palatial apartment by now, but instead, "It's been seventeen years and we still rent," she says. Rather than having her own country house, she visits her parents in the suburbs when she wants to escape the city. She and her husband are now debating whether to remove their kids from the private school whose steep tuition has become an enormous burden.

To avert such unwelcome sacrifices, he is trying desperately to live up to her demands. "He's scared out of his mind now; he knows I'm at the end of my rope with him," Greenberg says. "He knows he's got to deliver."

But as the financial stress escalates, Greenberg is sorry only about her husband's inadequate performance, not about her own decision to give up her earning capacity. A second income would obviously help to sustain the family, but Greenberg says, "I'm glad I stayed home with the children."

Her regrets are directed elsewhere. "If I had it to do over again, I would not have married this man," she says grimly.

Although she continues to pride herself on what she's given her children, Greenberg does admit to a growing fear that they don't respect her. "My thirteen-year-old daughter says, 'I'm not going to wind up like you. You don't have a job; you can't buy me a Juicy T-shirt! I'm going to be a plastic surgeon, and I'll have a condo on Fifth Avenue!'" Greenberg reports. "When we didn't have any money, she said, 'Why don't you go out and get a job?' She's saying, 'I think you're less of a success because you don't have a career.' I think she sees there's a whole part of me I never pursued. She sees the frustration."

Perhaps Greenberg shouldn't be surprised if her daughters reject her as a role model; she herself spurned her own mother's advice. "When I was thirteen, my father lost his job and had to take a huge pay cut," Greenberg reports. "My mother went back to work out of anger; she said, 'I'm never going to let this happen to me again.' When I grew up, my mother said to me, 'You shouldn't depend on a man,' but I didn't heed that."

Even now, Greenberg can't imagine a life determined by her own choices rather than by those of her spouse. She has already learned the hard way that husbands can lose their jobs or mismanage the family finances, but when I point out that husbands can also become ill or even die, Greenberg sounds like some Jane Austen heroine whose horizons are irrevocably circumscribed by her marriage prospects.

"What would I do if he died?" she asks, looking at me incredulously, as if I were a particularly dim bulb. "I would get married again."

Greenberg's own mother has been baffled by that attitude ever since Wendy got married. At seventy-five, Hilda Rothstein* still works as a real-estate broker in Connecticut, and she intends to keep doing so until she drops. "I stayed home for twenty years and raised my children," Rothstein says, "but in 1973 my husband lost his job. I was devastated; in my mind my whole identity was my husband's job. We went many places, we had this great lifestyle—and all of a sudden it was over."

The seeming disaster forced Rothstein into the workplace, and she became very successful. In retrospect, she has realized some surprising things about her years as a full-time mother. "When I wasn't working, I felt that I was a nonperson," she confesses. "As a non-working spouse, I remember standing in a group and not being spoken to. When I did get the chance to talk, I had nothing to say. I wasn't doing anything that anybody wanted to talk about, except other women. There's a big difference between working women and nonworking women: Working women have more to say. They're not searching for something to talk about. Today every man in the room wants to talk to me. It's not because I'm beautiful; he wants to pick my brain about real estate!"

Because her family endured such a painful upheaval when her husband's career hit the skids, Rothstein finds it hard to believe that her own daughter failed to draw the obvious conclusions. "I expected her to work," Rothstein says indignantly. "I'm annoyed that she doesn't work. I keep telling her to get a job! I want her to be independent; I don't want her to depend on a man. I think it's important for a woman to earn her own money."

In Rothstein's opinion, the lure of a rich husband seduced her daughter away from a promising career into a lifetime of dependency. "Wendy was halfway through law school when she met her husband," Rothstein recalls. "She had never known anybody to make that kind of money. Marrying a man who was so successful—I think she just gave up all thoughts of having to think about anything financial ever again. She doesn't look at the checkbook; all she does is go to the pot to get the money. I keep telling her, 'You're spending all your time watching your daughter dance.' I say to her, 'You never know. Something could happen to your husband. You have nothing!' But she's not interested."

Rothstein's opinions about the infantilizing effects of dependency have been sharpened by the clients she meets as a real-estate broker. "Women who don't work can't make up their minds," she says. "They have a very hard time deciding what they want; they need a husband to tell them what to do. Give me a working woman any day to buy a house! I don't care if they're married or single, they're entirely different—very decisive. They know what they want; they know what they can afford. They're wonderful to work with."

Having been a working mother herself, Rothstein doesn't underestimate the difficulties of the juggling act, but she sees firsthand how devastating the alternative can be for a dependent woman whose breadwinner doesn't live up to his end of the bargain. "When I went into the real-estate business, I saw these women who had to sell their houses because their husbands left them for a girlfriend," she reports. "I saw how the children suffered, because they had to leave their homes, lose their rooms. The women who are working while they have little children are struggling, but these women who stop working to become stay-at-home moms—when they try to go back into the workforce later on, they don't get good jobs. I don't think these women who stay home are being realistic about what can happen in life."

The list of unfortunate possibilities is a long one. The wife of one Wall Street tycoon was shocked when her husband, a master-of-the-universe type who had always assured her that she could depend on him, suddenly fell apart. "He was traveling constantly and never sleeping, and he had a nervous breakdown," she confides. "He was having panic attacks, and he was at a hotel in London, and he couldn't get out of bed. I nursed him back to health, but it was touch and go for six months. I thought, 'Holy shit—he's not going to be able to work! What will I do?' I had left my career, and I was really scared that we were going to lose everything. I freaked out."

At such junctures, stay-at-home wives face tough questions about the choices they have made. But by the time they realize the dangers, it can be too late to reclaim the options that were open to them in the past.

For many women, the realization that they have made choices that permanently circumscribed their future opportunities can come as a shock. Those who are struggling financially may find themselves genuinely trapped, unable to afford either the money or the time necessary to improve their situation.

Sophie Curtis,* a fifty-year-old mother of two who lives in Ridgewood, New Jersey, used to work as a sales representative for a clothing manufacturer and then in a television-syndication sales job that required extensive travel. But her frequent absences became untenable after she started a family with her husband, a restaurant manager and bartender.

"I took a six-month leave when I was pregnant with my second child, and after six months I said, 'I can't go back,'" Curtis recalls. "When I had my kids, I had no idea I'd be so madly in love with them;

my kids were only going to be young once, and I was not going to miss the first five years of either of their lives. I was making more money than my husband was, but at that point I felt very confident about his ability to support the family."

That confidence was tragically misplaced. Although her husband moved on to an excellent position as a union business representative, he developed a serious drinking problem and, despite several stays in rehab, ultimately lost his job. "I really needed to get back into some kind of work, but my problem was that I could not leave the children with my husband, because he drank and passed out," Curtis explains. So she took a low-paying job as a teacher's aide at a day-care pre-school, where her hours were compatible with her children's school day and she could get home in five minutes if necessary.

Curtis's husband eventually left her, and they have been separated for three years. "I literally can't afford to divorce him," she says. "The money I make has to go to the bills." Her husband has remained unemployed throughout those three years, and several months ago he was diagnosed with cancer, which has since become terminal.

Supporting herself and her children continues to be a terrible struggle. Curtis is now in her seventh year at her day-care job, where she started out making $8.50 an hour and has worked her way up to earning $13 an hour. But the job offers no benefits, and although she has managed to secure health coverage for her children through Medicaid, she herself has been turned down because she makes more money than permitted under the program's regulations. "It's the working-poor syndrome," she says. "So I have no health coverage."

Trying to make ends meet, she has already sold the family's home. "The hardest thing I ever had to tell the kids was that we had to sell our house because we couldn't afford to stay there," says Curtis, who is currently living in a rental. "You can't imagine the devastation."

Looking back on her choices, Curtis has many regrets. "I should have gotten up off my ass and gone back to work a lot sooner," she says. "And my husband should have said, 'I can't carry the ball by myself.' He was playing the male role, but my decision to stay home put tremendous pressure on him. The bills continued to mount, we got behind, and we couldn't catch up. It has only come to me in the last couple of years that it's not fair to say, 'I'm the mom; I'm staying home; you pay the bills!' I said that, only to discover later that my husband resented me because of the pressure he was carrying by himself. It was just too much for him, but I failed to acknowledge that, purely out of wanting to deny it. I think that as women we have been far too willing to say, 'Well, if he can pay the bills, I can stay home.' In a twenty-first-century partnership, I don't think any of us has the right to take that much time out. I don't care if a husband is making millions of dollars—it's about equal responsibility."

Although Curtis's financial situation is dire, she can't figure out a way to improve her earning capacity at this point. She never graduated from college, she doesn't have a teaching certificate, and "there's no money for me to go back to school," she says. She wishes she had prepared herself better for financial self-sufficiency when she was younger. "Knowing what I know now, I would have given work a lot more thought than I did," she says glumly.

Back then, however, she didn't understand the risk she was taking when she let herself depend on her spouse. "Because we were financially able to manage on my husband's income, I thought my place was at home," she explains. "There was no doubt in my mind where I wanted to be, and I didn't let myself think about what happens if it all falls apart. But it did."

When I ask how she sees her future, Curtis sighs. "I see a blank wall right now," she says. "I walk a very thin line every day, and I am absolutely terrified, but I can't let myself think about it. I have managed to hold up, but if I ever allowed myself to acknowledge how petrified I am, I would stop in my tracks, and I can't do that. I have to keep moving. I'm the only one these kids have, and it's very scary. I pray a lot."

CURTIS'S OPTIONS ARE severely limited by her income, but even wealthy women can find themselves dealing with many of the same problems when their life circumstances change unexpectedly.

As a young woman, Marilena Greig worked as a stockbroker at Lehman Brothers for eight years. "I loved it," she says fervently. "I lived, breathed, and ate my job. I would have a hundred-and-three-degree fever and I would be in the office because I loved it so much!"

But when she married a broker from her company's London office, her husband suggested she leave her job and devote herself full-time to volunteer work for the American Cancer Society. "He was making seven figures; I was making six figures; and I had never taken a day off," Greig recalls. "We were living in the city, and I thought the next move was to have kids and move to the suburbs. So I quit my job, and we moved to the suburbs. On the drive from New York to New Canaan, I was bawling my head off, saying, 'What the hell am I doing? Am I nuts?' I cried the whole way."

Like so many other women who recall their life-changing choices as if they were programmed to follow some script they didn't even understand, Greig is still trying to figure out all the reasons she gave up the career she loved so much. "I felt pressure from my husband," she admits. "He was saying, 'Just give it up—give it up!' He was saying, 'You don't have to do this anymore.' I wasn't satisfied and happy giving it up, but there was a lot of persuasion from my husband, so I threw myself into the American Cancer Society. I thought, 'We're a team, he's going to make seven figures and I'm going to raise money and cure cancer.' It was as if my work with the ACS was a career, except that I wasn't getting paid for it."

After Greig had two children, she became the classic suburban mom. "My life is driving to football, to lacrosse, up to Yale for a tournament, taking my daughter to horseback riding and dancing and gymnastics—it's nonstop," she says. "I live in my car; I call it my office."

The family lives in a seven-bedroom house on five scenic acres in New Canaan, a wealthy Connecticut community. For more than a decade, Greig never thought about the potential downside of economic dependency. "The vulnerability thing did not even cross my mind," she says. "After I got over my hysteria, I thought it was great. I had the kids, the house, the husband—I thought it was the perfect life. Women grow up with this ideal, and we drop everything for it. We thought this is what we're supposed to do. It didn't matter if we had great careers; our husbands were going to do well, and we really believed this was forever."

But after eleven years as a suburban wife, Greig found herself divorced. Now forty-four, she lives alone with her two children; her ex-husband travels for weeks at a stretch and rarely sees them. "Being a single mom in this town is tough," Greig confesses. "There are times I do feel alone and isolated. That's the way it is in the country."

Greig is also having second thoughts about the privileged lives of other stay-at-home mothers. "Even though everyone puts on this happy-family facade, they could be miserable in their lives, but they would never get divorced, because they don't want to give up their material things," she says. "A lot of these women identify themselves with their husband's paycheck, and it's too important to them. The money all comes from the husbands, and the women don't want to lose their things: their house, their car, their lifestyle. Most of these women are stuck in these horribly abusive marriages where they're emotionally or physically abused or neglected, but they won't leave. They'll stay in therapy and be miserable and go buy a new Range Rover SUV. I don't know if they're afraid that they're not going to be able to support themselves or they just don't want to lose their status.

But there's a lot of drinking; the AA meeting at the church is jammed, with cars parked around the block. A lot of people smoke pot. The men do drugs and cheat. There's also some messy stuff happening, like 'key parties.' People get bored and they swap."

As an insider, Greig has developed a jaundiced view of what passes for full-time motherhood in affluent suburbia. "Everyone's got help—nannies, baby-sitters, au pairs, housekeepers," she says. "One of my friends has got a cook, a driver, and four baby-sitters for four children. The women exercise, they play tennis, they love to lunch, they shop like mad, they go to this party and that party. Their values are to look great and make sure they have the latest things and are in the right clubs. But these parents do not keep their fingers on the pulse of what their kids are doing. That's why there's so much alcohol and drug abuse among the teenagers; it's rampant at the high school."

Greig's divorce was amicable, and she feels she earned the money she receives from her ex. "I took a role in my husband's business, and I was really proud of that," she says. "He's a genius in business, but he's shy and quiet, so I would go and hold court with some of the richest men in the world, in Singapore or Hong Kong or wherever. His business has grown and grown and grown. He's the first one to say that without me he couldn't have done what he did."

And for another decade or so, Greig will continue to reap some benefits. "My alimony ends next year, but I'm not really concerned," she says. "I still get child support and a piece of his business until the kids are twenty-four." When I point out that she will then be in her mid-fifties, with no further support due from her ex-husband and no prospect of earning a substantial income on her own, Greig looks stunned. Having invested a large amount of time and energy in her husband's business, she still thinks of it as partly her own—but the bottom line is that it's his business, not hers. Once he stops paying her a percentage of the profits, she will have no further rights to the asset she helped build.

When the subject turns to what she'll do next, Greig—an animated, high-energy woman whom one could easily picture as a top corporate executive if she had made different choices—becomes subdued. "If I have to, I'll get a job and make money, but it's hard at my age to break in to things," she says uncertainly. "I feel that whatever I put my mind to, I can do. But the barriers to reentry on Wall Street are tough. I can't go back there."

As her children approach adolescence, she finds that her perspective has changed dramatically since she first got married. "Knowing what I know now, I would never have given up my career," she says wistfully. "I loved my career, and I loved the financial independence. I don't want to say I made a deal with the devil, but I kind of compromised myself. It was my dream to get married and have kids, and my mind-set was that I couldn't do both. Maybe I could have kept clients and wound it down so I wasn't working full-time, but my husband was the real genius."

And so Greig bought into the idea that the big strong man would take care of her forever. "Women have grown up believing in this fairy tale, and nothing and no one is going to change them," she says sadly. "My closest friends all had great careers, and we all left our careers for this fucking fairy tale. It's only when the fairy tale crumbles that we go, 'What the fuck were we thinking?' We've grown up to believe, and it's blind faith. I thought: You leave your job, you move to the suburbs, you have kids, and you live happily ever after. The reality is, I left my job, supported my husband in his career, and now I'm divorced and feeling like, 'Shit, I hope I can survive after my alimony's done!' It didn't even cross my mind to get assets in my name. I had so much trust in my husband. Now he gets the twenty-five-year-old who says, 'What are we going to name our son?' on the first date—and I'm done."

And yet the power of the fairy tale is so enduring that women whose lives have diverged from the ideal often feel like freaks. "They

think, 'I'm the only one out here for whom it's not all working perfectly,' " says Elizabeth Warren, a professor of contract law, bankruptcy, and commercial law at Harvard Law School. But financial
anxiety, emotional isolation, and anguished regrets are all too common
among divorced wives in wealthy communities. As one divorced New
Jersey mother put it, "I feel as if I'm living on Noah's Ark, and I'm the
only one without a partner."

Yet, while most people still think of marriage as the norm in American society, the truth is that women who don't have partners have actually become the new normal. In January 2007, *The New York Times*
reported that for "the first time, more American women are living
without a husband than with one." A *Times* analysis of census data revealed that "in 2005, 51 percent of women said they were living without a spouse, up from 35 percent in 1950 and 49 percent in 2000."

The figures are startling: In 2005, nearly 60 million women were
single or living without their husbands, compared with 57.5 million
women actually living with a spouse. Such data indicate that for many
women, "the institution of marriage did not hold the promise they
might have hoped for," concluded William Frey, a demographer with
the Brookings Institution.

But all too many are still acting as if the promise is more real than
the reality.

## CHAPTER FOUR

# OPTING BACK IN

## "NO ONE TOLD ME IT WOULD
## BE SO HARD!"

N ow that her children are five and seven years old, Diane Miller is thinking about going back to a full-time job. But when she mentioned her interest to an old friend who is a headhunter, Miller was stunned by the response.

"My friend said, 'How old are you?'" she recalls. "I told her I was forty-four, and she said, 'You're right on the cusp—you're young enough to get back into it, but you'd better do it now.' She had a client who was forty-eight, and her sense was that this woman was too old to get back in. I had never thought about age discrimination or having difficulty reentering the workforce, and I was shocked. I just assumed I could start working when I wanted to, but I guess I'm not exempt from all that. Agencies might want somebody who's younger than me, who they think they can pay less. There are all kinds of things that could work against me. It's very depressing."

That realization can come as quite a shock to stay-at-home wives. Like most women with elite credentials, Noreen Sullivan always assumed she could go back to work whenever she chose, but recently she read some labor-force statistics that prompted an upsetting doubt. "I think I can go back to work, but what if I can't?" she says. "It had never occurred to me that I couldn't find a job if I wanted one, but the article I read gave me the shivers. I always figured, 'Someone's going to want me somewhere'—but that's probably so naive."

During her twenty-year marriage, Donna Chatsworth* made many of the same assumptions. With a four-bedroom New York apartment, a country estate in northwestern Connecticut, children in expensive private schools, and lavish vacations to exotic destinations, Chatsworth appeared to enjoy more than enough privileges to compensate for the career she gave up.

But she never anticipated how severe the long-term consequences would turn out to be. Her professional sacrifices began when she married and quit her job as a financial reporter in New York and moved to Washington because her new husband had landed a high-profile assignment as a political aide on Capitol Hill. That was only the first of the demanding jobs that required him to work long hours and travel constantly. "He was very successful very early," says Chatsworth.

After she had her first child, she continued to do freelance writing and to work part-time, but she gradually scaled back her career in order to accommodate her husband's busy schedule and her family's needs. "I didn't put myself first, or even second," she says. "I had always had dreams of writing something wonderful, but fundamentally I didn't think I would be able to do it, so I married someone who could do it. I was so scared about trying and failing at something that I put myself in a secondary position in relation to him. I always thought of myself in some kind of support role."

That view was encouraged by her husband, even as Chatsworth wrote and published five books. "He referred to them as 'your little books,'" she recalls. "He also wrote books, so there was some competition around those issues; he always pointed out that my books never made the bestseller list, but his books didn't either. He always considered the stuff I had to do annoying, because it inconvenienced him and because he made so much more money. Whatever money I did make was not considered very important and was not respected. All those years, he made me feel like a piece of shit because I wasn't making hundreds of thousands of dollars. Even though I was writing books and magazine pieces and doing radio shows and raising children with an absent and uninvolved spouse, he made me feel that my accomplishments were slight and I was a failure. I was keenly aware of being valueless because I wasn't earning enough money to support the family."

When their second child developed learning disabilities and emotional problems, his time-consuming therapies were added to Chatsworth's schedule. "Our son needed so much attention that I listened to my husband when he said, 'I make more than enough money, and Jamie really needs you now; do what needs to be done for him,'" Chatsworth says. "So I gave up what I'd been doing. That was so incredibly stupid, because once you give up your little perch, even if it's part-time, you can't get it back after some time away. In a high-profile business, you lose what you're doing. But I felt like my 'little' career was in trouble and it didn't matter; I had nothing to offer anyone professionally, and I should just crawl into a hole. Because I never made a lot of money from what I was doing, I had no sense of the value of it, and I allowed myself to be defined by my husband's valuation of me."

For Chatsworth, that retreat had terrible consequences. During her years as a stay-at-home mom, she says, "I was really, really, really depressed. I was drinking too much and feeling like, 'Who am I? Can I do anything?' I felt like I was in quicksand and I would never get out. I felt that if I ever wanted to end my marriage, I wouldn't have anything. I felt totally trapped, like a smart serf. I felt awful."

Chatsworth rationalized her growing desperation with the thought that she was doing what was necessary to help her child. "I felt I had to do it, but at the same time I was either too frightened or too lazy to sustain a life outside the family," she says. "It was one of the biggest mistakes of my life."

When Chatsworth was forty-five, her husband left her. "He said I was too involved with the children, and he needed to be with someone who was more successful, someone whose professional achievements were worthy of a great man like him," she says. "In essence, he saw me as a useless hausfrau. I was absolutely hysterical. I didn't have a career, I didn't have a nest egg, I didn't have anything. I had been a total doormat. I had prostrated myself on the altar of the family and of a difficult child, and I was just being thrown away. I used to refer to myself as a Kleenex wife—'just use her and discard her.'"

By this time, her husband had made millions of dollars, but he wasn't prepared to share them, and he placed little value on her contribution to their partnership. "He offered me a hundred and ten thousand dollars for twenty years of marriage—a hundred and ten thousand dollars to live on for the rest of my life, and that was it," Chatsworth reports. "I realized, 'I don't deserve this treatment,' so I hired a lawyer, and we had a horrible four-year battle."

Chatsworth ultimately won eleven years' worth of alimony and the ownership of her New York City apartment; her husband got their country house and the flourishing career she had freed him to cultivate while she took care of all the domestic and child-rearing responsibilities.

Although she quit drinking and pulled herself together, she was rebuffed at every turn when she tried to get a job. "People treated me like I was too old to do whatever it was," says Chatworth, who was in her mid-forties at the time. "I was an object of humiliation. The rejection was very hard. Every person who turned me down was one more somebody who didn't want me, just as my husband didn't want me."

Although Chatsworth had never intended to leave the labor force permanently, the time-out to care for her son's needs turned into forcible retirement. Now sixty-two years old, she has not earned any significant income since her divorce. She has done some freelance writing, but she has been unable to find a professional job in radio, television, or the print media, despite previous experience in each field. Her alimony has ended, and the money she has saved will have to last her for the rest of her life. Her mother died at ninety-three, and Chatsworth wonders how she will support herself for another thirty years if she, too, lives that long.

"I'm nervous about my financial future," she admits. "I may have to sell my apartment so I have more money to generate income." Anticipating the loss of her home, she has reluctantly begun to clear out a forty-year accumulation of possessions.

When Chatsworth was a young wife, a well-known feminist slogan of the 1970s cautioned women that they were "one husband away from welfare." More than thirty years later, she doesn't think that much has changed with regard to wives who relinquish their income-producing capacity. "Who in her right mind would put herself on a perilous edge like that?" she says bitterly. But she already knows the answer. Like herself, she says, "Sometimes women are lazy; sometimes they're eating the lotus leaves. They live in this illusion of 'happily ever after, till death do us part.'"

Chatsworth sees her biggest mistake as having opted out of the labor force rather than continuing to work, at least part-time. "In the end, it's possible to build something from something—but it's a hell of a lot harder to build something from nothing," she says. "Women do not realize that they have to be self-sufficient; that's the most important lesson of life, and the most important thing you have to teach your children—how to take care of themselves."

THE FACT THAT Chatsworth, a former financial journalist, was shocked by her economic problems and the barriers she encountered in trying to reenter the workforce attests to how unprepared many women are for the difficulties of opting back in. One of the few publications to examine this issue in depth is the *Wall Street Journal,* whose conclusions were sobering indeed. "Many professional women who quit their jobs to raise children are trying to go back, and they're finding it harder than they ever imagined," the *Journal* reported.

Among the women it profiled was a former prosecutor in the Manhattan district attorney's office. When she tried to go back to work, she got in touch with more than a hundred employers in a search that proved fruitless; she was even rejected for a job as an executive assistant. Another woman gave up her teaching job to stay home with her children. After she and her husband divorced, she found that the only position she could get was a minimum-wage, entry-level job at Starbucks, which she was forced to take. For most of today's affluent stay-at-home wives, an impoverished future in which they're divorced and working as seven-dollars-an-hour baristas at Starbucks is hardly what they've envisioned for themselves.

Economist Sylvia Ann Hewlett, founder and president of the Center for Work-Life Policy in New York, is a leading expert on what she has called women's off-ramps in exiting their careers and the on-ramps they attempt to find for reentry. At any given time, she says, "Two-thirds of all women who quit their career to raise children are seeking to re-enter professional life and finding it exceedingly difficult. These women may think they can get back in, but my data show that it's harder than they anticipate."

In 2004, the Center for Work-Life Policy formed a task force called "The Hidden Brain Drain: Women and Minorities as Unrealized Assets" that generated a study of highly qualified women and their career paths. "Off-ramps are around every curve in the road, but once a woman has taken one, on-ramps are few and far between—and extremely costly," Hewlett wrote in her report on the survey results in the *Harvard Business Review.* "Among women who take off-ramps, the overwhelming majority have every intention of returning to the workforce—and seemingly little idea of just how difficult that will prove."

The study's findings were devastating. "Unfortunately, only 74% of off-ramped women who want to rejoin the ranks of the employed manage to do so, according to our survey," reported Hewlett, who is also head of the Gender and Public Policy Program at the School of International and Public Affairs at Columbia University. "And among these, only 40% return to full-time, professional jobs. Many (24%) take part-time jobs, and some (9%) become self-employed."

Women with elite credentials often assume they will be immune from such penalties, but in fact the opposite may be true. There is indeed a class factor affecting women's prospects for reentry, but it seems to work against privileged women rather than in favor of them, according to Barbara Ehrenreich, the author of *Bait and Switch: The (Futile) Pursuit of the American Dream*, who found that employment gaps caused by child rearing were particularly damaging. "The prohibition on gaps is pretty great," Ehrenreich told *The New York Times*. Returning to work "was certainly fine in the blue-collar world, but there was a total blank silence in the white-collar world," she added.

For qualified women who had well-established careers, the barriers to reentry can come as quite a surprise. Toni Young is a special-education teacher who lives in Fishers, Indiana, with her husband, a heating and air-conditioning technician, and their two children. Like many women, Young has varied her work schedule to accommodate the needs of her family. "I stayed home with my daughter for a year, then worked half-time for two years, then worked full-time for two years, then half-time, and then I stayed home for three and a half years with my son, and then I went back to work half-time," she reports.

Now that their older child is thirteen, the Youngs are getting nervous about the family finances. "I've been requesting a full-time contract for two years, but I can't get a full-time job," Toni says. "My husband doesn't make a huge amount of money—not good enough for us to plan for college or retirement while I'm at home. We're looking at each other and thinking, 'We've got a kid going to college in four years, and we need to plan for our son, too!' Now that we're forty-five and forty-three years old, we're starting to worry more about the amount of money we have saved. I assumed there wouldn't be a problem with me getting back on a full-time basis, but there's a hiring freeze. And teachers are a dime a dozen; there are a lot of kids getting out of school and looking for positions, and they're young and energetic. There are a hundred applications for every position that opens in my township. Being older and more expensive, I think that weighs in to my situation, too. I had a little anxiety attack when they told me I wouldn't get a full-time contract this year, but I'm not as nervous as my husband. He's getting a little anxiety-ridden about the future."

While part-time work often enables women to manage their family responsibilities with greater ease, many are equally unprepared for how dramatic the financial toll can be. "I want my daughters to know that people who work forty-four hours a week make, on average, more than twice the pay of someone working thirty-four hours a week," wrote Warren Farrell, the author of *Why Men Earn More: The Startling Truth Behind the Pay Gap—and What Women Can Do About It*, in an essay published in *The New York Times*.

When women opt out for even a brief while, the monetary consequences can be permanent. The women surveyed in Sylvia Hewlett's study took relatively brief periods of time away from the labor force—an average of 2.2 years, and only 1.2 years in the business sector. "However, even these relatively short career interruptions entail heavy financial penalties," Hewlett wrote. "Our data show that women lose an average of 18% of their earning power when they take an off-ramp. In business sectors, penalties are particularly draconian: In these fields, women's earning power dips an average of 28% when they take time out. The longer you spend out, the more severe the penalty becomes. Across sectors, women lose a staggering 37% of their earning power when they spend three or more years out of the workplace."

In an interview about her findings, Hewlett bemoaned the fate awaiting such women. "Are they going to live to the age of eighty-three and realize that they opted out of a career?" she asked.

Like Donna Chatsworth, many women make that discovery long before they reach old age. Even workers who remain in the labor force must often deal with the ugly but pervasive reality of age discrimination. If you're over a certain age—and it's a sliding scale, depending on your field, the current economy, and other variables—you're just not what most employers are looking for, even if you're a male.

In an AARP-funded study, the "résumés of equally qualified job applicants with identical skills were sent to 1,000 of the largest U.S. companies. Half the applicants were age 57, the other half were 32," the *AARP Bulletin* reported. "The companies weren't even interested in interviewing older workers," said labor economist Marc Bendick Jr., who conducted the survey.

Such findings aren't news to many older employees. Recently a very talented man I know was demoted from a job he loved and did brilliantly, in favor of a younger peer whose abilities were widely viewed as inferior. "Why are you doing this?" my friend asked his boss. "I'm better at this job than he is."

"Yes, that's true," said his boss, "but it's about potential."

When you're thirty, you still have what employers see as potential. When you're fifty—or, if you're female, maybe merely over forty—you don't. And staying home for a period of time only exacerbates the problem.

"If you've not kept your skill set up, it's not just about being smart," Carol Evans, the chief executive and founder of Working Mother Media, commented in *The New York Times*. "They are up against competition that is brutal and work that is changing very quickly in every industry. No one is going to say, 'Thank God you're back. I can't wait to hire you after fifteen years.'"

As Tory Johnson, the chief executive of Women for Hire, told the *Wall Street Journal,* "If an employer uses the criteria, 'We will hire the best person for the job,' I think it's very difficult to choose someone who's been out of the work force that long."

But how long is too long? "Even people who have been out of the workforce for six months have found it difficult to step back in," reported *The Times.*

Like the women in Hewlett's study, Vicki Gault never imagined that a yearlong time-out might fatally damage her professional prospects. Having enjoyed an impressive career at a series of high-tech and communications companies, she didn't worry about her future marketability when she accepted a buyout package in order to take a break from the strains of juggling work and family. "My plan was to give myself a one-year sabbatical, to just rest and see how the other half lives," says Gault, a New Jersey mother of three.

She had always been ambivalent about the work pressures that impinged on her family time. "After my children came along, I definitely felt that tug to be home," she says. "I felt that I was losing out; it was very difficult to leave the babies, and I felt like, 'Do I really want to be in the office when I could be playing with them?' I had a good nanny, so I didn't worry about child care, but I also thought, 'If I were at home, maybe I wouldn't be so incredibly exhausted.' The stress level for working mothers is incredibly high, and there were many times when I just wanted to opt out. On Saturdays, when you saw the working mothers, they just looked glazed. We were at the children's games with our BlackBerrys and phones, thinking about the laundry that needed to be done."

Although Gault's husband, an accountant, worked at home, "he would vaporize the minute I walked through the door, so I would start the second shift," she says. "The weekend was when I did the grocery shopping, went to the cleaners, got the Halloween costumes and the stuff for the next school musical, went to Barnes & Noble for the books for the reading list, took the kids to play dates, got the leotards for dance class. . . ."

As any working mother knows, that list goes on forever. "I was very stressed," Gault admits with a sigh. When her company moved to Pennsylvania, adding a ninety-minute commute to her daily schedule, she finally quit. "The first year and a half was wonderful," she says. "I really enjoyed being home, because it was so novel. I went from leaving the house at six A.M. to still being in bed at six A.M. I wasn't as tired; I was more relaxed with the children; I was doing things I had always wanted to be able to do, like go see an exhibit. And my ego was still very intact, because I had just quit."

But the stay-at-home life soon lost its charm. "In the last year, I've enjoyed my time less," Gault says. "The novelty factor is gone, and I'm bored. I have felt bored with myself, and I feel I'm more boring to others. In so many professions, your working exposes you to so much that's going on, to so many more people and issues. Those are the kinds of things you talk about, and I just find I have less to talk about."

Gault also became disenchanted with the fanatical pursuit of domestic perfection she saw among the stay-at-home mothers in her comfortable community. "Some of the pressures we put on ourselves don't matter; the activities are a waste of time," she says. "There are mothers who spend hours making spider cupcakes for Halloween. I think these women do these things to justify being at home. You don't have to make cupcakes that look like witches and goblins; I went to the bakery and got brown cupcakes with orange icing, and my kids are just as happy. But women at home become these übermothers who get super-involved in the children's day-to-day lives. At the elementary school, this woman was obsessing about mandatory seating arrangements in the cafeteria, and about how it was an outrage, and the kids should be able to sit wherever they want. This was a big subject of discussion among the mothers, but the school is just trying to maintain order, and I don't think this is going to be a turning point in these children's lives. But for some of these mothers, the question becomes, does your kid take violin at three and go to the Johns Hopkins program and get perfect SAT scores in seventh grade? It's just too much. What they don't realize is that you get to a point where your kids are in middle school and you have to pry stuff out of them; they just push you away. At this point, my kids would die if I visited their school once a week. When we displace our ambitions onto our children, we are not helping the children. We are making the children neurotic."

As the appeal of her stay-at-home life diminished, Gault's anxiety grew. "I have felt much more pressure to get back into the workforce," she says. "Even if I have time to read a book, I'm still tense, thinking, 'I have to find a job!' It takes the enjoyment out of a lot of things."

Already worried about her future, Gault then had to deal with a tragic loss. Six months ago, her husband went into the hospital for an aortic valve replacement. "He had a heart murmur, and he had always known he would have to replace the valve," she explains. "But he took very good care of himself—he exercised, he meditated, he did yoga. Other than his heart, he was in perfect physical condition—no smoking, no drinking, and he was a vegan—no dairy, no meat, no wheat, sugar, or flour. Heart surgery is always serious, but there was a high expectation that he would be fine."

The procedure seemed to go well, and Gault's husband was discharged from the hospital. But he was suffering from internal bleeding, and doctors gave him medication that resulted in a blood clot. "Two and a half weeks after the procedure, he was admitted to the hospital, and within twelve hours he had a massive stroke and heart attack," Gault says. "He was in a coma for a week, and then he died. He was fifty-two years old."

Gault is now an unemployed widow trying to figure out how to support her family. "I've been job hunting off and on for two years," she says. "It's awful. Now I'm actively looking for a job, but reentry is extremely difficult. And my self-esteem has suffered, because I have applied for jobs I have not gotten. That's very tough. I've been surprised that it's been so difficult. I was naive; I thought I'd still be viewed as marketable; I thought my résumé would speak for itself. But the easiest time to find a job is when you've already got a job. People don't like hiring unemployed people; they want to hire employed people. When you're trying to come back as a senior vice president, there is concern about how fresh you are. Even after a year out, employers look askance at you. They're wondering, are you up to speed? Are you current? As strong as your track record and recommendations might be, you become stale very quickly. The headhunter tells you you're overqualified and won't recommend you for certain jobs. These Harvard M.B.A. types who drop out of the workforce—when they try to go back, I don't think they realize they wouldn't even be considered for the jobs they were offered as recent Harvard graduates."

The mommy factor can be a particular impediment. "To many men, the fact that I left to spend time with my children is suspect," Gault reports. "It raises questions. They're thinking, 'Could she not cut it? Did she crumble from the pressure?' Since I'm an executive, I'm interviewing at a level where a higher proportion of female executives don't have children, so they're looking at me like, 'Oh, God, it's a mommy! She quit this great job, and now she wants to go back. Am I going to have to hear about who's got a fever or has to go to the orthodontist?' And volunteer work is not valued by hiring executives, who tend to be male; there's not one person I've talked to who gives a hoot. As far as they're concerned, it's just another pink ghetto experience."

Gault is not being paranoid in suspecting a bias against hiring mothers. A study by Cornell University sociologist Dr. Shelley Correll found that "mothers are 44 percent less likely to be hired than non-mothers who have the same resume, experience and qualifications; and mothers are offered significantly lower starting pay (study participants offered non-mothers an average of $11,000 more than mothers) for the same job as equally qualified non-mothers," according to *The Motherhood Manifesto*.

In another study, "the researchers found college students would be less willing to hire a woman with two children than they would be to hire a woman with identical qualifications who had no children," New York's *Daily News* reported recently. "Moreover, the woman with two children was judged as a lesser candidate for promotion compared to a childless woman with the same qualifications."

"People are setting higher standards for mothers than for fathers because they expect that mothers will be less committed to their jobs and will need more time off to take care of their children," explained Kathleen Fuegen, co-author of the study and assistant professor of psychology at Ohio State University's Lima campus. "Because of these expectations, people demand better qualifications from mothers."

Many women are profoundly shocked by the extent to which such penalties prevail in the workplace, particularly when it comes to getting rehired after a hiatus. "I was truly unprepared for the ageism and sexism; I did not understand how difficult it would be," says Gault, who is now fifty. "A forty-six-year-old male executive is considered a young leader, but in the business world, as in Hollywood, age works against a woman. For women, the early forties equal a man's fifties. They're always looking for someone younger and perkier. They're looking at the road ahead of you, and your runway is shorter. They're investing in you, and they're thinking, 'How long is she going to work? This is a lot to invest, to have her leave in five years.'"

By now, Gault has used up her severance package, and money is a major concern. Her husband had a "very modest" life insurance policy, she says, and the family is living on her savings. "It's tough. I'm worried. I have three children I have to put through college."

And Gault's problems with reentry are all too common. "It's tough when people come back; I'm not very encouraging about it," says

Maxine Martens, the founder of Martens & Heads!, a New York executive-search firm specializing in the beauty, fashion, and luxury-goods industries. "The whole work thing is tough these days; it's just not a slam dunk. There is no such thing as security; companies have no loyalty; everyone is very results-oriented. People pay us a big fee to get someone who's doing it now. As executive recruiters, we are getting half of the first year's salary from our clients, and it is a very hard sell for them to think about paying that much for someone who is not currently employed. The women might be interviewing with men whose wives are doing the same thing, but these men do not cut the women any slack. They say, 'I want somebody who is doing it now and who knows the people who are doing it now.'"

Martens nonetheless believes that women's chances for returning to the labor force would be significantly improved if they planned their time away with more foresight. "In my experience, people who have taken time off neglect three things that are critical to any job market," she says. "The first is to stay connected to the business; keep your network up. The second is to stay informed about what's happening. And the third is not to lose the fire and passion that are required to succeed in business these days. What we have found with people who have taken time off is that they come in and they haven't done their homework, in terms of knowing what's going on in the business they're trying to reenter. I have seen quite a few women who totally get into living in Westchester or Connecticut or wherever, and they just get removed from the business they were in. Organizing charity events and functions at your children's school does not necessarily keep you sharp. The people who are hiring are not looking for women who can organize the school book fair; it's not relevant. They're looking for someone who can show them how to get people—consumers who have too many things already—into their stores to buy their merchandise. Everyone is looking for immediate results now and relationships now. That's hard to do if you haven't kept up with your business."

But even if you try to keep up by continuing to network, reading trade journals, and maintaining or improving your technical skills, your age alone may nonetheless be considered an insurmountable problem by potential employers. "They're not running around looking for older people," Martens acknowledges. "Over fifty-five, it's very difficult to get into a corporation, because it's harder to fire you if you don't work out. And fifty is hard, because if you've taken more than ten years off, there's a generational factor. People are looking for someone young, hungry, and less expensive, and older people are more expensive. Things are changing so fast, and not keeping up with the technology is a big detriment to reentering the workforce. The ones who opted out till their kids go to college have a very tough row to hoe, because the world has changed distinctly in those years. Nobody's going to hire anyone who's been out for anything over five years except in an assistant role or an entry-level role."

Even women who try to keep up can be left behind by a rapidly evolving workplace. Madeline Wheaton* was a successful television executive and broadcaster who had one child when she was forty-one years old and twins when she was forty-three. She soon decided to take a professional time-out. "I felt gypped; I wasn't seeing my own children growing up," she says.

Then her husband left her for a younger woman, and Wheaton found herself alone with three children. In her New Jersey suburb, where everyone else seemed to live in matched pairs, she felt extremely isolated by the combination of single parenting and stay-at-home motherhood. "I had no adult interaction whatsoever," she says. "It was very lonely."

When she tried to get a new job, she discovered that her age had become a prohibitive barrier in the industry where she once wielded so much power. "I'd been out of the game for a decade and people don't remember what you've done, and I've been shocked that the barriers are so much more difficult for women than they are for men. You work all your life to gain experience and gravitas, and the men sail on with their intelligence and acuity, and the women don't. For the most part, women still have to be babes. It's sexism, pure and simple."

The truth of her assertions was confirmed for me when I ran into a female executive at a network where Wheaton was once a prized talent. When the executive told me to give Wheaton her best, I glared at her. "Why wouldn't you people let her back in?" I asked indignantly. "She can't find a job. You know how good she is! What's the problem?"

The executive shrugged. "She's an older woman, and they don't want older women," she said. "It's as simple as that." We both knew that by "they" she was referring to the men who run the corporation.

Wheaton finally got a part-time assignment that pays one-tenth of what she was earning in the late 1980s at her last full-time job. Supporting her children is a constant struggle, and she is deeply worried about their financial future.

Chatsworth, Gault, and Wheaton are smart and talented, but all three were utterly unprepared for the long-term consequences of sacrificing their careers to accommodate their families. All face a perilous and uncertain future as a result. Whatever one's views about the value of the stay-at-home life, it's hard to avoid the conclusion that women who opt out are not being adequately informed about the workplace realities that may circumscribe their options in years to come. It's nice to be at home when your child loses her fourth tooth, but is it worth the price you might pay if your breadwinner dies or divorces you, and you end up losing that home entirely?

Of course, it's not impossible for women to leave the workforce and return successfully, although many have to settle for lesser jobs or lower incomes. Nor am I saying that it's always wrong to stay home; women of independent means can enjoy that luxury with no fear, and many wives lucky enough to be supported by devoted, healthy, well-to-do husbands might well argue that economic dependency was an excellent choice for them. But millions of women are not so fortunate, and no one can know ahead of time whether the future will bring good luck or bad. In order to protect themselves, women must become more realistic and plan more effectively for the challenges they will face if they quit the workforce, intending to return later on.

"If you're going to exit, you've got to have a reentry strategy," says legal scholar Sylvia Law. "You can't just walk right back in. Even men can't."

WITH A COMBINATION of good instincts, good work, and good luck, however, some women succeed even in fields that are notoriously inhospitable to working mothers. Ann Lewis was a corporate attorney working in the pharmaceutical industry when she had twins and scaled back her work schedule to half-time. After a couple of years, she increased her hours to work three days out of five. "It was an ideal situation, except that there's no such thing as an ideal situation; it's a constant struggle," says Lewis. "My schedule enabled me to keep up my career and also spend time at home, but when you're at home, you realize all the things you could do with your kids, and when you're at work, you realize how much more there is to do at work. It was the classic feeling that you're never giving either job the full attention it deserves. I enjoyed the work, I contributed to the family income, and I didn't want to walk away from my career, but when my job got transferred from New York to New Jersey, I also had a long commute. I was just feeling too fragmented."

One night she left work late and telephoned home from the train station. "My daughter had a hundred-and-five-degree fever, and the doctor's office was telling the baby-sitter that she didn't have to bring her in, and I just felt so frustrated," she says. "I knew that no matter what I did, I couldn't be home for an hour and a half."

Already overwrought about managing her conflicting responsibilities, Lewis finally cracked one evening when she came home and picked up her eight-year-old twins at a play date. "It was around eight thirty P.M. on a pouring rainy night, and one of the kids informed me that I was 'snack mother' for class the next day," she recalls. "I just burst into tears. It was late; everyone was tired; and it was a stupid thing, but I wanted to be a good snack mom, and I couldn't do it. I didn't have time to make cupcakes; I didn't have the ingredients in the house. I felt like I was going to fail at being a mom."

Lewis was already concerned about whether her children's emotional needs were being met. "They were very rambunctious, and my baby-sitter was very passive," she says. "I felt like they needed more guidance. One day, I went out to lunch with my son and said, 'If you had one wish, what would it be?' And he said, 'That my mommy was home all the time.' That was all I needed to hear. It was an instinctive thing—I can't keep up this commute, my kids need me, I need to be with them."

So Lewis, who was then forty-one, quit her job and spent the next three years at home. "Giving up my career didn't bother me at the time; I was just very focused on my family," she says. "It was great. I picked the kids up from school every day; we went to the park and to museums; I got to know all their friends; I took them to visit their grandparents."

Although she enjoyed her new life, she says, "I was amazed at how quickly each day went by without my getting anything done. I had nothing to show for it." And so—in a move that would later prove invaluable in enhancing her marketability—Lewis created a freelance project for herself. "I had been doing pro bono work with refugees, and it became clear that there was a need for a manual on political asylum," she explains. "I applied for a grant to do it, I got the grant, and I did the manual. It was quality work, and it had a lot of social value, so it gave me a sense of purpose and accomplishment, and it kept me connected to my profession. I always realized I would eventually go back to work, and this was something concrete I had to show people—something meaningful I had done with my time while the kids were at school."

Lewis also upgraded her technology skills, a second smart choice that served her well. "When I stopped working, lawyers were not using computers; they had assistants who had computers," she says. "While I was at home, I learned how to use a word processor."

Realizing that she shouldn't let her knowledge base become obsolete, Lewis kept up with professional developments in her field as well. "In the three years I was out of the industry, a lot of stuff was changing, and it was complicated," she says. "I was absolutely determined to understand it."

Lewis showed equal wisdom in making a realistic assessment of how long her full-time domestic role was genuinely helpful to the family. As time passed, she began to worry about growing too invested in her children. "They were getting older, and I realized that I would find myself in the position of living vicariously through them if I didn't go back to work—that their accomplishments would just become too important to me," she says. "I had this vision of myself sitting around waiting for them to come home from high school; it made me feel that this was not going to be a healthy thing for me, and consequently for them. They should not be living to validate my existence."

Family finances were another factor. "I felt it wasn't fair to put the entire burden of the children's education on my husband," Lewis says. "My son made a crack that really brought home to me how the kids saw things. He compared me to a vacuum cleaner: He said, 'Daddy puts money in the bank, and Mommy vacuums it out from the cash machine.'"

And so, after three and a half years away, Lewis decided to go back to work. "I felt it was time," she says. "I felt it was going to become indulgent to stay home after a while, rather than just being what the family needed. In the back of my mind, I always knew this wasn't forever."

When she began her job search, her skills were up to date, and she was able to show prospective employers the asylum manual she had created. "It was very helpful, because it gave me something to talk about in interviews," she says.

Lewis was also realistic about her expectations. "I accepted the fact that I had lost ground and that when I came back, I would be behind where I would have been if I had kept working," she says. "I hadn't worked full-time for more than a decade, so I was grouped with people who were ten years my junior, but it didn't bother me. My philosophy was, you can't have everything. Even so, I was very lucky to find a job. I think I owed it to a couple of things. I had done reasonably well before; people knew I had worked hard; and I had taken on a project while I was at home."

But her new job turned out to be an unsatisfactory experience; Lewis was denied a promotion she felt she deserved, and younger people with what appeared to be lesser qualifications were being promoted over her. Instead of giving up, however, she turned her efforts in a different direction that ultimately proved her professional salvation. Recognizing that the pharmaceutical industry was under tremendous pressure to keep up with an exponential increase in regulatory enforcement, Lewis began to specialize in the growing field of compliance, where the need for experts was becoming ever more acute. "I spoke at conferences and took part in industry groups that added to my workload and didn't necessarily get me any points at my own company, but that gave me a great perspective on what was going on in the industry, in terms of the broader political issues," she says. "That's how I got a larger reputation. If you have the opportunity to become an expert on a particular subject matter, you have something that's your own, no matter what the politics are. Even when I was out of favor at my own company, people had to come to me, because I knew something they needed to know."

And finally, at the age of fifty-five, she was offered her dream job at another pharmaceutical company, where she is now a highly valued executive with an industry-wide reputation in her area of expertise. Because she avoided certain pitfalls and made some smart choices, Lewis ended up as a textbook example of how women can adjust their careers at various stages to address their family's needs while continuing to maintain their professional viability. But her attitude has always been pragmatic and flexible, another important element in her long-term success.

"People are spoiled; they think they can have everything, and the way things are structured now, you can't have everything at the same time," Lewis observes. "If you want to be a top partner in a major law firm, you're on call all the time, but there are many jobs in between that and nothing at all. A lot of women have a very narrow view of what success is. You may have to settle for something a little less glamorous, a little less lucrative—but there are jobs. Be more flexible about what it is you want, and compromise on your reach, because you want other things, too."

Lewis enjoyed the luxury of choosing when to leave work and when to return, but other women find such decisions forced on them by traumatic events. Sarah Portnoy, a labor lawyer who left her career to stay home with her two children, had been a suburban homemaker in New York's Westchester County for more than a decade when her husband, a stockbroker, was diagnosed with terminal heart disease.

After he died, Portnoy, who was then in her late forties, returned to work full-time. Two years later, she was named the third female partner in the history of her law firm, Proskauer Rose. Her ability to recapture a high-profile job was greatly enhanced by her previous success over more than a decade as a lawyer. "If you can postpone childbearing until you're really solid in the skill area and have built a little reputation at someplace that knows what you can do, that's a help," she says.

Portnoy also believes that the workplace bias against volunteer work doesn't necessarily apply to areas with specific professional value. "One of my volunteer positions was as human-rights commissioner for the city of White Plains, and when I went back to work in the 1970s, the labor lawyers at Proskauer were beginning to cope with discrimination laws. I had qualifications in areas that were becoming important," she says.

Portnoy recommends that women interested in reentering the workforce keep that in mind when choosing volunteer work. "What can help them is work in their area of specialization, particularly at the board level of well-known organizations, or work that involves new ideas, such as helping to start things," she says. While acknowledging that time out is still a liability, she adds, "I don't think bake sales will overcome it, but I do think real achievement in a legal volunteer area will be a big help."

Until the age of eighty, Portnoy continued to facilitate volunteerism as chair of a committee called the Public Service Network at the New York City Bar Association, which matches people who want to volunteer with organizations that need them. "We have well over a hundred fascinating things for people to do, and most of them are part-time. While you're out of the workforce, you should do things that demonstrate your continuing interest in the skill and the activities. The point is being smart about where you put your time and energy," Portnoy says.

But in order to implement such strategies, women have to be focused enough to know what they want. Those who enjoyed their careers and wish to resume them therefore have a tremendous advantage over women who never found work they loved and don't know what to do next. The result can be the stay-at-home mom's version of a classic midlife crisis.

"I think there's a lot of fear with women my age," says Diane Miller. "They're afraid of not being wanted or needed; they're afraid of not finding something they care about doing; they're afraid of failing. A lot of them took silly jobs while they were waiting to find husbands; they thought it was just going to be a short-term thing, something to do while they pursued the ultimate goal of getting married and raising kids. They don't want to go back to those jobs, but they don't know what else to do. So where do they fit? They end up taking jobs that are not that satisfying. I think there are a lot of lost middle-aged women who don't know what to do. It's really sad, because some of these women were brilliant."

Those lost women remind Baby Boomers of their mothers' generation. During the 1960s and '70s, many stay-at-home moms of the 1950s lapsed into depression after their children grew up; without meaningful work to sustain them, they often felt useless and purposeless. The divorce rate also skyrocketed during the 1970s, and when breadwinner husbands departed, their wives were frequently deprived of the financial support they had assumed they could always count on. Seeing their mothers' anguish, a lot of Baby Boomers vowed that they would never let themselves be that vulnerable.

"I saw what happened to my mom, and I learned my lessons from the negative," says Kris Myers, a fifty-five-year-old school administrator who lives in Indianapolis. "My mother put my father through medical school, but after he became a neurosurgeon, she was a stay-at-home mom. Money is power and control, and he could pretty much control what my mother did or didn't do. When I was about seventeen, they had a messy divorce in which my father had all the power; when he wanted to leave, he left. My mom had absolutely no choices. I don't think my mother ever protected herself at all; she didn't think the marriage would ever end, and she had not done anything to keep up a skill so she could work. If you don't have anything of your own, you're dependent on somebody else for what they're going to give you. But what my father paid my mother was nowhere near the lifestyle we were having, so she had to sacrifice. I thought, 'I'm not going to let anybody play that game with me.'"

Myers has been married for thirty-three years to her husband, a heating and air-conditioning contractor, but she has always guarded her autonomy. "I felt that my mother wasted a lot of her life being our mom and my father's wife, and I knew that I had to have my own identity separate from my spouse and my kids," she says. "I control my own money. All my credit cards are in my name only; my checking account is in my name only. I always wanted to make sure I could buy a car, buy a house, do whatever I wanted to do without needing to have a cosigner or a spouse, because I was self-sufficient. Love is great until it's not there anymore, but there are no guarantees that someone's going to love you forever, and I've watched too many people fight over every last dime and stick of furniture when they got divorced. If you don't think it's going to happen to you, you're a sitting duck."

Observing younger wives who voluntarily gamble their futures on a form of security that will prove illusory for too many, Baby Boomers are often astonished that they have failed to absorb this message. Didn't these women ever hear of the philosopher George Santayana's famous dictum that those who refuse to learn from history are doomed to repeat it?

## CHAPTER FIVE

# RISKY BUSINESS

## "HOW AM I GOING TO LIVE?"

I f you were to imagine some ideal version of a contented middle-aged homemaker, she might well be Ruth F., a churchgoing Midwesterner who has devoted her entire adult life to her husband and children and has never wanted anything more. At fifty-seven, Ruth has been married for thirty-five years, ever since she graduated from college. Early in her marriage, she held jobs as a typist and an office worker to help put her husband through law school, but she quit as soon as she had her first child.

"That was our goal, to have the mom stay home with the kids," recalls Ruth, who lives in Michigan. "I grew up in an era when we had our mom home with us, and I was not interested in being a career lady. I wanted to stay home with the kids, and my husband thought that was important to do. I wanted to raise my children and mold them, and I loved doing it."

Ruth never worried about the economic implications of her decision. "I knew I was going to be dependent on my husband, and I was thrilled that we didn't have to have two incomes," she says. "He was always so respectful of my abilities. I never feared that I wouldn't get my fair share."

Life being what it is, even Ruth has confronted challenges over the years. Like most long-term relationships, her marriage wasn't always easy, and there were periods when Ruth worried about her lack of self-sufficiency. "When we went through rocky times, I would say, 'Can I hold this together? Is this good for me? Is this good for the kids?'" she recalls. "If the marriage broke up, I would have been real scared. I would not have known what to do."

But when Ruth's father died, he left her an inheritance that afforded some security. "My father was adamant that you don't know what's ahead," she says. "He said, 'I want you to keep what I give you in your name only.' So I had money I could get to if I had to. It was always a safety net, so there isn't as much of a fear factor."

Nine years ago, Ruth's husband, a corporate attorney, was fired from his job. "He was out of work for a year and a half," she says. "Then I got scared, and I did have feelings of inadequacy. I can't go get a good job to pay the mortgage; given the technological revolution, my job skills were not up to date. We had significant resources to fall back on because of the inheritance I got from my dad, but we did have to cut back a lot."

And yet after her husband began working again, Ruth slipped back into her old routines, grateful the crisis was over. "I did not take it as a shove to go do something about it," she admits. "Part of it is that I was lazy." But the larger reason was that she believed she could count on her husband to resume their financial support. "We felt it was all going to be okay," she says.

Both of Ruth's children are now grown and gone, but she still defines herself in terms of her former role. "I'm a typical 1950s mom—all the errands, the repairs, the cooking, the housework," she says. "I'm the one that keeps this household running."

Ever since her younger child left home, however, Ruth has harbored some vexing doubts about her place in the world. "I have struggled for a couple of years," she admits. "I got through the first year; I had a long church project that sort of filled my time. The second year, I'm going, 'Uh-oh!' I thought, 'What am I contributing to society? What worth do I have now? What is my value at this point?' I start looking at my own home; I'm not needed here as much. There have been days, usually in winter, when I go, 'Hmmm—what am I going to do today?' I'm not bored, but I sometimes think I don't use my brain enough."

She finds some consolation in teaching adult-education classes four or five nights a month. "I work with kids who have dropped out and come back to get a high-school degree," she explains, "and I have drawn some real strength from making a difference in their lives."

But she hasn't been motivated to get a more substantial teaching job, which would require her to go back to school first. "I could probably pursue it, but I haven't felt the kick in the butt to do it," she says. "I'm a little afraid."

As things stand now, the income Ruth earns at her part-time job doesn't alter the financial picture appreciably. "This is pin money," she says, "with no benefits." But bad luck has never caught up with her, and she is not troubled by the fact that she has been dependent on the income-producing efforts of two men—her husband and father— throughout her adult life. She believes that the decision to rely on her husband has worked out well, and the rough spots were eased by her father's bequest. Nor does she regret having forgone a career in favor of staying home. "I'm really happy about the way I did it," she says. "I'm thankful I had the choice."

LIKE RUTH, SOME women get away with the high-stakes gamble of economic dependency; for a fortunate minority, the traditional female assumptions about being able to count on a husband's financial support forever will turn out to have been a good bet. "Everyone I know is perfectly happy with their life," a Chicago wife says indignantly when I broach the subject of dependency. "This has worked out very well for them."

Beautifully dressed and impeccably groomed, she enjoys an affluent lifestyle, thanks to the substantial income earned by her husband. Her friends are equally lucky. "Their marriages are happy, and the women are very busy; they do charity work, they have projects," she says. "There will always be women who want that, and it works out well for a lot of people."

There is a moment's pause as she ponders what she has just said. "But if you're the person it doesn't work out for, it's bad," she concedes.

"Being a mom is a temp job, and if you take that temp job and become completely dependent on your spouse, that makes you so vulnerable," says Sylvia Law. "The odds that your spouse will die or fall in love with a younger woman or have a midlife crisis are pretty good. Of course you can't depend on a guy—just read the divorce statistics!"

Although I always wonder why anyone would predicate her entire lifestyle on such a roll of the dice, women in well-to-do households typically feel protected from financial jeopardy even when they themselves don't earn an income. That sense of security can be a dangerous illusion, however. "Marriage is not an equal financial partnership; women assume almost all of the economic risk," observed Dr. Anna Fels in *Necessary Dreams: Ambition in Women's Changing Lives.*

Having failed to secure their financial autonomy, stay-at-home wives may learn too late how serious the consequences can be. "They are putting themselves at great risk, which may never come to pass— but things can blow up," says Darcy Howe, an investment adviser at Merrill Lynch in Kansas City, Missouri. "I see young widows and divorcées who have to buck up, and they're scared to death. They're perfectly capable, but it almost takes that jolt to bring women to the table. After they got divorced, I've seen women who had to go back to work, and they're just humiliated. They didn't pick up where they left off; they didn't get the kind of jobs they would have gotten if they hadn't left the workforce. I'd say ninety percent of the time, the women aren't as well-off as the husbands after the divorce. They lack the skills to have the kind of earning power that could keep up their lifestyle, and half of the assets are unlikely to sustain you for the rest of your life. I see women having to scrape by, as opposed to the men. What you see among women after these divorces is underemployment, resentment, and fear."

Although such outcomes have been well documented for decades, younger women typically resist the idea that forfeiting an independent income could make them vulnerable to later hardship. "It's easier to deny it than to say, 'This is what I'm sacrificing,'" observes Stephanie Coontz, the author of *Marriage: A History* and a professor at Evergreen State College in Olympia, Washington. "Some of these women are making foolish, naive choices, and some are just kidding themselves. They don't want to count up the costs. It's about illusion and self-deception."

Indeed, the feminine mistake is so deeply ingrained in women's psyches that it tends to survive even the harshest assault by contradictory facts. The very suggestion that economic dependency might confer certain risks often elicits hostility, as I repeatedly discovered during interviews with young wives.

"I don't feel like I am approaching these choices expecting the worst," says Kathy Tanning, a thirty-two-year-old who expects to scale back her work life after she has children. Her husband's Wall Street career is extremely lucrative, and Tanning seems offended at the very mention of divorce. "I don't think that's going to happen to me," she says coldly. "I don't look at life in a defensive way. I'm not thinking, 'Ten years from now, my husband's going to leave me and I'm going to be living in a one-bedroom apartment, working at the Gap.' If I saw that coming, I would prepare for it, but I don't think I would all of a sudden be blindsided."

In formulating such optimistic expectations about the future, Tanning has her own family history to draw on. "My parents have a traditional marriage, and that arrangement has worked out for them," she says. "My mom has never worked, and if my dad decided to leave, my mom would be toast—but they have a great, stable marriage. I don't think that many people in my group of friends think defensively; we don't feel like the other shoe is going to drop."

I have always been puzzled by such attitudes; no matter what one's circumstances, that kind of blind optimism strikes me as highly unrealistic. Although I have been married for nearly two decades, I have never felt it was safe to depend on any man for financial support, for a host of reasons that have nothing to do with my husband as an individual. To me, it is only sensible to think about financial contingency plans, just as it's sensible to protect yourself and your family with medical insurance or home insurance.

And yet to young women like Tanning, the willingness to plan defensively would be an unseemly indication of cynicism and negativity. The product of an exclusive prep school and an Ivy League college, she has enjoyed a privileged lifestyle, and the misfortunes that can afflict adult life—from divorce to job loss, illness, or a husband's untimely death—have little reality for her. As they plan to scale back or give up their careers, such fortunate young women typically assume that their husbands will always be ready and able to subsidize their comfortable lifestyles.

But the facts would indicate that these fortunate young women are unlikely to sustain their economic dependency over the long haul. *Money* magazine has estimated that 90 percent of all American women will be in charge of their own finances at some point in their lives.

"It's a very uncertain world, and everyone should be prepared to take care of themselves," says attorney Harriette Dorsen. "Life presents a lot of unexpected turns."

But very few stay-at-home mothers do much contingency planning to prepare for the possibility of unwelcome developments. "These women are playing without a net," says Paulanne Mancuso, a Connecticut mother of two who recently retired as CEO of Unilever Cosmetics International. "They're not only putting themselves in an extremely vulnerable position—they're putting their kids in an extremely vulnerable position. They're setting themselves up for a potentially very ugly fall."

To many observers, the most heartbreaking thing is that they're choosing such vulnerability voluntarily. "Women's impoverishment is nothing new, but in the past, women didn't have other options," observes sociologist Kathleen Gerson. "Now they do."

The dangers are manifold. "Dependent wives have built lives that are entirely dependent on another person, and that's a financially risky undertaking," says Harvard law professor Elizabeth Warren. "These are women who have made themselves entirely vulnerable to the financial whims of their husbands."

Any number of events can turn that decision into the worst mistake they ever made, starting with motherhood. "Having a child is now the single best predictor that a woman will end up in financial collapse," Warren reported in her book *The Two-Income Trap: Why Middle-Class Parents Are Going Broke.*

Mothers typically suffer a severe earnings penalty. "It is well established that women with children earn less than other women in the United States," Jane Waldfogel wrote in the *Journal of Economic Perspectives.*

And that differential is considerable. "Right now the wage gap between mothers and non-mothers is greater than between men and women—and it's actually getting bigger," reported *The Motherhood Manifesto.* "Non-mothers with an average age of 30 earn 10 percent less than their male counterparts; mothers earn 27 percent less; and single mothers earn between 34 and 44 percent less."

Over the course of a lifetime, the financial consequences of that disparity are enormous. In *The Price of Motherhood,* Ann Crittenden estimated that the "mommy tax" effectively paid by mothers in reduced earnings typically adds up to a lifetime penalty of more than $1 million for a college-educated American woman.

Even with two earners in the family, maintaining a comfortable lifestyle is far more difficult than it used to be. "It is not possible for most median-earning families to have a place in the middle class unless they have a second income," Warren says. "It now takes two incomes to buy what one income bought just a generation ago. That is an extraordinary change in one generation. Real wages for a fully employed male have remained basically flat for an entire generation, while expenses for the basics have gone up, and aspirations have risen even higher. Middle-class families can't manage this; in 75 percent of the major metropolitan areas in America, police and firefighters can't qualify to buy a home without a second income."

These pressures are steadily increasing. *The Motherhood Manifesto* states, "A study released in June 2005 found that in order to maintain income levels, parents have to work more hours—two-parent families are spending 16 percent more time at work or 500 more hours a year than in 1979 just to keep up."

In this economy, the financial picture can quickly become dire when stay-at-home wives lose their breadwinners. Divorce is obviously one of the biggest risk factors. "Too often women find themselves in a bait-and-switch situation: suddenly one party decides to breach the agreement," Dr. Anna Fels wrote in *Necessary Dreams.*

WHEN LIZ PERLE was forty-two, she quit her job and followed her husband to his new assignment in Singapore. Five weeks later, he told her their marriage was over, dropped her and their four-year-old son at the airport, and gave her fifteen hundred dollars in cash to begin her new life alone with no job and no home. "Prince Charming had left the building," Perle observed in *Money, a Memoir*, the book she wrote about her disastrous experience with economic dependency.

Although stay-at-home wives often act as if divorce were a remote possibility, the numbers indicate otherwise. The most commonly used statistic—that one in two American marriages ends in divorce—is often disputed, particularly by conservatives, as well as by full-time mothers anxious to reaffirm the security that marriage supposedly provides to traditional wives. There is reasonable support for such statistical challenges, but reliable numbers are difficult to pin down, since these figures are estimates based on future probabilities. Politically as well as mathematically fraught, such statistics are the subject of considerable debate. Many analysts are nonetheless willing to stick with the conventional figure. "Divorce statistics are projections, but I still think it's fair to say that, on average, half of all marriages end in divorce," says family historian Stephanie Coontz.

Some estimates do suggest a declining divorce rate for college-educated women, who may ultimately endure as few as half the divorces suffered by women without a four-year college degree, if current projections hold. The marriages of female college graduates "are becoming more stable," Coontz explains. "Educated people tend to have more egalitarian values, and these are more egalitarian marriages."

But many experts believe that even these caveats will ultimately have little effect on the overall divorce rate. "About half is still a very sensible statement," Dr. Larry Bumpass, an emeritus professor of sociology at the University of Wisconsin's Center for Demography and Ecology, told *The New York Times*.

In my interviews for this book, stay-at-home mothers often cited such statistical disputes in challenging the idea that their marriages have a fifty-fifty chance of ending in divorce. I understand their desire to believe that the risk they face is far lower, but quibbling over numbers like this has always seemed beside the point to me. If someone proposed a game of Russian roulette and handed you a gun, would you agree if half the barrels were loaded? If only a third of them contained bullets, would that change your perception about the wisdom of pulling the trigger? It certainly wouldn't be enough to reassure me.

Proponents of conventional gender roles also like to argue that traditional marriages are less likely to end in divorce, but those assertions are highly questionable. "Do working women's marriages fail at a higher rate than those of homemakers? No," reported Rosalind Barnett and Caryl Rivers in Women's eNews. "In fact, as University of Michigan sociologist Hiromi Ono found in 1998, a woman is more likely to divorce if she has no earnings than if she does in fact earn money. Other researchers find that the higher the household income—whatever the source—the higher the quality of family life and marriage."

Even when the marriages of stay-at-home wives endure, that fact may tell only part of the story. In a survey by *Woman's Day* magazine and AOL released in January 2007, 36 percent of 3,000 married women said they would not marry their husbands again, and another 20 percent were not sure they would. "Given that women initiate two-thirds of divorces, if traditional marriages stay together, that doesn't mean they're any happier; it means they have more to lose if they have to send their kids to bad schools and put everyone in a one-bedroom apartment," explains sociologist Barbara Risman. "In traditional marriages where women are economically dependent, the consequence of divorce is often a dramatic decrease in the standard of living. In the no-fault equal-rights era, the traditional woman is likely to get child support until the child leaves home, but the marriage is no longer presumed to be a lifelong contract that guarantees her a paycheck for the rest of her life. She's going to be thrown back into the economic sphere, where she may or may not land on her feet. The consequences of divorce are nowhere near as devastating for women who have remained in the labor force. The options are different when women are economically viable."

Stephanie Coontz says, "Women who do not have financial resources are more likely to put up with things they don't like. But if your marriage does break up, you are worse off and take much longer to recover financially than the woman who does work, so it's a big gamble. The economic penalties of the decision to drop out of the workforce are enormous, even if it's only for a little while. You almost never get back to where you would have been if you hadn't taken that time off. So the chance of not getting divorced is not worth the much greater chance that you will be terribly bad off if you do get divorced."

And those odds are increasing. "Women following divorce are in worse economic shape than ever before, because today it takes two incomes to do what one income used to do," says Elizabeth Warren.

Women's standard of living drops 36 percent when their marriages are disrupted, whereas men's standard of living rises by 28 percent. Divorced women are also more vulnerable to complete economic collapse. Women raising children alone have twice the bankruptcy rate of married couples with children, according to Warren, and four times the bankruptcy rate of single women, single men, or married couples with no children.

But stay-at-home wives rarely incorporate such risks into their decision to give up work. "People don't think about death and illness, because they hope that if they don't think about it, it won't happen to them," says Warren. "I think the same thing goes on in terms of thinking about economic fragility. Economic failure is so laden with stigma and moral opprobrium; who fails in America? Either you were a crook or you were really stupid. In the Depression, people understood that things could go wrong that can cause you to fail, even if you're a good person and careful with your money. Today I think that most people say to themselves, 'I work hard, I play by the rules. Please, God, let me believe that will keep me safe.' But women play by the rules, and the rules are not designed to keep them safe. The rules are changing, and families are not adapting fast enough. It is possible to play by all the rules and still end up on the economic trash heap. You don't need to do anything extraordinary to go broke."

With the proportion of American households headed by females growing steadily, women are particularly vulnerable to those changes. During the quarter century from 1970 to 1995, the number of families maintained by women with no husband present rose from 5.7 million to 12.2 million. And yet 23 percent of custodial mothers reported that they did not receive child-support payments in 2003.

"The media fan fears about what will happen to your kids if you work, but a much more realistic fear story is what happens if the husband dies, leaves you, or loses his job, and you have no earning power," says Stephanie Coontz. "A lot of the problems of divorce are the result of downward mobility. When you have a sudden income loss, you have to change residences; kids have to change schools, and there's the loss of their peer groups. These things are very risky for kids."

More than 14 percent of households headed by divorced women were unable to repay bills, versus 10 percent of households headed by divorced men and 8 percent of households headed by married couples, according to "The Ability of Women to Repay Debt after Divorce," a study presented at an Institute for Women's Policy Research conference in 2003. Such economic vulnerability is apparently exacerbated by a double standard that discriminates according to gender: The survey also reported that creditors demanded repayment from more households headed by divorced women than from those headed by divorced men or married couples.

"A woman raising children alone is a financial high-wire act," says Warren. "She may make it, but only if the wind doesn't blow."

Marna Tucker, a matrimonial-law expert who has been called "the grande dame of Washington divorce" by *Washingtonian* magazine, has seen all too many wives cast on the rocks after choosing dependency. "Let's look at the consequences," she says. "Those little children you're giving up your career to take care of—how are you going to take care of them when your husband leaves you? So many of my clients are former professional women who left the job market. The smart ones stay on top of the family finances and help with the investments, but a lot of them say, 'My husband handles that.' In their minds and in their husbands' minds, making money and dealing with finances is a man's role, and dealing with kids is a wife's role. I don't think women want to think about marriage as an economic unit, but I see the end results."

And Tucker is intimately familiar with the many ways a marriage can go wrong. "There are a lot of divorces where people say, 'It's never worked since the beginning,' but then there are people who say, 'I didn't see this coming—he just came in last week and said, "Goodbye, I'll see you later,"' and they're totally devastated," Tucker reports. "I think denial plays a large role. During the child-bearing years, baby comes before husband. The husbands are put on the back burner, but husbands and wives don't talk about it. It's very hard, and the marriage just sort of dwindles away. Most affairs come from a relationship with people you're around, like people working together."

The dissolution of a marriage is painful for anyone, but working women have another role and an independent income to fall back on, whereas a dependent wife's entire existence has been shattered. "The wife is left saying, 'Oh, my God—I'm forty-five years old,' or 'I'm fifty years old, and I don't know what I'm going to do! My whole life has been demolished—the future I had planned is gone! I can't believe it!'" Tucker says. "The men have the options. The women have forgone so many options—of continuing to work, of getting promotions, of earning more and more money. They have also forgone the options that youth brings you, including the other men they could have had; the market is better when you're in your twenties than in your forties."

Ironically, even as popular culture glorifies the resurgence of full-time motherhood, the legal and financial supports that once provided a safety net for that choice are eroding. "Things are changing in the courts," says one stay-at-home mother who recently began divorce proceedings. "Lifetime alimony is becoming a thing of the past; now they're talking about 'rehabilitative alimony.' Judges are much less likely to say, 'You poor little lady, we'll make sure he takes care of you.' And in the long run, alimony isn't even an answer; alimony still means you're financially dependent on the man. If he dies, if he gets laid off, if he has financial reverses, you're still in the dependent mode where your fate is tied to what he does."

Legal experts confirm the trend toward awarding short-term support, which makes it far more difficult for stay-at-home wives to recover financially when their breadwinners move on. "What rehabilitative alimony means is a term limit, to allow the woman to get back on her feet—as if in two or three years life will be just as it has been," Marna Tucker explains. "I have to tell them, 'Even though you've been out of the job market for seventeen years, the expectation is that you've got an Ivy League education and the kids are going off to college, so the most a court is going to do is give you a couple of years to get back up to snuff.' If she's in her forties and her husband leaves her, she's going to say, 'I need to have a hundred and fifty thousand dollars a year to live.' The court says, 'We'll give you a hundred thousand dollars for three years, and that's it. After that, you are capable of earning enough to support yourself.' The women are terrified. They have to figure out how to support their kids, and the men go on to the next wife."

Court-ordered child-support payments don't necessarily solve the problem; the U.S. Department of Health and Human Services estimates that 69.7 percent of child-support cases had arrears owed in 2005, a figure that rose from 53 percent in 1999.

According to many legal scholars, even reforms aimed at equalizing the impact of divorce have had a disproportionately negative effect on women. "The law doesn't recognize that they're in very different circumstances," says Martha Fineman, a professor at Emory School of

Law in Atlanta and a leading authority on family law. "You take the rules that say you're entitled to fifty percent of the property—that's devastating for the average Jane where the marital equity is tied up in the house. She might get to use that house till the kids are grown, but then the child support stops, the house gets sold, she gets half, and she ends up substantially disadvantaged. Our society is not structured to accommodate caretaking, and there's no accounting for the work she's done. That's what the equality revolution has done—the law says, 'They're equal partners, so we're going to treat them equally.' But no matter what class they're from, stay-at-home mothers are tremendously disadvantaged. Women put an up-front investment into the marital relationship when they have children, which entails a disengagement or withdrawal from their careers that causes a decline in their earnings and in their earnings potential. If divorce occurs, the woman has produced children, which are a joint asset—but the man has produced his career, with all the perks he got from her contributions. He walks away with his career and his future earnings capacity. The end result is that the standard of living of the custodial parent and the children declines; you can document that across the board, at every income level. For working-class women, it's a disaster, because they have no assets."

Divorcing men typically underestimate or discount the long-term financial value of their wives' contributions to the marital partnership, but those contributions are significant. A recent study by the Massachusetts-based compensation experts at Salary.com found that stay-at-home mothers would earn $134,121 a year if they were actually paid for the 91.6 hours of domestic work they provide every week. (These calculations assume an average pay of approximately $22 an hour.) The survey also found that employed mothers put in a weekly 49.8 hours of domestic work in the infamous "second shift," which would earn them an extra $85,876 on top of their actual wages if they received additional pay for those services.

Other surveys value women's domestic contributions at even higher rates. "One financial planning company, Edelman Financial Services, has in fact added up the annual salaries of workers among seventeen occupations engaged in by a busy mother (pet care, house-keeping, etc.) and come up with an estimated $707,126 annual pay-check," *The New York Times* reported.

Even among the wealthy, few men would consider paying their wives an annual $134,121 for running their households and raising their children, let alone $700,000. And when divorce looms, their val-uation of the women's contributions only goes down. "The men have been a success all their lives, and they always talk about it as if 'I'm giving her this' or 'I'm not giving her alimony'—as if it's all their money," Tucker observes. "The law has a partnership view of mar-riage, so it shouldn't be that way, but it's very hard to get the men to see it that way. If they earned it, they feel it's their money, so why is she entitled? They always say, 'She's a wonderful mother, and the kids are terrific, but I've already paid for that.'"

Those attitudes are all too familiar to families who have lived through such an upheaval. "My father came home one night and said, 'I'm leaving,' and that was it," says one young mother who lives in Illi-nois. "My mom went after my dad for support, but he didn't feel like she deserved what was equal. He was like, 'It's my career; I've worked hard; this is mine.'"

And when the breadwinner plays hardball, a divorce can turn ugly indeed. "One of my clients is an artist who makes a little money; her husband makes two hundred thousand dollars a year, but he said, 'I'll stop working before I'll pay you one dollar of alimony,'" Tucker re-ports. "All the money has been used up by fighting, and he's claiming he can't work anymore. I see people claiming disability, and the minute they get divorced, he's going to be back working."

In order to avoid the worst economic consequences of a bad divorce, experts recommend that women who leave the workforce must be more practical about protecting their financial interests. "The women who do see the long-term come to me for prenuptial agreements," Tucker says. "They know they may have to take off a few years of their career, or move from New York to Seattle for his career, and they're worried. They're saying, 'What do we do?' So we do things like say, 'For every year she was out of the job market, she will get so much more money in the event of divorce.' But prenups are very hard for engaged couples to talk about. Ninety percent do not think about the consequences, because they're in love and getting married, and their spouse says, 'We'll work it out, and it will be fine.' It's very difficult for men and women to talk about these issues."

For those who failed to obtain prenups, Tucker offers another strategy. "I came up with the idea of a postnup for situations where people want to correct the financial issue in their marriage while they're still married," she explains. "It's a solution short of divorce for a lot of people. I see a lot of women who have had careers who are not happy with dependency. They say, 'I've always had my own money, and now I can't buy him a present without him knowing.' They say, 'I hate having to ask him.' So we try to set up a little nest egg, but they're still dependent. I had one client who was married to a wealthy guy and raising four kids. She missed being able to have her own money, and it was becoming a real bone of contention. We worked out an arrangement where he would give her a percentage of his income while they were still married, and that money would be hers to do whatever she pleased."

But such arrangements are the exception; in most cases, women continue to trust their partners until the worst happens. By the time they realize how much danger they're in, it's often too late to do anything about it. Jane Morgan* had been married for twenty-seven years when her husband, the foreman at a car manufacturing factory in the Midwest, suddenly left her. A stay-at-home mother who got married at the age of eighteen ("Dumb move," she says), Morgan had focused all her energies on providing a good home for the family.

"I enjoyed being with the kids, and I thought it was a great idea," she says. "I wanted to be there so they could come home for lunch; I wanted to be involved in school activities; and at the time everything seemed to be going good. I just thought, 'We're going to be married forever, and this is great.' That was a big error. I thought he loved me. I certainly loved him. I was real naive."

When I mention the risks of financial dependency, Morgan sighs. "I honestly never thought about any of those things," she says. "Not until he walked did I start thinking about those things."

But one Saturday morning, her husband came downstairs and calmly made an announcement. "He said he needed some time to think; he needed to get on his own for a while. He picked up some things and left," Morgan says. "I was just devastated. This was out of the blue; it was like he walked in one day and threw a bomb in our living room and blew everything up. I had no idea he was having an affair—none. I was so dumb! I used to say, 'Oh, a wife would have to know.' But I just didn't have a clue. I really trusted him. I couldn't believe he was having an affair; I think I was the only one who didn't realize it. It was someone he worked with—a woman who was fifteen years younger."

At first the whole upheaval seemed utterly surreal. "I walked around in a fog," Morgan says. "I couldn't believe it was happening to me." Indeed, her husband had given her every reason to expect that he would always take care of her. "When our sons were in high school, I didn't have as much to do; you can only clean your house so many times," she says. "So I got a job at a medical-supply company, but my husband wasn't thrilled about me working. He thought I should be home."

And Morgan was used to obeying her husband. "He was the domineering factor in our relationship," she says. "In the time I grew up in, you were programmed; you went to school, and you got married, and your husband was the boss. When he raised his voice, it scared me, and I would fall right into line. But after he left, I went to counseling. When he would raise his voice, I said, 'Shame on you—that doesn't work anymore!' Then I knew I was getting better."

Although her emotional health gradually improved, Morgan was horrendously unprepared to take financial control of her own life. "I was scared to death about what was going to happen to me," she says. "I wasn't building a pension on my own. He had control of everything. His name was on the checkbook; he handled all the financial affairs. Everyone said, 'You've got to see an attorney.' I thought, 'How am I going to pay for an attorney? How am I going to live?'"

Then came another blow. "The fellow I was working for retired, and the medical-supply company closed," Morgan says. Finding another job seemed an insurmountable challenge. "I'm not a great typist; I had no computer experience; I didn't really have any skills. Our economy is just awful around here. The factories and plants are closing; they're laying off thousands of people. Even with a degree, you could walk in to look for a job and there could be twenty people with the same degree and more experience. Employers have their pick."

Although Morgan once lived a comfortable middle-class life, she was so desperate that she began to clean houses and office buildings for a living. "It's hard work, and I work a lot of hours," she says. "Sometimes I'll have four houses to do in a day. Sometimes I start at five A.M. and work until five at night. If a job comes up on the weekends, I'll take it. I work my fanny off."

She is surviving financially as a cleaning woman, but her situation is precarious. She has no health insurance, and she has had to give up many cherished aspects of her former lifestyle. "I can pay my bills," she says. "Some months are better than others, but I'm not on public assistance. When I was married, we took vacations, which I rarely take now; I had more money to spend on clothing and extra things like skiing, which I could do then. But when my husband left, I thought, 'I've got to do something to get out all this frustration,' and I started walking. He had always told me I wasn't an athlete, and I believed him, but after I started walking, I started running, and then I started doing marathons and triathlons. I was very amazed at myself, after being told for so many years, 'You can't do this; you can't do that.' I bloomed into something I had never been before. Racing became a social thing, and it kind of kept me sane. But I don't enter races anymore; they're sixty dollars or seventy dollars to enter, and it's too expensive."

Morgan and her husband were separated for six years before they finally got divorced, after thirty-three years of marriage. "He got a better attorney than I did," she says. "I got alimony, but I lost most of it when he retired. Right now, I'm getting six hundred and fifty dollars a month in alimony, but he has gone back to court asking for all alimony to be stopped."

As her arthritis worsens, scrubbing floors on her hands and knees has become a painful challenge, and Morgan wonders how she will support herself into old age. "I say a secret prayer every night," she says. "I've never been one to complain, but I'm now sixty years old, and there are times when I get up in the morning and say, 'Jeez, I don't want to do this!'"

Her ex-husband has married his girlfriend, and Morgan still can't get over what happened to the partnership in which she invested her entire life. "It was like the whole family just blew up," she says sadly. "If I had it to do over again, I wouldn't have been a stay-at-home wife. I could have worked all my life, retired, and had a pension and not worried about it—but I didn't."

When she talks to young women, Morgan understands their desire to stay home with their children, but she worries about their obliviousness to the risks of dependency. "I hope it all works out for everyone; I wouldn't want what happened to me to happen to anyone. But I would tell them always to keep it in mind that it could happen," she says. "If you cover yourself a little bit, you wouldn't be in the position I was in. Relying on your husband, thinking he's always going to be

there, thinking he's not going to have an affair, thinking he's not going
to walk out on you, thinking he's not going to die—that's not a good
thing. I'm amazed at the women who don't see that. Everything has
changed so much since I was young, but obviously this hasn't."

From Morgan's vantage point, economic dependency doesn't look
like such a great deal anymore. "I really am amazed that there are
women out there who still do that," she says.

Too late, Morgan now understands that the most compelling arguments against a stay-at-home lifestyle have nothing to do with the
needs of children or the values of their mothers. No matter what your
social class or circumstances, your politics or opinions about women's
role in society, the crucial issue is financial self-sufficiency. Any clear-
eyed assessment of the harsh economic, social, and actuarial realities
of contemporary America makes it obvious that financial dependency
is no longer a safe choice for any woman.

DURING EARLIER ERAS—when divorce was stigmatized and men
worked for the same company for forty years before retiring with a
gold watch—most middle-class families could count on relative stabil-
ity in their home and work lives. Those days are long gone. Real job
security is increasingly rare, as are comfortable pensions from stable
corporations that you can count on until you die. The American pension system, both public and private, "is broken," as *The New York
Times* recently put it.

The pension systems that do remain solvent typically benefit men
to a disproportionate degree. Women aged sixty-five and older are half
as likely as men the same age to have income from pensions; only 22
percent of women receive pensions, as compared with 44 percent of
men, according to "The Effects of the President's Social Security Proposal on Women," a report on the proposal to privatize Social Security
that was released in March 2006.

"And when women do have pensions, they're much less, because they've worked less and earned less per hour," says economist Heidi Hartmann. "The amount of the pension is about half. Even for married women, when a man dies, they may lose his pension, and her Social Security will usually go down."

Older women also have less savings than do men. "The typical woman's 401(k) balance is 40 percent lower than the typical man's ($10,000 vs. $17,000)," the *AARP Bulletin* reported recently.

Women are therefore more reliant on Social Security for economic survival. Social Security payments account for an average of 74 percent of the retirement income of nonmarried women aged sixty-five or older, compared with 66 percent for nonmarried men in the same age group, according to the same Social Security report. Social Security is the only source of income for more than a quarter of all women aged sixty-five or older.

Today it's every wage earner for himself, and most men understand that they are dealing with a radically different world from the one in which their parents lived. Noting that his own father retired at fifty-eight with a generous pension that gave him a comfortable lifestyle for another thirty years, editor William Falk wrote in *The Week* magazine, "That era is gone. We're all free agents now, and the moment you stop producing, you're dead wood. By choice or by necessity, most of us jump from job to job and reinvent ourselves three or four times before we're 60 . . . No point in griping. Corporate paternalism and the nanny state are so 20th century. From here on in, God bless the child that's got his own."

Because women have been slower to recognize the implications of these changes, they continue to be disproportionately penalized. Even when both men and women are working full-time, the wage gap remains significant. "For year-round full-time earnings, women make three-quarters of what men make," Hartmann reports.

But those figures don't tell the whole story, because so many women work part-time or move in and out of the labor market. When such interruptions are taken into consideration, the gender penalty rises dramatically, as demonstrated by Hartmann's study "Still a Man's Labor Market." "I looked at men and women over fifteen years, and found that the typical woman who worked made 38 percent of what the typical man earned in the same period," Hartmann reports. "The decision women are making is to work quite a lot less than men. They're also earning less per hour, which means that women are definitely at risk financially, both when a marriage breaks up and at older ages when they will likely be alone."

Or, to put it succinctly, "The more time you spend taking care of children, the less you earn," says Ellen Galinsky, president of the Families and Work Institute, a nonprofit research center.

Compounding the economic problem is the fact that female life expectancy is steadily increasing. On average, American women outlive men by five years, according to the National Center for Health Statistics. Women also tend to marry older men, another factor that has led experts to predict that seven out of ten Baby Boomer women will outlive their husbands. In 2003, 27 percent of sixty-five-year-old women were expected to live to the age of ninety.

Such statistics prompt many middle-aged women—even married ones—to joke nervously about their prospects of ending up as bag ladies eating cat food. But the common female fear of a destitute old age is no joke. Fourteen percent of women aged seventy-five and older now live in poverty—nearly double the 7.7 percent of men the same age living in poverty. The risks are particularly great for women who end up alone. "Only five percent of aged married women are poor; in contrast, twenty-two percent of divorced, twenty percent of never-married, and eighteen percent of widowed women age sixty-five and older are poor," said Jane Ross, the deputy commissioner for policy at the Social Security Administration, in testimony before the Senate Special Committee on Aging in 1999.

These numbers may well rise in years to come. "If women hold back on working and opt for family, and the family doesn't pan out for them, then we'll see the poverty rate for women in old age go up, because they will have neither the labor-market exposure nor the family," Hartmann says.

The current projections are daunting. At a White House Conference on Aging in 2005, Paul Hodge, chairperson of the Global Generations Policy Institute and director of the Harvard Generations Policy Program, testified that more than 30 million of America's 40-million-plus Boomer women will not be able to afford to retire, will fall below the poverty line, and will experience poorer health in their later years with limited aid from traditional safety nets.

Women also have a far greater chance of ending up alone than men do. The average age of widowhood in America is only fifty-five, according to a keynote speech delivered at an AARP event last year by Ted Mathas, executive vice president of the New York Life Insurance Company. Citing U.S. government data, Mathas also told the audience that four out of five widows living below the poverty line had not been poor before their husbands died.

Among people aged sixty-five or older, 43 percent of women are widowed, versus only 14 percent of men. "There are 1.4 million aged widows who receive Social Security benefits and have family incomes below the poverty line," Ross reported.

In a highly volatile job market where American workers are competing with the impact of globalization, unemployment is a common risk factor. When the husband of a nonworking wife loses his job, the family is suddenly stripped of its only income. "Two-thirds of all families that file for bankruptcy do so following a job loss, and half do so following a serious illness in the family," reports Elizabeth Warren.

My own husband, a writer and editor, lost his job without warning when the financial backer of the magazine he was working for suddenly decided to close it down. My husband received two weeks' severance pay; it took him six months to find a comparable full-time job, during which time I was profoundly grateful to be able to support our family. That period of financial instability also sharpened my sense of women's vulnerability when they are not prepared to earn a living. The feeling of accomplishment you get from running a school bake sale or making a child's Halloween costume is lovely, but the feeling of empowerment you get out of saving your children from losing their home or their education is a different order of magnitude entirely.

Job loss is only one of the perils that can traumatize families; other common risk factors include illness and disability. What happens when the breadwinner husband gets sick or is injured and can't work? I know one woman whose husband has battled multiple cancers for nearly a decade. He hasn't been able to work for years. Another husband I know is an electrician whose wife refuses to get a job; when a broken leg put him out of commission, his family's income evaporated. A neighbor's husband was hit by a car while walking the dog one night. Although he survived the accident, he is severely brain-damaged and will never be able to work again. Unable to provide adequate care, his wife had to institutionalize him.

No one anticipates such catastrophes when they're young and healthy, but lives are full of unforeseen challenges, and it seems foolish not to plan for any contingencies.

And yet few of today's "new wives" bother to do the math. Assuming that their marriages will always remain the way they are in the early years of hope and optimism, they scoff at the idea that things could go wrong in the future. At a parents' function at my children's school, another mother asks me about the book I'm working on, and I tell her that it's about women and economic dependency. A stay-at-home mom, she laughs ruefully. "My mother is always telling me I have to make sure some of our assets are in my name," she says.

Has she taken care of doing so?

"Nah," she replies nonchalantly, as if ensuring her share of the family's net worth were less urgent than making her weekly pedicure appointment.

To more seasoned observers, this willingness to relinquish control of one's financial destiny bespeaks a breathtaking complacency about the future. Having made the classic "feminine mistake" of thinking that a man will take care of them forever, too many older women have learned, too late, what it's like to end up on the wrong side of the odds.

SALLY ROBERTS* ASSUMED that her adult life would be spent as a wife and mother, so she didn't bother with college, working instead as a keypunch operator at an office-furniture manufacturer until she got married at the age of twenty-five. She and her husband had two children, and Roberts followed unquestioningly as her husband was transferred from one Michigan location to another during the early years of his career in bank management. "It was important to both of us that I was able to stay home with our children, and I loved it," she says.

After both their children were in school all day, Roberts worked part-time as a salesperson in a clothing store. "I was home when my daughter got home from school," she says. "I had the best of both worlds."

But then her husband got transferred again, and Roberts had difficulty finding another job. Although her husband's career had always dictated the family's choices, Roberts didn't perceive herself as an economic dependent who was sacrificing her own interests to those of her breadwinner spouse. "I never thought about it, because I thought we would always be together, so it was not something I ever worried about," she says. "We always felt our life was a partnership. He was earning the money, but I was the one keeping things running, and he appreciated what I did. The only time I ever worried about it was during one period when he was unhappy and I thought, 'What would I do?' The thought of supporting myself or the children was scary; I didn't have a college degree, and I didn't have a lot of skills. Up until that point, I never had even thought about being vulnerable. He went through a period when his job was very stressful, and we were in marriage counseling, but after that I felt things were very good between us again."

When her children were teenagers, an aunt died and left Roberts her stock portfolio, but she and her husband used the money to make repairs on their house, buy a motor home, and put their children through college. And then, after the kids were on their own, the unthinkable happened.

"My husband moved out," she says. "One day, he said he was not happy with his life. He said there wasn't someone else, but I think there was. I asked whether he would go talk to someone in counseling, and he refused; he had already made up his mind. He didn't love me anymore. I had no husband and no job. I was devastated. I was like, 'What am I going to do?'"

Her husband offered a simple proposal. "He said, 'You can keep the money you have, and we'll split the house and the motor home equally,'" Roberts reports. But their assets had been enhanced by the money she inherited, and he was entitled to an equal share—whereas Roberts would receive no compensation for having sacrificed her own career to his over more than three decades. "I actually had to go to court to get spousal support and half his pension," she says.

Roberts's husband remarried ten days after their divorce came through—"someone he knew from work who has long, curly blond hair and lots of makeup and wears miniskirts," she says. During that period, Roberts was consumed by grief and anger. "I went through two years of a lot of sadness, a lot of tears, a lot of yelling, a lot of swearing," she says. "It was awful. I don't use the F-word, but one day I went to my sister's house and she opened the door and I said, 'That fucking asshole!' My sister said, 'I wondered when you were going to get to that point.' My sister got divorced after twenty years of marriage; she had three children, one of whom has cystic fibrosis, and her husband did not pay her any child support. He was supposed to, but he moved out of the area, and it was so hard for her to collect the money that she got it very seldom. He just kind of cut himself off; he'd see his kids maybe once a year. If it wasn't for our parents and me helping her whenever we could, her gas would have been turned off many times."

As long as Roberts's ex-husband continued to work, she received $17,000 a year in spousal support. "But then he lost his job, because the bank he was working for moved, and I went from getting $658 every two weeks to getting nothing," Roberts reports. "I was sick to my stomach. I felt like, 'What am I going to do?' When he did get back to work, he was making $40,000, and then he was out of work again. Then he got another job at a bank, and he just got let go again. He's lost three jobs since our divorce."

Having based her entire life on the assumption that she could count on her husband to support her, Roberts still finds it hard to explain what went wrong. "I always felt that he was a trustworthy person, but something happened to him," she says. "It truly surprised me. I didn't think my husband was going to change into a different person; I never thought he would be someone who would walk away—but he did. I thought our whole family life was too important to him. I think that's what surprised me most, that he was able to end the whole situation. But he got tired of domestic tasks; he was tired of cleaning the pool; he was tired of cutting the grass. The person he is now is not the person I was married to."

These days, Roberts works as a loan officer at a credit union; she is able to support herself, and she sees no point in second-guessing her past. "I'm very happy with my life now, but it's not the life I thought I was going to have at this point," she says. "It's very easy, in hindsight, to say, 'I wish I had gotten a college degree,' but when I graduated from high school, there wasn't really anything I wanted to do."

Despite the hardships she has endured, Roberts doesn't regret the years she spent at home with her family. "To me, raising children is as important a job as any anyone can have," she says. "If I had my choice, I would love for every mother to be able to stay home for the first few years of her children's lives. I think it's a very special time to watch your children grow. I truthfully don't know how you protect yourself, except to have an education and life skills. I think if you have an education and work before you have children, it's easier to get back into the job market."

Her own daughter, who has two children, has heeded the painful lessons provided by her mother's experience. "I feel sad that my daughter has to go to work every day," Roberts says. "In a perfect world, she could work maybe three days a week, but it's not a perfect world, and you do what you have to do. I'm very glad my daughter has a college degree and a good job. I think it's extraordinarily important today for anybody, male or female, to have some type of education or trade. I went into marriage with the idea that I was going to be married for the rest of my life, but I think it's very important for a woman to have skills that will sustain her if something happens. I have a good friend whose husband dropped dead when she was forty-five; I have three or four friends who have gotten divorced. In one couple I know, the husband owns his own business, and it went through a couple of really bad years, so she worked."

Such friends are struggling, and the women who are alone have seen their standard of living decline in comparison with what they were used to. But they work hard to avoid self-pity and accept their lot in life.

"We're a strong breed," Roberts says. "We have to be, don't we?"

CHAPTER SIX

# THE FIFTEEN-YEAR PARADIGM

## "IT REALLY DOES GET EASIER!"

Recently I met a thirty-eight-year-old friend for lunch and found her in an agitated state. Maintaining a demanding career while juggling the needs of two children, one with serious medical issues, Alicia Hobson* was feeling exhausted and overwhelmed. Her husband had been working on a project that required constant travel, which put tremendous pressure on Alicia to take up the slack at home.

"I just can't do this anymore," she wailed.

So Alicia had decided to ask her boss if she could work part-time. Knowing that I am an extremely committed and engaged parent, she asked my opinion, clearly expecting me to agree that she should reduce her job responsibilities and concentrate on the home front.

Instead I told her I thought it would be a terrible mistake. Alicia's husband is a freelancer whose income is variable and insecure. Their family derives its health coverage and other benefits from her job.

"I understand how torn you feel right now, but what about your long-term future?" I asked. "Derailing your career could make you very vulnerable financially. Have you ever thought about what you'd do if something happened to Matthew and you had to support your family? In five years, your kids will both be out of elementary school, but if you've sidelined your career, it may be very difficult to catch up by that time."

And then I told her about the fifteen-year paradigm.

For most working women, adding children to their already busy lives creates stresses that can seem intolerable. Whipsawed by the conflicting demands of job and family, they often feel as if they're coming unglued. The most obvious solution is to give up the juggling act. "If the question is, do I want to be totally stressed out and unhappy or not?—it seems like an easy decision if finances are not a factor," says Vicki Gault, who quit her job for similar reasons.

While they're in the middle of the maelstrom, however, few women consider the relatively finite nature of such conflicts. When my children were young, I, too, felt overwhelmed. My job allowed me to work from a home office, but it also required me to travel all over the world. At times, I found myself on another continent, frantically juggling the inevitable complications at home by long-distance telephone. Such crises are familiar to virtually every working mother. As I was writing this, I got an e-mail from an executive I know who lives in New Jersey but is currently on assignment in Kansas City. Her husband is at work in New York, but their daughter just started vomiting at her school back home in New Jersey.

And so—from half the country away—the mom is desperately trying to find someone to pick up her sick child. Logistical challenges like that are always daunting, and sometimes they're so discouraging that you feel you can't bear the pressure anymore. But when things got bad, I always consoled myself with the reminder that the acute phase of mothering wouldn't last forever.

For me, it ultimately came down to a question of simple arithmetic. I joined the full-time labor force even before I graduated from college at the age of twenty. As a writer, I intend to continue working indefinitely, but if I retired at the relatively young age of seventy, I would already have worked for fifty years. With two children who are three years apart in age, I spent close to fifteen years feeling pressed by the demands of running our household and being an attentive parent.

But as my children got older, the domestic pressures on me began to lessen. The kids' days grew longer and longer; they left the house at 7:30 A.M., and with after-school activities, music lessons, sports, and play dates to fill up their afternoons, they often didn't return home until 6:00 P.M. By the time they were old enough not to need a baby-sitter, they were also old enough to shoulder some of the household chores.

My kids are now seventeen and fourteen, and the last few years have been comparatively easy for me. On the way home from school, my daughter or my son stops at the grocery store on the corner to buy milk, fresh fruit, and other daily staples—an annoying daily responsibility I am happy to delegate. I can't remember the last time I felt as though my head were going to implode from the strain of competing obligations, although this used to be a fairly common occurrence. But the really difficult period amounts to fewer than fifteen years out of the fifty-plus I will spend in the workforce overall—a relatively short period, if you take the long view. In exchange for staying the course, I've been able to enjoy an immensely rewarding career—not to mention an income that has sustained my family during some really difficult times when my husband's employment was interrupted.

"I know how stressful this phase is, but it doesn't last forever," I told Alicia. "Instead of feeling that you're going crazy and you can't stand it anymore, try to look at it as a fifteen-year marathon. You're running a race, and it's hard—but you're already more than halfway to the finish line. You've made a brilliant success out of it thus far, and this is no time to give up. The consequences for your later life could be too risky."

During their children's formative years, the conflicts felt by working mothers are often agonizing. But Alicia had a wonderful baby-sitter, and her own job was flexible enough that she could be on hand whenever her children really needed or wanted her. As we discussed the logistics of her workday, Alicia realized that she really didn't have to derail her career on a part-time mommy track. She could simply rearrange her schedule to work from home more often; her boss didn't care, as long as she got her work done. Alicia lives in New York City, only a fifteen-minute taxi ride from her office; armed with a cell phone, she can remain in constant contact and be available for impromptu meetings whenever necessary.

But Alicia's children go to school with lots of privileged classmates whose stay-at-home mommies make her feel guilty for working. Exhausted from the pervasive cultural pressure of the stay-at-home ideal, Alicia had been seduced into thinking that the only solution to her present angst was to give up her career.

For many women, such conclusions reflect the natural human tendency to believe that the grass is greener on the other side of the fence. "In the 1950s, my mother's generation looked longingly at work and thought about how much better it would be, whereas people in today's workforce look longingly at *Ozzie and Harriet* and think, 'Wouldn't it be nice to quit!'" says family historian Stephanie Coontz. "That's the illusion that's fed by sitcom images. The media fans the fears about what will happen to your kids, and there's frustration with the work world, so women think maybe they should quit. There's this wishful thinking that everything will be fine if you make this decision."

But that's not the only solution—nor is it necessarily the best one. In previous eras, women had more children and were unable to control their fertility, but in today's world childbearing and child rearing represent a shrinking proportion of women's lives. Because people are living longer and having fewer children, the period of time we spend as parents of young children is decreasing, in real terms as well as in relation to our life spans.

The consequences of this shift are profound. "Both men and women can have both a family and a high-powered work life, and there are many ways to do it," says Sylvia Law. "One way is to do everything simultaneously, which is the way I did it. You have to be healthy, and you have to be willing to give up sleep, but you can perform at a high-powered job and be a good parent. But there are other models."

Although Law acknowledges the difficulties of reentering the workplace after opting out, she knows many women who have done so, with varying degrees of success. "You can take time out and go back. You can have kids when you're still in graduate school, because academic life is more accommodating to families than the workplace is. By the time you graduate from law school, your kids are ready to go to school. But the false message that the mainstream media are putting out there for women is that it's either all or nothing. That's wrong. Most of my students don't buy it; they have many role models on the faculty and administration of women with families who do serious jobs. How do we do it? We juggle," she says.

The inevitable hardships of the juggling act nonetheless weigh heavily on young mothers daunted by the challenges they're facing. "It's really hard; it's my life struggle," says Jennifer Friedman, who has one child and is expecting another, but continues to work as a public-interest lawyer. "I love my daughter, and I want to be a really good mother and be there for all the most important things—but I'm also very passionate about my work. I'm very committed to accomplishing goals for my clients and for my programs. I'm trying to achieve balance and compromise, but it's very difficult to balance working and parenting in the early twenty-first century. America is not set up for parents who want to be able to do both. People are pressured to work more and more in today's world."

But the long-term rewards of the juggling act are well worth the short-term sacrifices that may be required. "I see all these talented women who went to law school, who are having children and working fewer hours, and they're fine with it; at some point they'll be able to be valuable," says attorney Marna Tucker, who raised two children.

Tucker's version of the math is slightly different from mine, but she makes the same point. "Your career is forty years. Your stay-at-home years are ten to twelve out of the forty, but a lot of these young women don't see it," she says. "It's only ten years they've got to make this adjustment to afford the other thirty years, but they just think, 'This is what I want now.'"

In order to make it through those ten or twelve or fifteen years, flexibility is key; your plans may change repeatedly in response to evolving circumstances. "There is no one path you can take that's going to be either right or wrong," says Tucker. "But you always have to realize that you're building both your family and your career, and some things are going to take more energy than others at different stages. Look at your career as part of who you are, and look at your family as part of who you are, but understand that their needs are going to change over the years, just as your career is going to change. If your employer wants you to meet certain expectations that may be in conflict with your needs at a certain time, look around at how many other people there are in your situation. They may not want to lose all those people, and you can negotiate a pretty good deal if you realize that."

And yet younger women who view institutions as immovable often don't even attempt to negotiate solutions to their problems, whether individually or collectively. In a given situation, this may not be possible, but it's always worth a try. "At the end, what you want to do is be the boss and do what you damn please," Tucker says. "Recently I wanted to cut back on my workload and write a book, and my firm said, 'Do what you want to do; bring in the business and we'll do the work.' I felt so powerful with that. I felt like everything I had done mattered. The work has given me the confidence to do anything I want to do, not just to work."

Of course, Tucker's success in rearranging her schedule is her reward for being such a valuable asset to the firm. Achieving such flexibility earlier in your career can be difficult. You may have to give up some things in order to meet the needs of your children while managing the demands of your job, and these sacrifices are often frustrating. "I'm an ambitious and competitive person, and I have colleagues who choose to work more than I do and who have been promoted past my level," says Jennifer Friedman. "It's definitely an issue for me, but I can't work those hours right now. I have the rest of my life to do that later."

But this sort of realism is often lacking among women with grand expectations. In 1998, Joyce Purnick, then the metropolitan editor of *The New York Times*, caused a huge controversy with a graduation speech she delivered at Barnard College. "If I had left *The Times* to have children, and then come back to work a four-day week the way some women reporters on my staff now do, or if I had taken long vacations and leaves to be with my family, or left the office at six o'clock instead of eight or nine—I wouldn't be the Metro Editor," said Purnick, who supervised 150 people in the largest news department at the world's most influential newspaper.

She herself had married at the age of forty-two but remained childless, free to stay at work until midnight when breaking news demanded. But in general, she added, "Women who have children get off track and lose ground."

Both as a mother and as a former *Times* reporter, I found her assessment pretty accurate, but it generated heated attacks inside and outside the newsroom. A "damaging and demoralizing message," scolded Washington columnists Cokie and Steve Roberts. The editor of *Working Woman* magazine said she was "appalled." A major London newspaper accused Purnick of striking "a blow to women's hard-won equality in the work place." And at *The Times*, there were such angry protests from women who felt the speech devalued their worth that

Purnick had to call a special meeting to placate them. One woman accused her of believing that "because we're mothers, we contribute less."

A decade later, this issue remains just as inflammatory, as a prominent advertising executive recently discovered when he told an audience that women "don't make it to the top because they don't deserve to." After expressing his view that women's childbearing and caregiving roles prevent them from succeeding in top-level positions, Neil French was forced to resign as worldwide creative director at WPP Group amid an angry uproar.

To me, the cynics who maintain that mothers might just as well forget about high-level success are as guilty of simplistic thinking as the willfully obtuse Pollyannas who insist that mommy-track employees are as valuable as full-time careerists. In my opinion, you can find ways to build a successful career while also raising a healthy family, but you probably can't have every single thing you want at exactly the same time.

During my ten years at *The Times*, fourteen-hour days were routine, and I often came into the newsroom on Saturday or Sunday. Single and childless at the time, I had no one at home to miss me except my elderly dog, but the brutal work ethic at the paper was sometimes rough even for the unencumbered to stomach. When I was assigned, for the third year in a row, to work Christmas Day (a duty that was supposed to be rotated among the staff), I complained to my editor that perhaps it was someone else's turn. A hard-as-nails former marine, he had no sympathy whatsoever. "I haven't been home for a Christmas, a Thanksgiving, or any of my kids' birthdays for seventeen years," he snarled, clearly proud of being such a macho tough guy. Privately appalled, I worked yet another Christmas, glad I wasn't leaving any crestfallen children to mourn my absence.

But even before I became a mother, I was tailoring my career to enhance my prospects for building the family life I wanted in the future.

After I became a national political reporter at *The Times,* I was offered the job of a national bureau chief, which would have entailed moving to another city and covering the surrounding region. I didn't want to leave New York, and I didn't want to spend my life on the road—so I turned down the job, much to the surprise of the male editors who tried to harangue me into changing my decision. "How can you do this?" one asked incredulously. "We're giving you your shot at the brass ring! You'll be a national bureau chief, and then you'll be a foreign correspondent, and then you'll win your Pulitzer Prize. You can't turn this down! You're out of your mind!"

"But I don't want to be a foreign correspondent," I said calmly. "Those jobs mean you're traveling all the time; it's impossible to have a personal life, let alone a stable relationship. If I spend my thirties doing that, I'll end up unmarried and childless at forty-five, and that's not the life I want."

The editors were furious with me, and my obstinate refusal to capitulate certainly didn't help my career at the paper. In those days, male editors found it inconceivable that a young reporter wouldn't acquiesce to being treated like a pawn on a chessboard, regularly moved around the globe in the service of a larger plan. Such correspondents had almost always been male, and their wives had followed unquestioningly as they relocated every two or three years, uprooting their families for their husbands' careers.

But my personal goals were simply more important to me than the professional glory I might have achieved that way. When I got pregnant with my first child, I even changed careers in order to prepare for raising a family. After fifteen years as a reporter at daily newspapers, I went to work for a monthly magazine that not only offered more flexible deadlines but also gave me the option of working at home, which proved invaluable in permitting me to create the family-centered life I wanted for my children.

A year later, however, I made another professional decision that turned out to be foolish and unrealistic. Soon after delivering my first child by cesarean section, I was offered an enticing book contract with a leading publisher—an event that might have been cause for celebration under other circumstances. But given the realities of my life at that moment, the fact that I signed on to write a major biography might well have been proof that, in my hormone-addled postnatal and postsurgical state, I had completely lost my mind. First of all, I had a new job, which required intermittent travel. I was also thirty-nine years old, and I wanted desperately to have another child; my obstetrical chart read "advanced geriatric risk," so the baby-making effort clearly had to take precedence over other matters. During the next two years, I endured three more very difficult pregnancies, two of which ended in miscarriages and surgery. The last pregnancy finally produced my healthy son, also by C-section.

In addition to all the hormonal, physical, and emotional upheaval of those years, I was so sleep-deprived that I thought I was going to die. Tormented by gastrointestinal distress despite nearly a year of breast-feeding, my daughter screamed through the night until she was one (so much for colic ending at three months!) and didn't sleep more than forty minutes at a stretch until she was well over two years old. It was all I could do to drag myself through each day; coping with any additional burdens seemed unthinkable. Tortured by a guilty conscience about the book that didn't appear to be writing itself, I would lie awake at 3:00 A.M. in a cold sweat, horrified that I was failing to deliver on an obligation I had undertaken in good faith. But at the time, writing a book was simply more than I could handle while being an attentive mother and doing my job, so I finally returned my advance to the publisher—an acknowledgment of defeat, but a huge relief nonetheless.

Many years have passed, and when I signed a contract to write *The Feminine Mistake*, I knew it was the right time for me to take on such a challenge. In the months since then, I've spent a lot of time working.

But my daughter was holed up in her room studying for her eleventh-grade finals, the SATs, and the Advanced Placement Exams that dominate her current schedule. My son is usually in his room practicing guitar or working on his computer. We're all busy, and the time I spend at my computer is no longer time taken away from my family. I'm only a couple of rooms away, available whenever they need me—but when they don't, I'm free to do my own thing.

The professional sacrifices you may have to make in juggling family and career can require you to adjust your goals, your value system, your ego, your marriage, your sense of timing, and more. There's no question I'm not as successful as I might have been had I churned out bestsellers all these years. But the time I would have spent writing them has been devoted to raising healthy, well-adjusted children—and I wouldn't give up the relationships I have built with my kids for any amount of success. Besides, there's always tomorrow; my book-writing career may have begun late, but with luck it will continue in the years to come. It seems to me that deferring a few goals for a while is a small price to pay for achieving most of them over the long run.

"I don't view it as a compromise; I see it as sequential living," says Susan Mercandetti, an editor at Random House who has maintained an enviable career while raising her two children. Before she got married, Mercandetti held high-profile jobs in the television industry that required her to live and work "at warp speed," she says. "My life was all about work."

But after she had children, Mercandetti scaled back her career, limiting work to a series of part-time jobs that enabled her to pick up her children at school every afternoon and engage fully in their lives while still maintaining a professional presence. "Life is about living sequentially," she says. "You do certain things for a while, and then you want to do something else. It's okay to go full force on your career and then go full force on motherhood and then do half and half. You ratchet it up, and you ratchet it down. Everyone has to look at their own priorities. I had this incredible chance to be a mother, and I didn't want to give it up. For me, the overriding factor is that I don't want anybody else raising my kids, because I think I'm better at it than anybody. I thought, 'No one is going to take this time away from me.' I had enough confidence that I knew I could get my career back."

Mercandetti is a master of the juggling act, but her leverage was greatly increased by the credentials and contacts she accumulated during the long, successful career she built before becoming a mother. "When I started working as a part-time consultant at *Vanity Fair* and then at the *New Yorker,* I could do it on my own time, in my own way—on the playing field, at the jungle gym, wherever," she says. "I would sit up in the tree house with the kids playing below me. I worked in the park; I worked in the parking lot; I worked in the car-pool lane. I worked whenever I could. With my employers, I said, 'I work at home; deal with it.' I was too old to give a damn. That's an incredibly luxurious place to be in, to be psychologically and economically independent enough to say, 'I'm going to live my life. If you don't like it, tough!'"

While an outside observer might conclude that Mercandetti has succeeded in having it all, she is well aware of what she's given up. "I never feel like I'm at the top of my game," she says. "There's so much more that I could do professionally, if only I could devote myself to this. I could have been running a magazine, or *Good Morning America,* or had a book imprint. I could have had all those things—but so what! I chose not to. I don't view it as a compromise. I view it as different phases of my life. What I got was the opportunity to raise these two magnificent kids, and I'm so grateful. We have a wonderful relationship, and I take pride in that. You have to choose what you want. I had children late, at thirty-nine and forty-one, and I had a very full, interesting career, and eventually I might do something else. I've reinvented myself so many times; I can reinvent myself again. I will always find something to do. I live in the moment, and I don't look back. It worked out."

Although Mercandetti rejects the label, most of us would call this compromise. The requisite trade-offs may vary depending on the needs of the moment. When Mercandetti's children were younger, she says, "I made a lot less money, but my bonus was flexibility, and that was a lot more important to me, because I didn't want anybody to tell me at three o'clock on Wednesday afternoon that I couldn't go to my kid's play."

FINDING AN INSTITUTIONAL structure that can accommodate family needs—or becoming an entrepreneur and building your own— is crucial to many women's success at combining careers and children. "Nearly half of all businesses in the United States are woman-owned, and women are starting ventures at twice the rate of men," the magazine *Country Living* reported last year. "Why is it such a banner time for female entrepreneurs? 'Technology has increased flexibility,' says Victoria Colligan, founder of Ladies Who Launch, a network of women entrepreneurs. 'You can work anytime.'"

But when women look at mothers who seem to have managed both work and family with ease, they often don't realize how many adjustments had to be made along the way. Elizabeth Warren is now a distinguished professor who teaches contract law, bankruptcy, and commercial law at Harvard Law School, but the early years of motherhood were harrowing for her.

"I did it in a way I would never recommend," says Warren, who has three grown children. "I got married at nineteen, had my first baby at twenty-one, started law school at twenty-three, and had my second baby three weeks after graduation. I got a full-time tenure-track job when my second child was two years old, and I went through eleven child-care situations in seven months. There were people who never showed up, people who quit—it was just one thing after another. I was like the worst stories people tell about working women. I had spit-up on my shoulders and a pacifier in my pocket; I would agree to do things and then say, 'I can't do this, because the baby has an ear infection.' It was *horrible*! I finally called my elderly widowed aunt and said, 'I'm going to have to quit my job; I can't find any way that I can live with to take care of my children.' She arrived from Oklahoma City the next day."

Warren ended up buying one house nearby for her aunt and another for her parents. "That made it possible for me to work and have a family," she says. "It was the child care that almost did me in, but once I got that piece, the rest of it was never very hard."

For other women, professional demands ultimately necessitate a job change in order to accommodate family needs. Tanya Mandor was a department-store buyer when she had her first child. "I spent her first birthday in Hong Kong, and I was devastated," Mandor says. "That was a trade-off I was not willing to give up. I said to my boss, 'I have to quit. I can't do travel.' My boss said, 'Don't quit. I'll put you in cosmetics.' "

So Mandor kept her job and acquired Revlon as one of her clients—a move that later propelled her into a successful career in the cosmetics industry. "I ended up as executive vice president and general manager at Revlon Global Brands," Mandor says. "I worked for several women as well as several incredible CEOs. They had families, too, and they believed in having a life. I was able to raise my children and go to school events and plays; weekends were pretty much your own, and I didn't miss as many of the milestones in my children's lives as I would have if I'd stayed in retailing."

After many years at Revlon, Mandor left to become an independent strategic planning and marketing consultant, a change that gave her even more flexibility. "I really wanted to be able to go on vacation with my husband and to have the time I wanted, and I couldn't do that at the level I was at," she says. "It's not as lucrative, but I'm loving it."

Working women who manage jobs and children without undue trauma tend to have lucked into accommodating professions where they structured their work lives to suit their family's needs. "The work you choose will be a determining factor in whether it works or not," says Darcy Howe, a forty-nine-year-old mother of two and an investment adviser. "If you choose work where you have crazy hours and don't have flexibility in your schedule, what kind of life is that? My life works because I've chosen something that is completely flexible. How my day works all depends on me. I have friends who are the highest of executives, but they have no flexibility. If you realize you need to keep working, the structure of how you do that will be the make-or-break thing on whether it's going to work."

Young women lawyers frequently bemoan the brutal demands of major law firms, and many sacrifice their careers because they perceive their options as an all-or-nothing choice. Wiser women often compromise by finding more flexible opportunities.

Although Harriette Dorsen had three young children when she went to work for a small New York law firm, she soon became a partner and then a managing partner. "It never would have happened if I'd gone to a big law firm, where you have a certain structure and you have to pay your dues and start by doing very low-level work," she says. "You're in a big class at a big law firm, but I wasn't in a big class. We did work hard, but it was a humane firm, and we were partners in the best way. Everyone wasn't out to wring the last dollar out of every person's labor, which is what the big firms do."

No one is claiming that it's easy for women to forge legal careers while building their families; the law is, unfortunately, one of what Dr. Anna Fels refers to as the front-loaded professions in *Necessary Dreams*.

"Careers in law, medicine and business require years of often brutally intensive training. Women who choose these professions must agree to a painful trade-off: the loss of many of their potential child-bearing years, in exchange for the pursuit of their career," wrote Dr. Fels, a psychiatrist. "When women arrive at their mid-thirties, however, the relative gains and losses shift dramatically—career women are doing much better than the homemakers. A comparison of homemakers with married women professionals and with unmarried women professionals twenty-five years after their college graduations found that the homemakers had 'the lowest self-esteem and the lowest sense of personal competence, even including childcare and social skills.' Perhaps counterintuitively, this study also found the marital happiness of the career women to be dramatically higher by midlife than that of the homemakers. This enhanced marital happiness may be a direct benefit of the women's careers; it has been shown that for both men and women, the less time individuals spend on low-control tasks, the better the quality of their marriages." (Social scientists use the term "low-control tasks" to describe household chores that must be done, such as preparing meals, doing laundry, and housecleaning, as opposed to those that can be rescheduled or postponed, such as yard work—the kinds of tasks typically done by men.)

Even in the most inhospitable professions, however, many women find ways to circumvent obstacles and build their careers, often by going outside the more rigid institutions. "At a large firm, you never go home, and you have no control over your life," says Miranda Blake, a defense lawyer who was working as a prosecutor in the U.S. Attorney's office when she formed her own firm with another attorney. "We had tried cases together, and he asked me to leave with him," Blake explains. "I wanted a family, and he said, 'I understand what you want. We will always work it out.' And we do." That was twenty years ago; Blake's children are now fifteen and eighteen years old.

When my kids were small, child-related crises that interfered with work were a constant headache; someone always seemed to be throwing up or needing stitches. But such problems tend to become less frequent as the years pass, and professional women with older kids have generally learned to take the long view. During her career as a corporate executive, Vicki Gault was often sought out by other mothers who were upset about the conflicts between work and family. "It was so clear that women struggle with this constantly, and with each passing year, as I rose up through the ranks, other women would come to me as a mentor and a role model," Gault says. "When I talk to younger women, I talk about the phases of your life. I was ambivalent, too; there were days when I thought, 'I must be crazy—I wish I were at the playground right now!' But there were many other days when I thought about how exciting my job was. I had gone further than I ever thought I could go, I couldn't believe I was making the money I was making, and I felt an incredible sense of accomplishment and achievement that felt really good. So I could tell these women that it was achievable to be relatively successful and be a good mom, but I would say, 'Just be realistic. You're going to be exhausted for at least four years.' When your kids aren't sleeping well, you have to physically give them their baths and brush their teeth—in the early stages it's just physically exhausting to provide that kind of care for babies and toddlers. But none of these decisions are forever. You don't have to be home all day when the kids don't get home until three forty-five P.M. Pretty soon they go to school, and they're there until two or three or four in the afternoon. How much laundry and scrubbing is there to do in anybody's house? So then the question becomes, how will I keep myself busy? With volunteer work or tennis at the club? As they get older, your children need you in a different way. With teenagers, I have to be available to talk to them and to guide them. It's a different kind of mothering—and it's a bit easier to do by phone."

Most working women find it difficult to avoid feeling guilty when they compare themselves with stay-at-home moms who have time to volunteer at school, attend every play date, and micromanage each homework assignment. But as their children get older, both groups sometimes find that the tables have turned.

Cyndy Byrnes, a working mother of two, used to be keenly aware of disapproval from the full-time mothers in her Connecticut community. "There's a great divide between working mothers and stay-at-home moms," she says. "When I go to the cafeteria at school, I'm always standing by myself; all the stay-at-home mothers are chatting it up in a group. I feel like they say, 'Oh—she works,' and they have nothing in common with me."

Back then, Byrnes regularly found herself in tears when business trips took her away from her children. Recently, however, she started her own business dealing in art and interiors, which enables her to work at home. "I don't really want to stop working now, because I found something fun to do," she says. "I feel like I'm in a good place. I have freedom and flexibility; I feel so much more in control and so much more relaxed."

Her contentment provides a growing contrast with the stay-at-home wives whose children are growing up. "I'm getting paid back a little bit now," Byrnes says. "When I started my own business, the mothers came up to me and said, 'Oh, what a good idea!' I could just see the wheels turning, like 'I wish I had something to do at this juncture.' I think they're bored when their kids get to the point where they're pretty self-sufficient. Their husbands are never home, and the wives are on their own. When they go to a meeting at school, they're all decked out; there's not a lot to occupy them."

Darcy Howe has experienced a similiar evolution among her social circle, which leads "a typical country-club life," she says. "The husbands play golf, and a lot of the women in this environment don't work."

But Howe is different. As the first vice president for investments at Merrill Lynch's Private Banking and Investment Group in Kansas City,

Missouri, she manages a billion dollars' worth of clients' assets in a high-powered career that has long set her apart from her friends and neighbors—just as her domestic concerns have set her apart among her male colleagues.

Howe doesn't pretend it was easy to be a good mom while doing her job well. "I never thought I was good enough in either role," she says. "I had colleagues that were doing more business than I was, and I felt as if they were thinking, 'Why isn't she doing more?' But I wanted and needed balance in my life, so I wasn't going to be at the office until eight o'clock at night. Being a very competitive person, I didn't say, 'Oh, well, I'm going to allow myself mediocrity,' so it was very stressful when the kids were little; they came in and sat in playpens in my office on Saturday mornings. I wanted to be there for the first step; the mothers in parents' magazines are always drooling over all those great moments you're missing. At times, I felt completely inadequate as a mother. You feel like a failure that you didn't put all the pieces together better."

Those pangs were often exacerbated by the tight-knit community of stay-at-home mothers whose lives were so different from her own. "My friends who picked up their children at school were smugly saying, 'Oh, you didn't know this? The three kids in the back of the car told me this!'" Howe reports. "I felt like I wasn't doing enough as a parent. There are all these other moms who sit around the pool with their kids and go to swim-team practice, and I'm not there. I definitely feel that there are women who wouldn't invite me to things; either they think I wouldn't be available or they think, 'You don't live our life; you're not welcome in our life. You're not one of us, so we're going to make you pay for that in every possible way.'"

But, over time, Howe detected a gradual change in those attitudes. "I feel the longing and envy from the other women much more now than I did ten or fifteen years ago, when they felt very fulfilled, because they were very needed," she says. "Back then, I did all this stuff, trying to show them that I wasn't this totally derelict parent, but the stay-at-home moms felt very smug; I could take on little jobs, but they could take on big jobs. Now that their kids are in high school, some of them are totally panicking. Their kids don't want them doing everything with them, or for them, anymore. There is an identity crisis that they see I don't have. There's a certain amount of jealousy about it, too. When they see some of the accolades I get, I see that they recognize that their lives are different. No one recognizes them for their job, because they don't get the public gold star."

As Howe's children prepare for college, she is profoundly grateful that she made the accommodations necessary to sustain her career rather than giving it up. "I have to admit I could have been tempted by that other life; I might have done that, if money were no object and my husband had a very lucrative career," admits Howe, whose husband is a lawyer for a nonprofit organization. "But now that I look at becoming an empty-nester, boy, am I glad I've got direction! If I had given it up, what would I do at fifty? I'm at the pinnacle of what I'm doing. I'm good at it. I feel great about myself."

Howe wishes that younger women could receive more encouragement to take the long view in making such crucial life choices. "When I talk to young moms who are torn, I tell them, 'The hardest time in your life is the first month back at work, when you've just had this bonding experience. But you've got to look beyond that time and think that it's good for your child that you have balance in your own life,'" she says. "If women can just look beyond the moment and listen to people who have been there, maybe they would make different decisions."

For no matter what their circumstances, all mothers must ultimately cope with the fact that children get older. Deeply invested in the idea that they're indispensable, stay-at-home moms often fail to anticipate how finite their chosen role will prove to be. "Being a mom is a temp job," as legal scholar Sylvia Law put it. "To the extent that women are assuming they can just go home and depend on a guy—that's dumb, because being a mommy is not a lifetime career," she says. "Women who think they need to drop out of work life are going to discover that when their kids are a little older, they don't even want Mom at home all the time. That doesn't mean you stop being a mom, but it's not a full-time job."

While the empty-nest syndrome can afflict any mother, that transition is particularly painful for stay-at-home wives. "My son was my most important project, and as he started pulling away, I felt terribly bereft," says Geraldine Cochran,* a Chicago mother who started writing a novel while her son was in high school. "I missed having a little kid, but when they get to be teenagers, they don't need us the way they did. I don't know what I would have done if I didn't have my life as a writer; I would have felt totally useless. I'm still a mother, but my role has changed. What can you do? They grow up, and you have to find a way to get beyond the fact that the children are gone. If you don't figure out how to deal with the passage of time, you're in trouble."

That prospect is deeply worrisome to Tessa Sullivan,* the seventy-one-year-old mother of stay-at-home mom Noreen Sullivan. Tessa has long been perplexed by her daughter's decision to abandon her career as a lawyer. Tessa loved her own work, as her daughter well knows—but she also took her domestic responsibilities very seriously.

"My mother was a tenured university professor, and she felt very grateful to have found something she liked to do," Noreen explains. "She always made a three-course dinner for us every night of the week, even when she was writing her dissertation. I don't know how she did it, but she was very happy to be working. She knew very few nonworking women, but I always got the impression she thought they were unhappy."

Tessa found her career so gratifying that she can't help but wish the same satisfaction for her daughter. "I hope that eventually she will be able to do some sort of work she finds fulfilling and interesting,"

Tessa says. "Otherwise what does a woman do when the children are gone?"

Stay-at-home moms like Noreen Sullivan typically insist they live in the present, and they'll worry about the future when they get there. But such short-term thinking isn't necessarily the wisest approach. "People should take the long view," says attorney Ann Lewis. "You have kids for maybe one-third of your working life, but you need to look at the whole picture and consider the other two-thirds. If you leave work, what are you going to do to keep your hand in, so you can go back when you decide to go back? Don't make decisions that are going to lock you in for your whole life, because the kids *are* going to grow up and go away."

## CHAPTER SEVEN

# WHO SAYS IT
# DOESN'T WORK?

## "IT CAN BE DONE!"

A s the lunch program was called to order in the New York of-
fices of the global investment bank Lehman Brothers, the
room was packed with an overflow crowd of animated, attractive women. The National Council for Research on Women had
assembled a group of high-powered executives, academics, social scientists, and other experts for a program entitled "Opting Out—Myth,
Viable Option or Media Spin?"

The women in the audience were as accomplished as the speakers.
In fact, the contrast between the subject at hand and the lives of the
women in that room provided an ironic exercise in cognitive disso-
nance. If it's really impossible to combine work and family successfully, how to explain all these energetic, confident women buzzing
excitedly about their children, their grandchildren—and their own
fascinating careers?

During the question-and-answer period after the speakers' presen-
tations, a Lehman Brothers vice chairman stood up and told the audience that she had raised four children with her doctor husband while

advancing to her present level of professional achievement. "It can be done," said this paragon of having it all, "but nobody ever writes a story about us. Why isn't the media talking about the success stories?"

Why indeed? Ever since the 1970s, the mainstream media have harped endlessly on the downside of "having it all." Even as millions of women succeeded in combining work and motherhood, the news coverage focused obsessively on the logistical challenges of the juggling act, rarely exploring the rewards. Negative stories are generally deemed more compelling than positive ones by news editors, and our culture has consistently emphasized the difficulties of combining family and career while ignoring the disadvantages of the stay-at-home life. And yet the labor force is full of women who love their families and enjoy their jobs and who have somehow managed to combine the two—to the benefit of all concerned. So where are the glowing profiles illuminating the admirable lives of women who manage it with competence and relish?

Such women are usually too busy living those lives to worry about the chronic biases of the media. When ABC-TV newswoman Elizabeth Vargas returned from her maternity leave last fall, her first broadcast on *20/20* was promoted with a grim advertisement that read, "I grew up thinking I could have it all. I was wrong."

But when the glorification of full-time motherhood prompted a new generation of young mothers to reject the idea of work, many of us became alarmed. For years, we had struggled to balance the demands of our jobs and our families, enjoying complicated but deeply rewarding lives as a result. As far as we were concerned, "having it all" was the best idea since women's suffrage, and we were genuinely surprised to learn that our guiding credo had been discredited. Why on earth did younger women believe that it couldn't be done, or that it was too difficult to be worth the effort, or that the attempt would wreck their marriages and ruin their children? Our marriages were fine, our children were thriving, our careers had flourished. Why didn't these younger women understand that combining work and family was an immeasurable improvement over being confined to a purely domestic life?

The first problem might well have been the catchphrase itself. "Having it all" was an unfortunate misnomer from the outset; it struck many women as insufferably smug, reeking of an elitist self-righteousness that belies the messy realities of women's domestic lives. Although most of my friends are working women, many with noteworthy accomplishments, I have never once heard any of them talk about "having it all." None of us feels as if she has it all; our lives are imperfect and often chaotic, we have fallen short on many of our goals, and we've made countless compromises in order to maintain our capacity to work without slighting our families in any irreparable ways.

SITTING IN HER luxurious Manhattan office at CBS News, which boasts a spectacular view of the Hudson River as well as framed pictures of her children, Vicki Gordon might seem to be the ultimate exemplar of having it all. As the executive story editor of *60 Minutes,* she has an illustrious career as well as a wonderful family. A hands-on mother who spends virtually every nonworking moment with her kids, she lives a dozen blocks from her office and maintains an intimate connection to both of her daughters, who are fourteen and ten. Our conversation, which occurs on a weekday afternoon, is repeatedly interrupted by calls from one or the other girl about subjects that range from a shoe purchase to art supplies for a school project.

But even Gordon, who has worked at CBS for twenty years and is married to a fellow TV news producer, recoils from the suggestion that she has it all. "No one has it all—are you kidding me?" she exclaims. "You always look at people who have more, and I see people who have so much more than I do—people with bigger careers, whatever."

Instead Gordon describes herself as someone who has made many compromises in order to balance work and family. "I had opportunities that would have paid me more money, given me bigger titles, more responsibility, but I didn't want to take the risk of trying a new venture and having the venture fail, or having me fail, and having no income, and then chaos," she says. "I wasn't willing to take the risk. I never wanted to rock the boat. A lot of it was knowing that I could control my schedule more here. But you always wonder, 'How far could I have gone? What could I have done? What could I have mastered?'"

And yet Gordon is well aware of how fortunate she is. She has just spent a typically fascinating day at the office, and she's about to go meet one of her daughters at the shoe store. "What more could I ask for?" she says softly.

But it's always difficult for women to hold on to such feelings of self-satisfaction; for most of us, self-doubt and self-criticism seem to come a lot more naturally. We compare ourselves unfavorably with others we admire, even though we know that few are immune from the normal vicissitudes of fate. "Nobody's life is what it looks like from the outside. I've gone through ups and downs in my marriage, financial crises, kids with problems, illnesses and deaths among loved ones, administrative changes at work—you name it," says one professional woman.

Acutely conscious of our own shortcomings, most of the working women I know do a lot more commiserating than bragging. Our conversations include endless kvetching about the details that fall through the cracks. Our daily lives are a humbling exercise in the impossibility of truly having it all, let alone doing it all, and we rehearse the litany of our failings in our own minds far more often than our most scathing critics could ever do in public.

To me, all we're really talking about is having a full life instead of settling for half a life. "Love and work are the cornerstones of our humanness," according to Sigmund Freud—and while I disagree with Freud on many issues, it seems to me he was right on target there. The developmental psychologist and psychoanalyst Erik Erikson built on Freud's thinking to develop a similar concept, defining mental health in terms of the ability to love and to work. Those two complementary dimensions are the bedrock elements of a mature, fully satisfying adult life, no matter what one's gender.

To professional women who derive an important part of their identity from their work, the whole concept of "having it all" often seems ludicrous, because it is assumed to have relevance only to females. No one ever questions a man's right to have a family as well as doing meaningful work; nobody ever talks about men "having it all" just because they've managed to sire children and hold down a paying job.

The phrase also seemed to imply that there was a formula for a successful life and that feminists had figured it out. But every woman's interests, ambitions, and personality are different, and any solution to the challenge of combining work and family is necessarily individual. A domestic lifestyle that would feel stultifying to me might be deeply satisfying to someone else; a level of professional achievement that would thrill me might leave other women hungry for greater power and glory. There is no one-size-fits-all answer to the question of how to achieve the right balance between career and children.

It's also true that some people handle these responsibilities better than others—a fact that even the most ardent feminists admit. "Some of us managed well, and some of us didn't," says family historian Stephanie Coontz. Any honest assessment would have to acknowledge that the "you can have it all" ethos may wreak real damage when children's needs are sacrificed.

At a preschool picnic, I was startled when an acquaintance with three children told me that she had just accepted the job of her dreams—in another city. "I've stayed home with my kids for seven years, and I've had it," she said. "I can hardly wait to get back to work."

She didn't see any problem in leaving her husband and children in New York while she spent the workweek hundreds of miles away. "Oh, I'll just commute," she said with breezy nonchalance.

A year later, her husband was offered the job of his dreams—on the

West Coast. So off he went, to the other end of the continent. Some time afterward, I wasn't surprised to hear that this couple was divorcing. He stayed on the West Coast with the two boys; she remained on the East Coast with their daughter. A family was fractured forever, with each of the children deprived of one parent and at least one sibling—all because a couple of job offers seemed too good to refuse. Mom's and Dad's careers may be in fine shape, but the family they've lost is irretrievable—and that loss will have permanent consequences for their children.

Even when a marriage survives such strains, careerist priorities can take a terrible toll on children. A woman I know was offered an exciting job in another city and took it, leaving her husband and two small children in New York. When the kids missed her too much, she moved them to the city where her job was located, and Dad became the one who had to get on an airplane every weekend. Her job proved disappointing, and she finally quit—but by the time the family reunited in New York, the children were so clinging and needy, they could scarcely tolerate their mother leaving the room.

But most working mothers have the sense not to make such extreme choices, and those who give their children's interests top priority generally find that they don't suffer over the long haul. Marna Tucker, a senior partner at the Washington law firm of Feldesman Tucker Leifer Fidell, has enjoyed a long and distinguished career, raising two children while becoming the first woman president of the District of Columbia bar and the first woman president of the National Conference of Bar Presidents, among many other honors. "I went back to work because I didn't like the idea of making raisin faces in the oatmeal," Tucker says. "I loved practicing law."

Like most working mothers, she doesn't claim that the juggling act was always easy. "I came home early, and I tried to be home every night, and I had the best help you could have, but I felt guilty all the time," she says. "My daughter is thirty now, and I finally had the courage to ask her, 'Were you upset that your mother went to work all the time?' My daughter said, 'Well, when I was eight or nine and I went over to Kate's house, her mother would be there baking cookies, and I would think "Gee, I wish my mom were home baking cookies!" When we were thirteen or fourteen, Kate's mother was still baking cookies, and we were thinking, "God, I wish she would get away from us!" ' "

Tucker laughs. "So the answer is, things change, and there is no answer. I'm not a superwoman. If I do anything, I get a B-plus. I didn't set my goals to be the perfect mother or the perfect lawyer. I had a brain, and I wanted to use it."

Tucker's matter-of-fact acceptance of the idea that she's not perfect provides a striking contrast with the attitude of the Yale sophomore featured in the *New York Times* story about young women planning to give up their careers in favor of their families. Cynthia Liu said she believes that she couldn't be "the best career woman and the best mother at the same time," and that she therefore has to choose between those goals. I have to admit it's never entered my mind that I should try to be the best career woman in the world or the best mother; if I held myself to that kind of impossible standard, I'd be too intimidated to get up in the morning.

Those of us who have maintained a long-term commitment to both work and family have resigned ourselves to the reality that we may not be the best, but most of the time we're good enough—and that's fine. "I'm good enough" isn't the kind of slogan you want to emblazon on a billboard, however; the payoff is more like a quiet pride that usually remains unspoken.

And maybe this is the real problem. As we watch younger women rejecting the quest for a fully rounded adult life in favor of a portion of the whole, many of us wonder whether we ourselves might be partly to blame. Perhaps younger women don't understand the appeal of combining work and family because we failed to tell them how great it can be. Yes, we've all been harried and overburdened at times, but for most of us those strains were more than compensated for by immeasurable rewards.

Did we somehow forget to express our delight in those rewards? Have we failed to articulate the deep satisfactions of building independent lives and enjoying professional success as well as loving families?

Nearly thirty years ago, I made a close friend a generation older than myself. Although she had two children she adored, her marriage ended in a bitter divorce, and what professional success she achieved later in life was never enough to assuage her thwarted ambitions. Frustrated and angry, she often told me that women, if they were lucky, might be able to accomplish two out of three of their primary goals—namely, marriage, family, and career—but that they couldn't have all three. Arguing with her proved futile; my career was flourishing, but I was still single and childless. "You'll find out," she would say grimly. "Just wait and see."

Well, I'm now the same age that my late friend was when I first met her, and I still think she was wrong. Like me, most of my close friends have stable marriages, wonderful children, and satisfying careers. And yet such self-defeating, self-fulfilling prophecies still retain a powerful hold on women's thinking. Many of the stay-at-home mothers I interviewed for this book parroted the same depressing line I used to hear from my older friend so long ago.

When people don't succeed in getting what they want out of life, they often rationalize their own failures by claiming that the task was impossible in the first place. But it's hardly impossible for women, like men, to enjoy good marriages and exciting professional lives while raising healthy children. And communicating this essential truth now seems like a vitally important mission.

Female dependency has deep roots in Western culture, and the combination of a politically conservative climate and a resurgence of fundamentalist religion has helped to reinforce age-old stereotypes that idealize strictly circumscribed female roles.

But we Baby Boomers have spent the last three decades creating multidimensional lives that most of us have enjoyed to the hilt. As the pioneers of "having it all," shouldn't we have been able to offset those negative images of working women with the positive evidence of our own experience? Why hasn't the message gotten through?

"Women now don't want to be in the grind," Kate White, the editor of *Cosmopolitan*, told Maureen Dowd of *The New York Times*. "The baby boomers made the grind seem unappealing."

How on earth did this happen? The women I know certainly don't feel that way about their professional lives. "There's nothing more fun than being in business, making money, being successful," says Paulanne Mancuso, a Connecticut mother of two who recently retired after a thirty-four-year career as a retail and cosmetics executive. "But it's not just a question of finances. There's a tremendous amount of joy and satisfaction in being good at something. If you miss that, you really miss a big part of life. There's so much stimulation to working with smart people. At the end of the day, the questions people have to face are, did they raise great kids, and did they make a contribution? I think it would be really hard, at the end of the day, to say you bought great shoes."

To working women, the benefits of a professional life seem so obvious that we rarely stop to articulate them, but maybe this is a huge mistake. Perhaps we have neglected to explain, even to our own daughters, the innumerable ways we have grown and developed as a result of our work. Have I really communicated to my children how thrilling my professional life has been? How proud I am of my accomplishments? How much of my identity and my self-esteem are derived from utilizing my talents and achieving success in my career? More likely, I downplayed the exhilaration of my independent life in order to reassure my daughter and son that they were always my first priority. And they are—but they aren't my whole life.

"Because working mothers fear a backlash of disapproval against them for actually working, they are really reticent to talk about the benefits they get from working—to talk to their peers, to their families, to their children, to society at large," says New Jersey mom Vicki Gault.

"If I say, 'I love my job, it's so cool, I get to go to Germany for three weeks,' they think, 'Why did she even have children?' If you tell your children, 'I have this great new project, and I'm so excited about it,' they think you're saying, 'You're not as important as Mommy's job.' "

Guilt-ridden and afraid of making our kids feel like an afterthought, some of us fall into the trap of portraying our work as an obligation rather than an affirmative choice that yields exhilarating rewards. It's always hard for women to assert their right to self-fulfillment, and it's harder for mothers. When my kids were younger and I had to leave them, whether for a lunch meeting downtown or a business trip to Africa, they would ask me why I had to go. I always framed my answer in terms of necessity. "I have to work," I told them.

This was true; even if I'd wanted to stop working after I had children, our family couldn't have managed on my husband's paycheck alone. But with toddlers clinging to my knees every time I tried to get out the front door, it assuaged my guilt about leaving them, even for a couple of hours, to act as if I didn't have a choice.

And yet even that was only part of the truth. I've been a journalist far longer than I've been a mother, and the larger truth is that I have always loved what I do. My work has made me who I am; it has afforded me incredible opportunities to travel and meet extraordinary people and learn about the world I live in, it has been exciting and empowering and endlessly fascinating, and I wouldn't have given it up for anything, not even my infinitely precious children.

Because of my work, I have met kings and queens and presidents, movie stars and Olympic gold-medal athletes, murderers and con artists, Nobel Prize–winners and supermodels, pedophile priests and transsexual former nuns—as well as thousands of ordinary people with amazing stories to tell. After thirty-six years as a journalist, I never know, when I get up in the morning, what the day will bring. At a moment's notice, I may be asked to fly to Paris or Prague, to Napa or Nairobi.

That possibility lends every day a sense of excitement at its un-known potential. Most of the time, however, I'm at home. When the kids return from school, I'm working in my office next to the kitchen, eager to take a break and hear about their day as I start to prepare our evening meal. I have always cooked dinner for my family, and most nights the four of us sit down to eat together.

Certainly there have been moments when I felt overwhelmed, ex-hausted, or simply torn between competing demands. Once, when my children were small, I went to the airport to catch a flight to London, feeling very pleased with myself because I'd organized everything so meticulously on the home front. Every breakfast, lunch, and dinner the children would eat while I was away had been planned, cooked, and labeled. (Yes, I'm compulsive.) Every appointment was carefully charted on the family calendar. Every last detail had been taken care of, so my baby-sitter and husband could manage the children's lives without a hitch in my absence. As I stepped up to the ticket counter at the airport, I felt exceedingly smug about being such a superwoman.

"Your passport, please," said the clerk. Experienced world traveler that I was, I stared at her blankly. My passport? I had remembered to leave my husband detailed notes on every muffin to be defrosted while I was away—but I'd forgotten my passport.

So much for superwoman. My heart pounding, I called my baby-sitter in a panic and counted the minutes until she and my children ca-reened into the airport in a taxi, laughing and waving my passport at me. I hugged them again, made the flight, and flew to Europe, al-though it doubtless took a while for my blood pressure to return to normal.

The juggling act undeniably demands discipline and organization and energy and determination and flexibility. One friend still laughs about the time she saw me sprinting down the sidewalk, with one baby plastered to my chest in a Snugli and another in the stroller I was fran-tically wheeling in front of me, as I raced to get to the bank before it closed. Wild-eyed, I greeted her with, "What kind of money do they have in Amsterdam?" As usual, I was about to take off into the unknown and arrive in a foreign country at some ungodly hour before the currency-exchange bureaus were open. As usual, there were more items on my to-do list than there were minutes left to accomplish them.

In retrospect, however, those moments of stress make me smile rather than shudder. Sure, I've dreamed about winning the lottery so I could retire to a life of leisure—but even as I fantasize about lying in a hammock reading trashy novels, I know I'd be bored within a month. Quite apart from the loss of income, my life would be impoverished in innumerable ways were I to give up my career. How could I ever regret the amazing opportunities it's given me?

But that's not all. Long before I ever made it to Lahore or Amman or Dubai on assignment, my career had completely transformed my personality. As a child growing up in Manhattan and then in suburban Westchester County, I was shy and self-conscious, paralyzed with stage fright whenever I had to talk to more than one person at a time. The prospect of delivering an oral book report to my fourth-grade class made me sick with anticipatory panic for weeks ahead of time. Whenever I had to perform in front of anybody, even to sing a round with my brother for a visiting great-aunt (my mother was big on impromptu performances), it was all I could do not to faint on the spot. I spent much of my childhood in a state of excruciating anxiety, unable to assert myself in even the most egregious circumstances.

As a teenager, I remember sitting on a train, utterly frozen, while the man next to me furtively rubbed his hand along the outside of my thigh. It was like being caught in one of those nightmares where you try to scream but no sound comes out. After what seemed an eternity of shame, I finally managed to squeak out a quavering, apologetic, "Excuse me . . ."—hardly an adequate protest, but enough to make him jump up and flee into the next car of the train. Typically, I was left feeling guilty, as if I'd somehow been rude and unladylike, rather than outraged at having been molested by a stranger.

When I became a reporter, I seemed hopelessly unsuited to the tasks at hand. At the first press conference I ever attended, I watched Marci Shatzman, a reporter only a few years older than I was, firing off questions with a bold self-confidence that astonished me. I was racked with self-doubt; whenever I thought of a question to ask, I tortured myself with imagined criticisms. Was it a stupid question? Did everybody know the answer except me? Would I be humiliated in front of the entire crowd? Nothing seemed to intimidate the brassy woman in front of me. In despair, I figured I could never be like Shatzman and wondered whether I should give up my prospective career before I'd even gotten started.

Few people who know me today would recognize this self-description. After more than three decades as a journalist, I am generally seen as confident and assertive—not to mention tough and aggressive at times. Some years ago, when I asked a national leader an especially nervy question in an interview, one of America's most famous male journalists told me, "You have more cojones than any reporter I know." At the start of my career, the idea that anyone would ever say such a thing to me would have seemed about as likely as a mouse morphing into a lion.

When I think back on my early years, it's hard to believe I'm actually the same person I was then—but of course I'm not. The demands of my work have transformed me into someone else entirely—someone far better suited to cope with the rigors of life than the wimpy girl I used to be, I might add.

Many successful professionals have experienced the same kind of metamorphosis. Harriette Dorsen began adulthood as a full-time mother; although she had gone to law school, she didn't really begin her legal career until her third child turned three. "She was going to a little nursery school in the neighborhood, and one day she said, 'I don't want to go home with you. I want to stay at school with my friends,'" Dorsen recalls. "I thought, 'Well, I guess it's time for me to get a job.'"

When she went to work for a small law firm, she found her new role extremely daunting. "I felt terror the first time I had to stand up in court and speak," Dorsen says. "There were always times of doubt where I felt, 'What am I doing? I can't do this! I'm incompetent! I'm incapable! I'd better go home and bake another loaf of banana bread.' It's terrifying to take responsibility for things, but it gets less terrifying if you do it a couple of times. If you take responsibility, there's a slow accretion of confidence; you begin to feel you're intelligent, and you know how to get the job done. You know what you know, and you know what you don't know. You know how to get people to support you, how to find the right people, how to ask for advice and take advice and sift through advice and learn what's good and what's not. You learn who you can trust and who you can't. Over the years, it changes you. You become more certain, more secure, more able to deal with anything that comes up. You're not afraid to speak up, because you know that most of the time, the things you're going to say are reasonably intelligent. The confidence you get in yourself as you achieve things is very powerful and very satisfying. It makes you feel good."

After becoming a managing partner at her law firm, Dorsen ultimately left for a job as general counsel at Bantam Doubleday Dell. She finished her career in publishing as senior vice president and general counsel at Random House, where she supervised the design and construction of a new headquarters—an experience she found so fulfilling that she has since become a real-estate developer. "The conventional wisdom is that life is short, but it's not necessarily true," says Dorsen, who is now sixty-three. "I started working when I was thirty-five. If I stop at sixty-five, that's thirty years. You can do a lot of things in thirty years."

Having had at least four separate careers—as a full-time mother, as a high-powered lawyer, as a book-publishing executive, and as a real-estate developer—Dorsen has enjoyed extraordinary opportunities for someone who stayed home for so long before getting started. My own career followed the opposite pattern; I had been a journalist for nearly two decades when I finally had children, and my identity as a writer was firmly established, at least in my own mind.

But motherhood can rattle even the best-fortified identity, and like many other women, I find it difficult to assert my needs in the face of my children's more pressing ones. Submerged in the demands of maintaining the family and running a hectic household, I usually function like a well-programmed machine, racing from one obligation to another. All too rare is the chance to step back, take a deep breath, and stop worrying about what to make for dinner or whether we need milk, which we always do. Having an independent life has always given me the opportunity to disengage from my family, even if only momentarily, and reconnect with my own most authentic self—the writer I was long before I had kids, the writer I will be after they are grown. My work—particularly the intermittent travel it requires—provides a crucial opportunity to listen to my own inner voice. In a busy family, it may not literally be true that you can't hear yourself think, but it's a lot easier to get some clarity and perspective if you take a time-out once in a while.

"When my daughter was young, I had to travel sometimes, and I was gone maybe once a month for two nights," one business consultant recalls. "That was hard, but there were times when it was great to be in a hotel for a night alone. I could take a bath!"

Endlessly willing to sublimate their own egos and sacrifice their individual needs to those of their families, stay-at-home mothers often characterize working women as selfish for deriving any enjoyment from the parts of their lives that exist independently of husbands and children. A professional woman's admission that she enjoyed a hotel Jacuzzi or a foreign shopping spree is proof that she's the selfish cowbird who doesn't care about her children.

I don't find such criticisms especially surprising; many people have a need to justify their own choices with harsh indictments of alternative choices. Far more startling to me are the unforgiving attitudes of so many younger women. In my interviews for this book, I was often stunned by how judgmental some younger women can be about the normal imperfections in any life.

One thirtyish executive spent an hour telling me that it would be impossible for her to manage her current job after she had children, so she would probably give up the career she loved. "But what about Sarah* and Melanie*?" I protested, mentioning two older working mothers in her corporation.

"I don't consider them to be role models," this woman said with palpable disapproval.

"Why not?" I asked, astonished.

"Well, Sarah's husband left her—they were separated for a while, you know," she said.

"Yes, they went through a rough period—and then they got marriage counseling and got back together, and now they're very happy," I replied. "But I don't see what that has to do with Sarah's ability to do her job and be a good parent, which she is. And what about Melanie?"

"Well, her husband has problems," said the young woman. "He used to drink too much."

"Yes, but he stopped," I pointed out. "It's true that husbands sometimes have problems, but how does that nullify Melanie's success at maintaining a meaningful career while being a good mother?"

"I just wouldn't want my life to be like either of theirs," the young woman said primly. As far as she's concerned, there are no role models in her vicinity, despite the presence of some terrific senior executives with stellar professional credentials and families who are close and loving, despite their all-too-human failings.

Such young women apparently believe that they will be immune from the sorts of challenges that many older wives have contended

with at one time or another, whether in the form of a husband's substance abuse, a husband's affair, a husband's depression, a husband's
job loss, or any of the myriad other difficulties that beset ordinary
lives. They insist that their own futures will never be blighted by such
problems and that the families they build will be free from the flaws
that afflict other, less fortunate mortals. In the meantime, they dismiss
the achievements of older women because our lives are not perfect.
Well, it's true—they're not perfect. The real question is, why did anyone expect them to be?

THE WOMEN'S MOVEMENT never promised that life wouldn't be a
struggle. The women's movement never promised that it would be
easy to combine meaningful work with raising a family—only that it
should be possible for women, like men, to do so, rather than being
forced to make a draconian choice between the two major components
of a fulfilling adult life.

But somehow the entire idea of "having it all" has been discredited,
and the backlash against women's progress has been abetted by the
personal complaints of certain women who blame the empowering
ideology of feminism for the individual disappointments of their own
lives. If they concentrated on their careers and deferred motherhood
until it was too late for them to conceive, feminism was at fault. If they
didn't manage to marry a powerful alpha male and ended up alone,
they blamed feminism for making them believe they could have interesting careers as well as marriage and children.

In her recent book *Are Men Necessary?* Maureen Dowd—a Pulitzer
Prize–winning op-ed columnist for *The New York Times*—bemoaned
her status as a single, childless, fifty-three-year-old professional woman
and complained that "being a maid would have enhanced my chances
with men."

Although the book was a bestseller, many analysts scoffed at Dowd's conclusions, noting that her assertions were often based on specious sourcing. Women's eNews accused Dowd of relying on "flaky research and flimsy evidence." The *New York Post* reported: "Dowd cites one study that found women with higher IQs less likely to be married, but does not reveal—if she knows—that the study looked at women [who are now] in their 80's, not modern women, the authors said. Dowd uses another study suggesting males shy away from ambitious women, but that was based on college students—seventeen-to-nineteen-year-old guys. Dowd also cites a study that found high-achieving women aged twenty-eight to thirty-five were less likely to be wives and mothers—but fails to explain the same study found that by the ages of thirty-six to forty, the high achievers were slightly *more* likely to be hitched with kids than other working women."

Indeed, if anyone had analyzed my life at age thirty-five, when I was still single and childless, I could have been used as yet another statistic to buttress the sexist arguments against women's having careers. But I married at the age of thirty-eight and had my two healthy, wonderful children at thirty-nine and forty-two. A final verdict on my life that was rendered when I was thirty-five would have been misleading indeed.

That said, it's also true that some segments of the population face more difficult challenges than others. For African-American women, who become educated and professionally successful at higher rates than African-American males, the problem of finding a peer to marry is genuine and heartbreaking. African-Americans have the lowest marriage rate of any racial group in the United States, and twice as many black women as white women have never been married. But among middle-class white women, the problem is often self-inflicted. If men tend to marry down and women insist on marrying up, some of the most accomplished may end up without a resting place in the great cosmic game of musical chairs.

And yet for every woman I know who never married and claims the reason is that it's impossible to find a suitable mate, I know dozens of successful women who are happily married to peers. So if some women, emboldened by the visionary idealists of the women's movement, ended up disappointed, was it really the fault of the feminist leaders who looked at the deprivations of women's lives and argued that things could be better? The fact that some women make choices that result in disappointment doesn't mean an entire vision of social change was fraudulent; it only means that those particular people failed to achieve every part of the vision, for reasons that were likely to have been far more personal and individual than historical or political.

But when influential women attack the core ideas of the women's movement as some kind of hoax or failure, rather than taking responsibility for the consequences of their own individual choices, they lend credibility to the reactionaries who have always claimed that women shouldn't, or couldn't, enlarge their horizons. At the same time, those opposed to gender equity keep ratcheting up the pressure for women to conform to conventional feminine images and standards.

As a result, all too many American women are in thrall to increasingly deranged ideals of perfection. We live in a culture that constantly exhorts us to improve ourselves—and that assumes the perfectability of virtually everything. If you don't like your nose, get a nose job! If you don't like the color of your hair, dye it! If your thighs are lumpy, have liposuction! If you want abs of steel, go to the gym! Personal maintenance has become a national obsession that consumes a staggering amount of energy and resources; if American women put even a fraction of the time they spend on their appearance into working for social and political change, this country would be utterly transformed.

But they're too busy torturing themselves with the endless array of idealized images we're served up by the media, which delight in featuring surgically and digitally enhanced stars who seem to be flawless. If you don't work at perfecting every aspect of your appearance, your family, your home, and your life, you feel like a slacker. And when women feel bad about themselves, they usually assume that the problem is an individual one: If only I were thinner, prettier, richer, better organized, a better mother—then I would be happy. Frighteningly intolerant of ordinary human faults and frailties, we judge others as harshly as we judge ourselves.

But in order to maintain their sanity, working mothers have to be practical; perfection is an ideal you can use to berate yourself forever, but this takes a lot of energy that would be better directed toward more productive ends. Many of us ultimately find that the solution is to change our expectations rather than constantly flog ourselves to meet some impossible standard, whether of beauty or behavior.

For me, one of the defining moments of my dual career as journalist and mother came many years ago, when my son was almost two and my daughter was about to turn five. Ever since having kids, I had struggled with feelings of guilt that plagued me no matter what I was doing. When I was engrossed in my work, I always worried that I was slighting my children. When I focused on them, I felt guilty about neglecting my work.

I finally asked the writer Anna Quindlen, who has three children and one of the more successful careers in journalism, how she handled the guilt. "I don't do guilt," she said firmly. End of subject.

At the time, the contrast between her crisp, no-nonsense attitude and my own hand-wringing sense of inadequacy made me feel that this was just another way I didn't measure up—on a par with the fact that Anna roasted a Christmas goose while I struggled to get a turkey into the oven, or that her children took turns reading *A Christmas Carol* aloud by the fireside for weeks when my family could barely manage to find our battered copy of "The Night Before Christmas" twenty minutes before bedtime on Christmas Eve. It didn't occur to me back then that the refusal to feel guilt was a trait that could be cultivated, like patience or good manners or kindness.

Then I had an unusual stroke of professional luck. Early in the first term of the Clinton presidency, the so-called Whitewater scandal was raging around Hillary Clinton, who initially responded by refusing to talk to the press, although virtually everyone in journalism was clamoring to get an interview with her. But the day before my daughter's fifth birthday party, I landed an exclusive interview with the First Lady—a real professional coup. My time with her would be very limited, so I spent the flight down to Washington frantically preparing my questions to make the best possible use of our interview. When I arrived at the White House, I was escorted to the Map Room, where I was left to sit and wait for Mrs. Clinton to join me.

As the minutes dragged on, my mind wandered. After some time had passed, I suddenly realized with horror that my thoughts had drifted to the birthday party I'd been planning. Instead of rehearsing my interview questions, I'd been obsessively going over the party favors, children's games, and birthday snacks in my mind, absorbed in the eternal have-I-forgotten-anything drill of the ever-anxious mom. I was about to conduct an interview any other reporter in the country would have killed for—but, as always, my responsibilities as a mother exerted an inexorable pull. At that moment, I was appalled at myself. What kind of reporter was I? One with a head full of domestic trivia instead of the weighty subjects I was supposed to be focusing on!

Despite my self-flagellation, the interview went exactly as I'd planned, the story worked out fine, and the next day I threw a wonderful birthday party for my daughter. As they picked up their children, the other mothers congratulated me. "You give the best birthday parties," one said, "and you always have the best party favors!"

Planning ahead as usual, I had ordered the favors from a catalog months before the party, knowing that I might not have time for last-minute shopping, which of course I didn't. As a mom, I had delivered a successful party—and, as a reporter, I had delivered a successful story. Maybe neither one was as perfect as it might have been if I'd had an unlimited amount of time to focus on every last detail, but the greatest satisfaction ultimately came from having managed both sets of responsibilities competently.

Indeed, it's the combination of the two that has made my life so interesting. Yes, it can be stressful to keep all those balls in the air, but if I'm being really honest, I have to admit that it's also an incredible thrill. There are few experiences more exhilarating than living up to every bit of your potential. Being a working mom can tax you to the max, but it also gives you amazing opportunities to live life to the fullest and utilize all your abilities, not to mention discovering new ones you never even knew you possessed.

My work as a journalist has enhanced my home life in innumerable ways, just as my responsibilities as a parent have enhanced my professional effectiveness and my ability to relate to many different kinds of people. But whatever I'm doing, it's always hard to resist the impulse to torture myself with ridiculous standards of imagined perfection.

In the 1950s, the English pediatrician and psychoanalyst D. W. Winnicott wrote about the "good enough mother," saying that parents don't have to be perfect as long as they provide enough love and care for their children. In 1987, the American child psychologist Bruno Bettelheim expanded on this reassuring idea in his bestselling book *A Good Enough Parent.* But that sensible perspective seems to have gotten lost amid the current hysteria.

Haunted by the anxieties inherent in juggling work and family, women often assume that the way to resolve the problem is to give up one or the other. But when they sacrifice work to concentrate on family, they frequently put the kind of pressure on themselves that Judith Warner explored in her book about full-time motherhood run amok, *Perfect Madness.*

"I was surrounded, it seemed, by women who had surrendered their better selves—and their sanity—to motherhood," Warner wrote in *Newsweek.* "Women who pulled all-nighters hand-painting paper plates for a class party. Who obsessed over the most minute details of playground politics. Who—like myself—appeared to be sleep-walking through life in a state of quiet panic."

But perfection is a dangerous goal; not only is it unrealistic, dooming you to eternal feelings of inadequacy when you fail to measure up, but it can also be terribly damaging, particularly to female children who are already bombarded with cultural pressures to conform to impossible images. A couple of years ago, a teenager I know became anorexic. She got thin enough to be a fashion model—and then she got thinner. As she grew increasingly skeletal, her worried parents hovered over her, trying to understand the deranged ideal that was tormenting her. Their daughter had no trouble putting it into words. "I want to be perfect!" she wailed, pinching the shrunken thighs that were still, in her own eyes, too fleshy.

Misguided ideals of perfection are the bane of women's existence, and their pursuit inadvertently encourages women to limit their ambitions. Instead of accepting that life is an inherently messy enterprise and that the vast, complex sweep of it is a large part of the joy, they think it's better to narrow their focus to small segments that can be tidied up and wrapped with a big bow, even as they turn their backs on most of the wondrous possibilities that might otherwise enrich their existence.

Throughout their lives, my children have watched me manage a wide range of demands, both familial and professional. They've seen me confront obstacles, get frustrated, make mistakes, figure out compromises, and ultimately meet whatever challenges were thrown my way. No doubt they've learned many things from my struggles, not all of them flattering to my self-image. But whatever my flaws, I know they know I've tried my best. On my last birthday, my daughter, who was then sixteen, made me a beautiful card. Inside she wrote, "I could never ask for a better role model or more loving mother, and I want to thank you so much for always being here for me."

My own life is, in many ways, disordered. My apartment usually looks neat, but there are secret nests of clutter scattered throughout. My overstuffed closets are a disaster. Some items haven't made it off my ongoing to-do lists for years. The super-fit stay-at-home moms who spend a good part of their day in the gym all put me to shame; no one is going to ask me to pose for the *Sports Illustrated* Swimsuit Issue for the remainder of this particular lifetime. My wardrobe is pathetic; my idea of dressing adequately is finding something black and not too wrinkled to put on. Who has time to shop? Certainly not me, although I'll admit to snatching the odd moment when I'm on a business trip.

And I'll freely confess that some of my contributions to school bake sales were store-bought. So what? In the infamous opening scene of *I Don't Know How She Does It*, the heroine is frantically "distressing" mince pies at 1:37 A.M. so that her own furtively purchased donations to the school Christmas party will look homemade. As a scene in a novel, this was amusing, but in real life, why do women agonize about such things? No woman is entirely impervious to these pressures, but unless you're a professional pastry chef, the cosmetic perfection of your baked goods is not the best measure of your worth in the world.

Although my children are teenagers now, there are still days when I suffer over the inevitable conflicts between job and family. I have often taken the red-eye home from Los Angeles—an unpleasant experience that always leaves me exhausted—in order to make it back to New York in time for an important event involving my children. Such accommodations can be annoying, but the bottom line is that I have two fantastic children and a career that has given me financial autonomy as well as an independent identity, challenging work, gratifying recognition, the opportunity to learn new things and grow as an individual, and countless other benefits. I've been a working mother for nearly eighteen years now, and in all that time I've never once regretted the immeasurably rewarding life of a working mother. If combining work and family isn't worth the hassle, you sure can't prove it by me.

But in order to balance those dimensions of our lives, we have to revise our ideas about what's holding us back. Juggling jobs and children doesn't necessarily mean doing badly in either area of your life, but it does mean changing the way you evaluate what constitutes success.

The problem isn't that we can't manage both areas of our lives perfectly.

The problem is that we ever expected perfection in the first place.

## CHAPTER EIGHT

# THE JOYS OF THE FULL LIFE

## "IT'S HARD FOR ME TO IMAGINE WHO I'D BE IF I DIDN'T WORK."

After several years as a stay-at-home mom, Diane Miller was vaguely unhappy with her life. "I felt something was missing," says the Pennsylvania mother of two. "I've always been a hard worker, and part of me felt unfulfilled or unsatisfied." But she was nonetheless hesitant about returning to work. "I was really frightened," she says.

So when Miller, who was trained as a social worker, took a part-time job as a school therapist, she was astonished at her own reaction. "I couldn't believe how great it felt to be back in the workforce doing something professional," she says. "I cannot tell you how exciting it was. I was really surprised. It was just a completely different feeling, doing something you have a skill at, where your skill is recognized by other professionals. In my profession, where you're doing something for kids, you can see that it matters to them. I had built up a career before I had children, and it felt incredibly comfortable and satisfying and rewarding to exercise those talents. It was like, 'Oh, yeah—this is who I am!' Not that being a mom isn't who I am, but it wasn't enough."

Many women might consider Miller brave for even saying such a thing aloud. Our culture simply assumes that men will also have active, engaged lives outside the home, but when a woman acknowledges that life inside those four walls might not fulfill her every need, many people act as if she's a bad person as well as a bad mother.

Remember the stay-at-home mom who was so enraged by my essay on women's economic independence that she fired off a scathing e-mail to *Tango* magazine? "Shame on the women who will leave their kids with someone else just so they can 'have a life'—you're a bunch of cowbirds!" she wrote.

As an urbanite, I felt the need to fortify my knowledge of avian social mores in order to appreciate fully her point of view, so I did enough research to discover that cowbirds are the shiftless hos of the bird world. First of all, they have loose sexual morals: enature.com describes them as "promiscuous," noting that female cowbirds go into the woods with several male suitors and fornicate willy-nilly. Among cowbirds, "no pair bond exists." To make matters worse, these slutty females then perform the ultimate act of maternal treachery on the nests of more than two hundred other species of birds. The cowbird is a "brood parasite," in the accusatory phrase of the experts: Removing an egg from another bird's nest, she substitutes one of her own, leaving the faithful full-time bird mommy to hatch and feed the interloper's progeny while the feckless cowbird flies off into the blue to resume her whoring. Like the children of the town tramp, even the offspring of cowbirds are morally tainted by their mothers' bad behavior: "The young cowbird grows quickly at the expense of the young of the host, pushing them out of the nest or taking most of the food."

Whew. Faced with attitudes like these, many working mothers simply keep their heads down, remaining silent about their independent lives while judiciously refraining from public judgments about full-time mothers. As a result, however, much of what working women really feel about their choices remains unspoken. Afraid of disapproval, they rarely verbalize the enormous rewards of work and success, of money and power—not to mention the incomparable richness of combining those satisfactions with the joys of family life.

"It's so enormous I don't even know where to begin," says NYU sociology professor Kathleen Gerson, who has been married for twenty-five years and has one child. "My identity as a worker is the bedrock of all the other identities in my life. It's so huge and so profound and so important. It's certainly given me self-confidence, a belief in my own abilities, respect for myself, and the ability to work hard and achieve some meaningful things in life. I also think it's made me a better parent. I haven't poured all my identity into my child, and it's given me resources to understand that my child's life is her own—to be there for her and to nurture her but not to impose on her my ideas about what her life should be. It's given me the skills to protect her in institutional settings where parents need to fight for their children, like schools. It's also contributed to a happy marriage, because of the mutual respect my partner and I have for each other's abilities. I'm married to a man who couldn't imagine being married to a woman who didn't have her own career—not just a job but a calling. That's something we share; he's a professor, too, and that's kept us together as well. It's also given my daughter a wonderful father, because parenting her has been a completely shared endeavor. It's been genuinely egalitarian. I feel extraordinarily blessed that I have been able to live a life that would not have been possible in earlier generations. It's made me a more generous person; I've reached a point where I feel good enough about myself that I really want to be generous toward other people, in line with Erik Erikson's classic theories of life stages, which include generativity, where you genuinely want to give to others, to pass along what you have learned and help them reach their goals. The irony is that working women are cast as selfish, when I think that it is through nurturing yourself that you are ultimately able to nurture others.

Work has made me happy, and that's the greatest gift you can give the people around you."

Such testimonials could hardly be more fervent or sweeping, but in my interviews with professional women I was surprised by how many said that they had never talked about what work had done for them. "You ask me that question and I well up with tears," says television news producer Vicki Gordon, looking astonished at her own response. "Working is so important to me—it is just my essence. I don't know what I would do without it. It connects me to the world; it gives me a sense of accomplishment, of doing something important. I'm always engaged in learning about something new. It forces you to be disciplined when you don't want to be disciplined, to read, to think, to question, to confront what's going on in the world. And it's fun. I meet interesting people; I travel. It affords me a window on the world I would never have had otherwise. If you say to me, 'Would you quit if you won the lottery?'—the truth is that I wouldn't. It's not really work, for me. It's pleasure."

None of which diminishes Gordon's commitment to her children in any way. When her children were younger, she agonized over her choices. "After I had kids, I berated myself for not wanting to give up work. I kept wondering, 'Why isn't this mother thing, where you want to spend 24/7 with your children, overtaking you?'" she says. "I love my kids; my children are it, for me. But I spent nine months at home on maternity leave after I had Isabelle, and I got nothing done. It was a big deal that I could be dressed and showered by six P.M. I had some feelings about 'How am I going to go back to work and leave Isabelle?' but I needed a paycheck, and I liked getting a paycheck. It gave me a sense of independence and freedom. I didn't want to give up my work, and I didn't want to give up my paycheck. I didn't have to choose between my kids and my work—I did them both. I always had pangs, but in the last three or four years I made peace with it. I am proud of what I've accomplished."

The women of the Baby Boom generation have enjoyed unprecedented professional success. But, like Vicki Gordon, most working mothers remain as reticent about their accomplishments as they are hesitant to describe their passion for their work. In an essay for *The New York Times* entitled "The Silence of the Moms," writer Alison Frankel commented on that omission in describing her interactions with other suburban mothers. "The only thing we never discuss is our jobs. I know which soccer moms work—we're the ones most often scrambling for carpool help—but I have no idea what they think of their jobs. I don't even know what most of them do, let alone whether they like their work or are up all night worrying about deadlines. I don't ask, and they never volunteer."

Oddly, Frankel attributed this silence to the success of the women's movement, saying that "if feminism is about the freedom to make choices, true liberation is not having to discuss and defend those choices." But the mothers she hangs out with talk constantly about their domestic lives; somehow they feel entirely free to discuss their marriages, parenting issues, and homemaking practices. It's only work that remains a taboo. I find it very difficult to believe Frankel's assertion that this is truly a measure of freedom.

But I know that this silence isn't limited to suburban soccer moms. My best friend, whom I've known since we were seven years old, is a nationally recognized expert in her field, but when she calls to tell me about some new accolade, she whispers into the phone as if she were confiding a shameful secret instead of sharing joyful news with her biggest fan. In this culture, females are socialized to be humble and self-effacing, and braggadocio remains the province of blowhard males.

Dr. Anna Fels offered a telling anecdote about this phenomenon at the beginning of *Necessary Dreams*. A woman had agonized about revealing something she found acutely embarrassing to Dr. Fels, a psychiatrist. A journalist in her forties, the woman confided that she had hidden this secret since she was seven. "I haven't even told my husband about it," she admitted.

And what was this terrible transgression she had concealed for so long? As a child, she used to write a mysterious acronym on her notebooks and papers. "It was IWBF—I Will Be Famous," the woman confessed.

"Conveying their strengths and attainments to others is so far from the expected female style of self-effacement that women experience it as 'bragging'—in other words, socially unacceptable boastfulness," wrote Dr. Fels. "The linguist Deborah Tannen, in her book on language and gender, *Talking from Nine to Five*, concluded that soliciting or even accepting recognition is heavily proscribed. 'For middle-class American women, the constraint is clear: talking about your own accomplishments in a way that calls attention to yourself is not acceptable. . . . Girls are supposed to be "humble"—not try to take the spotlight, emphasize the ways they are just like everyone else, and de-emphasize the ways they are special.'"

Among professional women, the result is often a bizarre disconnect between their achievements and their social demeanor. During her twenty-three-year career at Merrill Lynch, Darcy Howe's effectiveness has always been indisputably evidenced by the bottom line. "In my business, the numbers mean everything," she says. "I know I'm good."

Recently Howe was named to an eight-person national advisory board for her firm—an achievement that constituted a major acknowledgment of her success. "I feel great about the public affirmation," Howe says. "That's a real validation for what I've done in my career. There's not a lot in my life that could replace that kind of feeling of accomplishment."

But Howe's social acquaintances don't know about the honor. "I haven't even told my friends," Howe admits. "I always feel I have to be careful about tooting my horn. That's just not what you do as girls; that's not who we are as friends."

It takes some probing for Howe to open up about her work—but when she does, it is obvious how much pride she feels in her own accomplishments. "I've always felt powerful, in my work and in my life," she says. "My identity is pretty clear in my community; beyond my own circle, people know who I am. Why is that important to me? It seems shallow, but it's really affirming when you have this experience with people who admire who you are. My career has done that for me, and because of that I feel good about myself. As I'm going into my fifties, people say, 'Oh, you look better than you did ten years ago!' I'm coming into my own; I'm less concerned about what people think. I admit that my work has given me all these things."

THE MYTHOLOGY OF motherhood often presumes that women should be content with a purely domestic role, which generally means forgoing public rewards in favor of private ones circumscribed by the family. When they're being honest, however, working women readily acknowledge how satisfying it can be to receive broader recognition for their talents. "I'm pretty well known in Washington, and when I go somewhere and people say, 'Oh, you're Marna Tucker! I've heard about you!'—I feel really good about that," says Tucker, a leading attorney whose pioneering career included her election as the first woman president of the District of Columbia bar. "Somehow I succeeded and got to the top of where I needed to go, and that made me feel I could do anything I ever wanted to do. I'm not afraid to take risks. I learned how to work with people in a very tough field where people would pay me ungodly amounts of money to deal with the most important parts of their lives. People trusted me, and that was more important than the money. It's also given me compassion for people who are not working and for people who are downtrodden. I think, 'There but for the grace of God go I.' It just makes me realize how lucky I am."

While women work for different reasons, many do so because the job of full-time mother is less satisfying than income-producing labor. "One investigation in which 201 gifted women were interviewed found that 'more women who worked reaped satisfaction from that experience than the homemakers did from their work at home,'" Dr. Fels wrote in *Necessary Dreams*. "Another study reported that only 21 percent of working mothers say that they would like to leave their jobs to stay home with their children, while 56 percent of homemakers, given the chance to start over, said that they would choose to have a career."

As the survey of gifted women indicates, many simply feel that being a homemaker fails to utilize the full range of their capabilities. "I cannot imagine myself not working," says Heidi Hartmann, founder of the Institute for Women's Policy Research and the mother of three as well as grandmother of one child. "I have a Ph.D. in economics; I love the work I do, and I want to keep on doing it. It gives me the sense of mastery and the sense of control you get from doing your craft well. My kids are great, but you don't really get that from raising kids; that's not something you control in the same way. I think everyone wants to make a contribution and be productive in some way. Women have always done that through having children, but there's a big difference between accomplishing something yourself, by writing a report or building a building or digging a ditch, and doing that through other people. Raising kids is a great activity, but it's a somewhat marginal one that doesn't necessarily use all your energy and talent. I don't want to belittle the women who say it does use all their talents, but for many women it doesn't."

When Hartmann gives speeches, she has been known to shock her audiences with provocative comments about the relative value of raising children in relation to other forms of achievement. "As wonderful as my kids are, and as much as I love them and would surely be willing to die for them were that necessary, I would have to say that the work I've done has probably been a more important contribution to the world than those four wonderful people and their future progeny," Hartmann observes. "As I once said at a conference, unless you are the mother of an Einstein or a Madame Curie, which most of us are not, your own work, if it is significant, is probably more important to society than raising your kids."

And the rewards of work are far more enduring than the presence of children at home. "I loved being a mother, but I also knew that the whole point was to raise children so they would grow up and leave, and I knew that I'd better have other things to put my energy into besides my children," says Harvard law professor Elizabeth Warren, who has three grown children.

The author of several bestsellers, including *The Two-Income Trap* and *All Your Worth,* Warren was named one of the fifty most influential women lawyers in America by the *National Law Journal.* "My children used to say, 'Good thing Mom worked!'" she reports with a laugh. "It lets me use all my energy; I don't have to hold back. If I didn't work, I'd smother a child and never mean to; it would be with the best of intentions, but having a job lets me be fully who I am. I have a job where there are really important things I want to do. Being a college professor is a great job. If I were doing data entry all day long, I might not find working so much fun."

Indeed, it's hardly surprising that women with intellectually challenging, creative, glamorous, lucrative, or altruistic jobs feel strongly about their rewards. But for millions of American women, work is not such an appealing enterprise, and when their jobs are mundane, repetitive, unsatisfying, or poorly paid, their life choices often reflect a corresponding lack of engagement.

Diana Cassity worked as a manager at McDonald's and as a cashier at Wal-Mart while raising her three children, who are now twenty, twenty-two, and twenty-four. At the age of forty-six, Cassity, who married at nineteen, is already a grandmother. She and her husband, a supervisor for a contracting company, live in Freedom, Indiana, a rural area offering few jobs that don't require an expensive, gas-guzzling commute. Now that her children are on their own, Cassity has opted to stay home.

When I ask why she doesn't work, she snorts. "Because I don't have to," she says. "It just seems like we can make it without me working now. I don't have to, so I don't. I like not working, because I can choose what I do. I crochet, I sew, I cook; I'm busy. I don't feel that I'm not fulfilled."

At the lower end of the socioeconomic spectrum, the goal may be simply to earn the money necessary for survival. "I've always worked; we need the income," says Corky Hall, who lives in Wabash, Indiana, with her husband, a mechanic. Married at the age of seventeen, Hall is now forty-seven, and her children are twenty-four and twenty-seven. Over the years, she has worked as a nurse's aide, in a fabric store, and at an office-equipment factory, among other places. These days she drives a school bus and runs a sewing alterations and mending business out of her home, although its revenues are limited by the fact that many people in her area can't afford to get their clothes altered.

"I didn't always like some of the jobs I had, but it meant income," Hall says. "There's no way we could have afforded two vehicles if I hadn't worked, and my son wouldn't have been able to do sports, and my daughter wouldn't have been able to do ballet. Around here, parents have to dish out a lot of money for a lot of things the school systems can't pay for, like schoolbooks and sports uniforms. Those are things we had to come up with the money to pay for, and my kids wouldn't have been able to do them if I hadn't worked."

Even with Corky employed, the Halls have always had a modest lifestyle; Corky made most of her own and the children's clothes, and going out to eat as a family meant a once-a-month trip to Pizza Hut. The Halls' vacations usually consist of trips to a state park to go camping and fishing, inexpensive expeditions that nonetheless wouldn't be possible if Corky weren't augmenting the household budget. "If I didn't work, we couldn't go on vacations, and my husband couldn't own his motorcycle," she says. "Most of the women around here work out of necessity. They're not able to manage on one income, just because it costs so much to live."

Of course, the exigencies of economic survival are not limited to women; men have always worked because they had to, often in jobs that were hard and unsatisfying. But because men know they must work, they tend to plan more effectively for lifelong employment, whereas women often find stopgap work merely to suit the needs of a given moment, rather than mapping out the long-term trajectory of their labor-force participation and preparing for advancement. This lack of commitment contributes to the erratic nature of women's employment patterns, which are characterized by frequent interruptions and job changes. Since women pay such a high price for those interruptions, in terms of both earnings and promotion, it seems obvious that they might fare better if they took into consideration the lifelong value of meaningful work and economic self-sufficiency. If women were encouraged from childhood to think in terms of building a career that offered increasing rewards and long-term potential, they might be far less likely to drop in and out of the workforce as frequently as they now do, and far less likely to suffer the resulting penalties.

Even when jobs aren't particularly satisfying, however, many working-class women retain a firm grasp on the value of employment. "I know a woman whose husband left her, and she was put into a terrible financial situation," says Corky Hall. "The career she had before she stopped working was no longer available, and she had to take a lower-paying job. She felt like the benefit of being home with the kids did not outweigh the circumstances it put her in. She nearly had a total breakdown over the whole mess."

But having an income is only one of the reasons women cite for valuing work. Work gives structure to their lives and discipline to their schedules; many stay-at-home wives admitted to me that they actually got more done when they worked outside the home, simply because they were forced to use their time so effectively. Being a homemaker can be isolating, and many women also appreciate the social benefits of working outside the home, even when their jobs aren't particularly interesting. "Sometimes it's a relief, when you have children, to have someone else to talk to, instead of somebody just saying 'Mommy, I want' all the time," Hall acknowledges.

"When I left Wal-Mart, I missed the interaction with people," Diana Cassity admits.

Whatever the relative satisfactions of their jobs, however, it's also true that nearly everyone who works consistently for many years will experience periods of weariness or burnout, although "working mothers may be most immune," as *New York* magazine reported last December: One study in the Netherlands found that "twice as many working women without children showed symptoms of burnout as did working women with underage children." In general, however, as women contribute an increasing share of the average family's income, the financial pressures on female breadwinners have come to resemble those traditionally experienced by men who feel shackled to their jobs.

At a recent birthday lunch for a friend, I found myself sitting next to a woman with a successful career whose financial rewards supply the bulk of her family's income. Her husband is a documentary filmmaker for whom employment is intermittent and monetary compensation is limited, even when he's working. "I'll tell you what you should write about in your next book," this woman said. "I know a lot of women who are the major breadwinners, and many of them are leading lives of quiet desperation. They would like to work less, or even to stay home entirely, but they don't have that option, because they have to support their families."

Such practical constraints can also curtail their freedom to explore new professional challenges or opportunities for personal growth. "I went through a period when I was aching to head in a new direction, but my financial responsibilities definitely narrowed my choices to jobs where I could be sure of making a salary above a certain level," says Connie Dunne,* a fifty-eight-year-old psychiatrist who lives in western Massachusetts with her husband, a consultant for nonprofit health-care organizations, and their teenage daughter. "When I was in my early fifties, I had a series of jobs that were flops, and I was just so sick of being a psychiatrist, of working in the mental-health field, and of dealing with all the problems in the system. My idealism had sort of run out, and I entertained the idea of going into a completely new field. I thought about alternative medicine, I thought about environmental studies—I even sent résumés to places like the Sierra Club. I had all these fantasies, but I felt trapped, and that threw me into a depression. I didn't want to work; I didn't want to go out of the house. All I wanted to think about was being a homebody, making cookies, being a mom."

Because Dunne had always earned more money than her husband, however, she couldn't depend on him to make up the difference should she reverse course or take time out of the workforce, which only added to her resentment. "I felt like, 'Why do I have to work so much? Why can't I take more time off?'" she recalls. "You want to go play, especially when your kid is out of school. You see somebody riding a bike and think, 'Why isn't that me?' In recent years, I have felt more of a yearning for the lighthearted stuff. It's the desire to not be working so much that has been increasing in intensity. There's definitely a sort of wistfulness, a longing I feel that can be quite poignant at times. It would be nice to have more time to pursue other interests, but I'm just not free to do so. I have to admit that at times this has prompted some thoughts about why wasn't I married to a rich man who could support me so I could do what I wanted."

If she were, Dunne might have given up her career entirely rather than addressing the root causes of her discontent. But, because of financial necessity, she was forced to figure out more creative solutions.

Over time, she resolved her problem with a series of measures that included enrolling in a yearlong intensive seminar in personal change and committing herself to a professional shift in direction that required new coursework and an expansion of her skills.

"I became certified as an adolescent psychiatrist," Dunne explains. "It wasn't as drastic a change as I might have envisioned, but it was significant enough to be okay. I was able to maintain my income while changing my focus in a way that allowed me to get recharged again."

Despite periods of disenchantment, Dunne realizes that her work provides important mental-health benefits that make a significant contribution to her general sense of well-being. "I'm a person who really needs structure, and I feel better when I've got places to go and things to do," she says. "I'm really nervous about the next stage of life, when you scale back on work because you're moving into retirement. I do better when I'm in a rhythm."

She also recognizes the extent to which her various jobs have broadened her horizons and brought her into contact with a diverse array of colleagues and clients. "It would be very easy, in retirement, to end up being with people who are just like you," she notes. "It's very enriching to go to a job and work with people you like to be with but who are very different from you."

Although she still fantasizes about working less, Dunne is well aware that her commitment to providing psychiatric services for troubled low-income adolescents has given her an enormous amount of personal satisfaction. "I definitely feel like I'm making a contribution to the world," she says. "I'm lucky, and I feel like I have to pay back. I'm trying to support kids who are in a very bad way, and feeling like I'm doing something that's important makes me feel more ethical, makes me feel better about being part of this country and receiving all the blessings I experience."

Like Dunne, women who enjoy challenging careers typically believe that work enhances their lives in countless ways. "I need to have a purpose in being here," says Tanya Mandor, a strategic planning and marketing consultant who previously had a successful career as a high-ranking executive in the retail and cosmetics industries. "To raise my kids, to be with my husband, to have a home—those are all purposes, but I also need a purpose that's going to keep me intellectually stimulated, and that's what work is all about. I love being involved with problem solving. There's problem solving at home, but it's different from figuring out what position a certain brand should have in the marketplace, which to me is much more interesting and challenging. That's why I'm still doing it; I find I still need that. I love being able to work on a project that interests me; I love learning new things."

Such accomplishments bolster any woman's self-esteem, no matter how self-effacing she is. "I am so much more confident than I used to be, because of work," says attorney Ann Lewis. "Work gives you the opportunity to master something. The challenge of the blank page, of the report that has to be done, of the statute that has to be analyzed, and the knowledge that you've done those things successfully—things like that give you a sense of self-worth, of using your brain, of problem solving, as well as being part of the world. I know my material, and I just feel a lot more authority. This has been a remarkable change for me."

Having opted out of the workforce and then opted back in, Lewis has also realized some unexpected benefits for her marriage. "When I was home, our lives were pleasanter in some ways, because we weren't both scrambling. There were things I could do for my husband that I couldn't do before I stopped working; there were home-cooked meals and other services—but it was not all a plus," she says. "He certainly felt more stressed about his responsibilities. Supporting a family is an incredible burden to put on one person. If marriage is supposed to be a partnership, it's not really fair to say, 'This is your job.' When you're out working, you realize how hard it is, particularly the pressure of keeping a job over the long run and performing satisfactorily. It makes you more sympathetic when your partner is stressed to know what that stress is like. Money is a great equalizer in marriage. It makes it easier to make joint decisions, because you both contributed."

Lewis also sensed a substantial change in the attitudes of others when she went back to work. "People just don't look at you the same way when you're home," she says. "When you say you're a lawyer, people sit up and take notice. When you stay home and take care of your kids, people just assume you don't have that much to contribute."

It can be painful for stay-at-home mothers to face this fact, but there is no doubt that work and the benefits that come with it—money, responsibility, autonomy, power, competency, self-confidence, knowledge, expertise, and wider renown—earn people's respect, both within a marriage and in the larger world.

"Work has made me a much more interesting person to be around," book editor Susan Mercandetti attests. "My job is about ideas, so I'm not the dreaded housewife; you can sit me anywhere at a dinner party. I'm also more interesting to my husband."

"Work has given me a tremendous sense of worth as a person," says family historian Stephanie Coontz. "The satisfactions of work have given me self-confidence and made me less dependent on having a man but more able to handle a loving relationship, because I'm less needy. When you're needy, you often cling, and you're not really loving. You're bribing; you do things to bribe people to stay with you because you need them, rather than because you love them. Having my own money means that I don't feel like I have my hand out all the time. There's an evenness. You don't feel like you're dealing with a parent; you feel like you're dealing with a friend."

And the benefits of work steadily increase with time, even as the disadvantages of managing a dual life begin to evaporate. Now that Ann Lewis's children are in their twenties, she is grateful to have a meaningful job. Her husband works long hours and often travels, but she minded his absences far more when she wasn't working. "If I hadn't gone back to work, I think I would be horribly depressed," she says. "When I wasn't working, I was lonely; my husband was away a third of the time, and I was less sympathetic to his being away, or to his being tired when he was home. You can't help it; if you're not working, you become needier. I was grown-up enough to know it was not logical, but I just felt sad. I missed him. I love him just as much now, but I'm energized by my own work. I feel less resentful when he's away, because I'm busy, too."

The gradual evolution from a life that revolves around finding or keeping Mr. Right into a life that revolves around your own individual agenda was exemplified by the change in Candace Bushnell's work in recent years. Her "Sex and the City" columns in the *New York Observer*, which were made into a bestselling book and then a hit television series for HBO, followed the romantic escapades of four Manhattan women as they tried and failed to find the Perfect Man. But in Bushnell's latest novel, *Lipstick Jungle*, the women characters are less interested in chasing Mr. Big than they are in becoming mistresses of the universe themselves. "Success and self-actualization was what really made women glow—they shone with the fullness of life," the author wrote.

In a subsequent interview with *The New York Times*, Bushnell—who was then forty-six years old and married to Charles Askegard, a principal dancer for the New York City Ballet—added, "The women in this book have realized that you can't completely rely on men. Women have got to rely on themselves."

By the later years of their careers, many professional women have resolved their ambivalence and become unapologetically enthusiastic about the work that has sustained them for so long. "I'm a very happy camper," says law professor Sylvia Law. "I have so many things I'm interested in. It's wonderful to be involved in such a rich diversity of different things. I like it all."

Law relished the challenge even when her son was young. "I was on

a board in Los Angeles that met four times a year, so four times a year
I'd take him and fly to Los Angeles, where he would spend time with
his grandparents—and then we'd take the red-eye home to New York
on Sunday night, and I'd go back to work," she says. "I didn't have to
do that, but it felt good. I knew I was good at what I did; I've been
successful in different ways for a very long time. The importance of
work in my life could not be overstated. It's hard for me to imagine
who I'd be if I didn't work."

At the age of sixty-two, Law also appreciates her autonomy. "The
job market is so unstable, and the marriage market is so unstable," she
says. "I grew up poor and never had any money except what I earned.
I find it extremely reassuring to earn my own money."

"If you don't work, you miss out on a lot of satisfaction," says Tilde
Sankovitch, who was a longtime professor at Northwestern University
in Evanston, Illinois, before she retired. "If I hadn't worked, I would
have been a doctor's wife, going to lunches and doing some good work
in the hospital. I probably wouldn't have felt that happy about it. For
me, psychologically, work was very important. It gave me a sense of
being my own person. The fact that you work gives you a kind of status that was important to me, too. For my mother, to be a wife of a
well-known doctor was more than enough, but the world has changed.
Having my professional identity gave me a certain standing, which I
loved. It made it easier for me to communicate with people and to
hold my own. I loved seeing my things get published. I liked having
my own colleagues, so you don't depend on your husband for all your
social contacts. It is good to have that variety of social milieus. It certainly expanded my horizons very much and gave me another take on
American society that I otherwise wouldn't have had."

In retrospect, even her dual responsibilities as mother and professor
seem minor to Sankovitch, who is now seventy-one. "It did require
some juggling, but I can't remember that it was terribly hard—
nothing that wasn't acceptable or bearable," she says. "I didn't find it

too difficult. My husband was helpful, and he would take over completely if I had to go out of town. He was always very proud of me and what I accomplished, and I think it's probably true that he respected me more because of my career."

In comparison with such benefits, the sacrifices required by the juggling act ultimately seem negligible to many working women. "When my kids were young, there was never 'me' time—time to get a haircut or do my nails," says Tanya Mandor. "But I had something that fulfilled me. I had a purpose in life; I contributed to something that was bigger than my family. I contributed to a business, I trained people, I mentored people. It's the same thing a man has. Why does a man go to work? Just to make money? I don't think so. Most men, given the option of staying home, would say, 'I'd rather die.' And yet women welcome it with open arms, because we were raised that way. To this day, we are raising women to be mothers and wives and housekeepers."

But in doing so, we are depriving them of the myriad rewards of meaningful work, which include a raison d'être that can last a lifetime. Although the women I interviewed for this book were employed in a wide range of fields, the happy ones shared at least one thing in common: They all felt a tremendous passion for their work. "You have to really love what you do," says sociologist Pamela Stone. "I do love what I do, and I think that has always kept me going. My work gives me the ability to think about topics I think are important. I do basic research, but I always choose subjects I believe have policy relevance. You always hope your work informs real-world policy decisions, and this is a wonderful opportunity."

Stone nonetheless made compromises to accommodate her family. When her children were younger, she served as chairman of Hunter College's sociology department for a decade. "It was a heavy administrative load, but one of the upsides of being department chair was that it did give me more control over my schedule," she says. Like many moms, she found that flexibility to be crucial in enabling her to take care of her family obligations.

Such trade-offs are often viewed as too difficult by stay-at-home mothers, many of whom conceptualize work as something that will only add to their burdens; as far as they're concerned, simplifying their lives and concentrating on the domestic sphere is the best way to protect themselves from stress and hardship. Working women often have the opposite view; well aware that their independent lives can help fortify them against major losses, they see work as a source of enormous strength and resiliency in times of need. "If something happened to my husband, what would be my lifeline? What a miserable, isolated person I would be," Ann Lewis says.

Switching back and forth between the parallel universes of work and family, most working women develop a perspective that helps them deal with both dimensions of their lives. The family provides a welcome haven from stresses on the job, but work can also offer respite from family stress. "When my husband and I separated, thank God I had an office to come to and a place to focus my attention on the larger world," says one working mother who later reconciled with her husband. "If I had been home with children and no income, I would have been powerless on every level. At least I knew I had a paycheck, and I could take care of my children and myself without him if he disappeared or couldn't give me any money."

When the outcome is divorce, work can seem like a lifesaver. One professor was devastated when her seventeen-year relationship with her son's father ended. "I would spend most of each day sobbing, and then I would dry my eyes, go teach my class, come back to the office, and start crying again," she says. "I think it's good having to get a grip. Work distracts you, because it's interesting. You realize that it's more interesting than wallowing in self-pity."

In *A Mother's Place,* her book about working mothers, Susan Chira described the importance of her routines as a *New York Times* editor when one of her children became seriously ill. "My child's life was in danger, and the crisis lasted many, many months," Chira wrote. "I discovered that work can be a lifeline, not only in normal times, but in dire times as well. I was lucky to work for a generous and compassionate employer, who allowed me to take as much time off as necessary to care for my child. There was no question in my employer's mind—or my own—about what came first. Going to work when I could, though, allowed me to visit a world far removed from the one of sickness and sadness that we inhabited. Working also signaled to my children that life could be normal and they could feel normal, too. Without my work and the restorative sense of identity and continuity it provided, I could not have mustered the strength to do what was indeed my most important job—nursing and reassuring my child. . . . Along with the support of friends and family, working helped me compose myself. It helped distract me from terror, and it helped replenish me so I could give again."

Chira's child eventually recovered, but others are not so fortunate—and when the worst happens, work can prove to be a woman's salvation. After Janet Rodkin's* husband and only child were killed in a horrific accident, she was virtually paralyzed by grief for several months. "As I started to come out of shock, I started to think, 'Thank God I have work to get back to!'" says Rodkin, a health-care consultant who lived in New Jersey at the time. "In the beginning, concentration was very hard; grieving takes a lot of energy, and I did get very tired. But I did see myself as capable and competent in my work, and eventually the part of me that needed that was rekindled. If my whole identity had been wrapped up in being a wife and mother, I don't know how I would have fared. But my role in life was not solely dependent on my relationship to my daughter and husband. I still was Janet the professional, and work represented normalcy to me. Having relationships, handling responsibilities, being accountable to other people were part of my routine, and working became a way of having some portion of my life be normal—which helped me to deal with the part of my life that would never be normal again. I felt very fortunate that I had work."

With luck, most of us will never have to deal with tragic loss of such unthinkable magnitude, but while Rodkin's circumstances represent an extreme, most working women readily express a profound sense of the ways in which work has nourished them in every area of their lives. "I feel I am a better mother because I work; it gives me a better perspective on everything, and it makes me enjoy being with my son that much more," says Barb Alexander, a project manager at JPMorgan Chase in Chicago. "I'm not just a mom and a wife all the time; I'm a professional, and it's something I'm very proud of. My career is a big part of who I am."

When working women acknowledge the pleasures of having their own independence, right-wing conservatives often blast them for being selfish in seeking their own gratification instead of dedicating themselves exclusively to the needs of their family. Despite the reactionary claim that women's autonomy threatens the family unit, however, research suggests that it may actually strengthen the marital relationship, according to Scott Coltrane, a sociology professor at the University of California, Riverside. Studies show that in relationships characterized by a more equitable division of household labor—such as dual-income marriages where both partners work and also share domestic tasks—the women are less prone to depression, more likely to be sexually attracted to their spouses, and more likely to enjoy improved sexual relations.

"Satisfaction with spousal help is positively associated with positive marital interaction, marital closeness, affirmation and positive affect," Coltrane reported in his study "Research on Household Labor." In contrast, he says, dissatisfaction with a spouse's help is correlated with "marital conflict, thoughts of divorce, negative affect, and depression."

Playing a subordinate role in marriage can even impair a wife's health. A ten-year study on women and heart disease demonstrated that wives who don't speak their minds to their spouses are four times more likely to die of any cause than are women who feel free to be honest about what's bothering them. Wives may feel they must muzzle themselves in order to sustain their marriages, according to Elaine Eaker, who presented her findings at the Second International Conference on Women, Heart Disease and Stroke—but these women suffer from a higher incidence of depression as well as life-threatening ailments. A woman's decision to avoid argument or conflict "may or may not preserve her marriage, but it seems to have a negative impact on her own health," Eaker told the *New York Post*.

Because working women are so often portrayed as being unbearably stressed out by the juggling act, one might presume that stay-at-home wives, having been "liberated" from those demands, would prove to be healthier. Surprisingly, however, the opposite turns out to be the case.

"Employed women are healthier than their homemaker peers, despite the pressure of their added responsibilities. They have lower blood pressure, lower cholesterol levels, and lower weight," reported Dr. Anna Fels in *Necessary Dreams*. "Rosalind Barnett and Caryl Rivers note in *She Works/He Works*: 'Few facts are as well-documented as the good physical and emotional health of women on the job. . . . Among social scientists, the question of whether work is good for women isn't even much argued anymore.' "

Dr. Fels added, "Psychologically, working women have less depression than their domestic counterparts, and they have, astonishingly, been reported to have less anxiety."

While such findings may seem counterintuitive, they are consistent. Last year, a longitudinal British study found that women who have full-time jobs as well as families are likely to enjoy better health than full-time homemakers do. Over the course of twenty-eight years, researchers from University College London surveyed the health of women born in 1946. By the age of fifty-four, those who combined multiple roles as employees, parents, and partners were significantly less likely to report ill health than were those whose lives did not include all three roles. The women who had been homemakers for all or most of their lives were the most likely to say that their health was poor, followed by single mothers and childless women. The study, which was reported in the *Journal of Epidemiology and Community Health*, also found that 38 percent of the long-term housewives suffered from obesity, in comparison with 23 percent of the working mothers.

"Combining work with family life is actually good for women's long-term health," reported Dr. Anne McMunn, a senior research fellow in the department of epidemiology and public health at University College London. "While it may be stressful for them at the time, their long-term health is better when they have a combination of roles."

One of the study's goals was to determine cause and effect: Did this multitasking actually produce good health, or were healthy individuals simply able to accomplish more? The findings suggested "that good health is more likely to be the result, rather than the cause, of taking on work along with family and child-rearing obligations," *The New York Times* reported.

Other surveys have produced similar results. "Sociologists Elaine Wethington (Cornell University) and Ronald Kessler (Harvard Medical School) found that women who were homemakers at the beginning of their three-year study and then went to work full time reported a decrease in psychological distress," reported Rosalind Chait Barnett, a senior scientist at the Women's Studies Research Center at Brandeis University, and Caryl Rivers, a professor of journalism at Boston University, on Women's eNews. "In contrast, women who were employed full time and then dropped out to stay home reported an increase in distress, regardless if they had children. Women who had a child but stayed in the work force showed no increase in distress.

But women who had a child and dropped out of the work force experienced a major increase in stress."

Such research provides a stunning refutation of the cultural propaganda American women have been subjected to for the last few decades. Despite the endless obsession with the difficulties of balancing work and family, little attention has been paid to the problems imposed by the absence of fulfilling outlets for a woman's intellectual and creative energies, the powerlessness that results from dependency, and the lack of options experienced by women who are not financially self-sufficient. But many social scientists suggest that our focus should be redirected.

In his book *What Happy People Know*, Dan Baker lists "the twelve qualities of happiness." In addition to such obvious elements as love, Baker gives high priority to "a sense of freedom," proactivity, and security. These qualities—familiar to working women who feel a measure of control over their own destinies—are described by Baker as making up "the emotionally enhanced life," in contrast to what he calls "the lesser life," which is characterized by fear, a lack of options, a narrow focus, a sense of purposelessness, anxiety, and depression. That dismal list describes the emotional reality of all too many dependent wives.

Some studies have actually been able to quantify the differences between how men and women react to marriage. For the past twenty years, researchers at Ohio State University have been studying ninety couples to learn more about how personal relationships affect health. Their work focuses on the way in which stress alters the levels of hormones in the blood and how that affects the body's immune system. When researchers revisited couples a decade after assessing their stress hormones, they found that elevated levels were the best predictors of eventual divorce.

But even among couples with happy marriages, the health benefits were not shared equally. "Men get a lot more out of marriage than women do in terms of an extra boost," Dr. Janice Kiecolt-Glaser, professor of psychiatry and psychology at Ohio State University, told the

*Miami Herald.* The study also found that an unhappy marriage takes a deeper toll on the wife than it does on the husband. "The broad message is that a bad marriage hurts a woman worse," said Kiecolt-Glaser.

Another factor may be the relative disparity between how either gender perceives its freedom to change the conditions that are causing distress. Men with thriving careers and excellent income-earning potential have a very different sense of their future prospects than do nonworking women who feel trapped in unhappy marriages by economic necessity.

In *What Happy People Know,* Dan Baker also discusses the work of Dr. Martin Seligman, a pioneer in cognitive psychology and the author of *Learned Optimism.* "Dr. Seligman believed that having options and making choices is the very foundation of human psychological health," Baker wrote. "Life can be brutal, he said, but if we always have options, we'll always have hope. . . . However, when we feel as if we've exhausted all our possibilities and are left with no viable choices, then our suffering really starts. . . . It creates depression, anxiety and apathy. It destroys the body, mind and spirit. . . . But choice can be reinstated, he said, and when it is, it is a veritable elixir for human happiness."

Such conclusions have been reinforced by the findings of other social scientists. Kennon Sheldon of the University of Missouri conducted several large studies aimed at discovering which events bring people the greatest satisfaction. "Dr. Sheldon's studies tested the validity of self-determination theory, a concept that says people are happiest when they're able to make their own choices," Baker reported. "The results were a stunning confirmation of self-determination theory. The main thing that made the events feel good was the sense of being in charge of them. This sense of being in charge included experiencing feelings of autonomy, competence and self-esteem. These feelings finished in three out of the four top positions, among eleven feelings that made people feel good."

Those of us who have faced up to the hard challenge of maintaining careers while raising families already know what social scientists are only beginning to prove: that work provides women with a multitude of rewards that constitute critical components of happiness itself. While the opportunities for such self-expression have increased exponentially in recent years, wise women have understood their importance in even the most repressive times.

When the celebrated writer Charlotte Perkins Gilman had her daughter in 1885, she was prescribed the "rest cure" recommended by Dr. Silas Weir Mitchell for "hysterical women" afflicted with "nervous disorders," including postpartum depression. This draconian "cure" mandated that the patient be confined to bed and prevented even from sitting up, let alone engaging in such useful activities as reading, writing, or sewing. Gilman later wrote a fictional account of that experience in her famous short story "The Yellow Wallpaper," which depicts a woman slowly descending into insanity.

But Gilman finally rescued herself from Mitchell's "rest cure." Half a century before Betty Friedan launched the modern women's movement with *The Feminine Mystique*, Gilman described her own liberation from the narrow confines imposed by Victorian gender roles and the transformational effect of finding something meaningful to do that transcended her domestic duties. "Using the remnants of intelligence that remained, and helped by a wise friend, I cast the noted specialist's advice to the winds and went to work again," she wrote in 1913, "—work, the normal life of every human being; work, in which is joy and growth and service."

# CHAPTER NINE

# IT'S THE MONEY, HONEY

## "GOD BLESS THE WIFE WHO'S GOT HER OWN!"

When Rachel Stein* got married twenty-two years ago, she seemed like a powerhouse in every conceivable way. Armed with a Harvard M.B.A., she had become the chief financial officer of a major corporation. But despite her credentials, she gave no thought to marital finances when she wed her husband, who was a lawyer.

"We both had respectable incomes, and the subject of money never even came up," Stein says. "It was a nonissue. I spent my own income as I saw fit."

After having three children, Stein quit her job, a decision she viewed as a lifestyle choice that had as much to do with nurturing her marriage as it did with taking care of her children. "I stopped working because Jake made more money and had many more interesting demands on his time around the world," she explains. "I concluded that I needed to spend time on living some part of Jake's professional life with him, entertaining his clients, and so on. All of which had its rewards, but it meant walking away from my own income. I gave up my day job for all the right reasons, but what I didn't anticipate was what it was going to do to my sense of self."

Although Stein made a few stabs at protecting her financial future, her husband dismissed such measures as unnecessary. "I remember saying, 'Should I put some money into a 401(k)?'" she recalls. "My husband said, 'I'm going to make so much money it won't matter.' It was just a 'trust me' routine. For fifteen years, it never crossed my mind what I was doing to myself. I was so into the 'trust me' stuff—we were married for life, and it didn't matter."

In terms of income, her husband proved as good as his word, earning millions of dollars. And yet Stein found herself reduced to the position of supplicant in dealing with her husband about the money needed to maintain their various homes. "When I wrote checks, inevitably I would get a spending lecture every month," she says. "Our lifestyle quadrupled; we had houses all over the place. He would say, 'We're having twenty-four people for dinner on Saturday night; I don't care what it costs.' It was impossible for me to know whether I was supposed to put on the brakes or keep spending, so I would spend and get a lecture, spend and get a lecture. This put catastrophic stress on the marriage."

But Stein's husband refused to share any information about their finances to help her maintain a realistic budget. "I would beg him to tell me what the cash flow was, and he would say no," she reports. "He'd say that if I knew what he had, I'd just go out and spend it all. I had no clue."

Stein recognized even then that these issues were largely symbolic. "When it starts out about money, it's really about many other things," she says. "This was about using money as a proxy for control—and it's a damn good proxy. As I became dependent, dependency was treated by my husband as me becoming childlike. I'm the one who had a Harvard M.B.A.; I'm the one who had been a CFO—and yet I got lectures as if I were a naughty child overspending her allowance. It's really a form of emotional abuse. My husband totally lost respect for me, and he put me down more and more."

The impact on their marriage was devastating. "The money issues simply ruined it," Stein says. "It was a combination of having no money of my own to spend independently, of getting nonstop lectures from my husband, and of his becoming so angry with me for our spending level that he simply withdrew. After two years of not speaking to me, he called one day and said, 'I want a divorce.'"

He has since changed his mind, but the Steins' marriage is poisoned with rage. Given their great wealth, Stein feels particularly bitter that their financial conflicts had nothing to do with any real need to economize. It took her a long time to realize that a dependent rich wife can have the same problems as a dependent poor one if her husband uses money as a means of exercising power over her.

"Whether you're worth thirty thousand dollars or thirty million dollars, it doesn't change the dynamic," Stein says. "It is totally a control thing, and it is totally destructive. Women put up with this emotional abuse because they don't have the courage to walk away from it. In a lot of cases, they stay together because they don't have enough money to separate. Many of us lose our sense of self and become tremendously depressed. I was hanging by a thread until my shrink started turning it around for me."

In a desperate attempt to impose a workable structure on their marital finances, Stein sought professional help of another kind as well. "We had a postnuptial agreement negotiated by a lawyer," she reports. "I settled for much too little. If we stay married, he doles out my allowance monthly, and it's the same old control thing." At this point, their relationship is so toxic that the damage seems irreparable. "We're still married, but just barely," says Stein, who is now fifty-four years old.

Looking back on her choices, she remains baffled. "I don't know what the right answer is about any of this," she says. "I wanted to have babies, and Jake seemed like the right type of husband. It never ever occurred to me that we would not stay married. I thought that was the one thing that was rock solid between us."

But she knows now that relinquishing her economic independence was a dreadful mistake. "Women don't realize how infantilizing it is," she says. "I think they come upon that realization very gradually. If you give up your financial independence, you've lost the only exit there was. The work is not just a paycheck; it's an independent identity, separate friends, being with people who respect you. When you give that up, you're totally at the mercy of your small family world; you're totally dependent on it for feedback and rewards. And if that family world doesn't give you the rewards you need, you're trapped. If you have to ask your husband for money, you're as trapped as if you were living in a trailer park, even if he's worth a hundred million dollars; you just have prettier clothes. And if you have kids, you're deathly afraid of ruining your children's lives by breaking up the family unit."

Although a patriarchal society encourages women to subordinate their individual needs to those of the family, Stein has come to see that as another classic female mistake. "There are a lot of women, like me, who are born to be pleasers," she explains. "For twenty years, I convinced myself that my life was truly wonderful, and all the other thoughts I might have to the contrary were trivial and selfish. All that mattered was the family unit. If you have a rich husband, nice friends, and beautiful houses, you just keep swallowing hard and saying, 'Everything I don't have doesn't matter'—even if you are living a life of total loneliness. I felt so hopeless in my sense of possibilities that I thought the only chance of having a life where I had any feeling of achievement or contentment would be if Jake died. It's hard to imagine that an intelligent person can get that low in what should have been a charmed life. But I didn't have a way out, because I'd bought into the whole package with a controlling husband—and with that had gone my self-esteem and any financial freedom I'd ever had."

After recognizing the price she paid for her opulent lifestyle, Stein came to view even her accustomed luxuries as tainted. "I was spending all this time trying to convince myself that the big fancy South Sea pearls were my reward for this life, so I should just shut up and enjoy it—which makes you feel like a whore," she says bitterly.

Even now, Stein doesn't necessarily believe that women must continue to work; although she knows that work is invaluable in helping women to create happy lives, she sees financial autonomy as the single most important issue. "You have to have your own money, but whether you earn it or not doesn't matter," she says. "There has to be a meaningful amount that is yours to spend as you choose. To me, having a division of assets where you control a reasonable sum of money is an absolute prerequisite for giving up your income. If you decide to stop working, the first thing you need to do is agree with your husband on the amount that goes into an account where you never have to answer to anyone for what you spend. If you can't do that, you're not an independent person, and you're no different from your own children who are getting an allowance."

Stein believes that such measures are crucial even for women whose marriages are good and whose husbands are tolerant about spending habits. "These women are optimists, but half of them will get divorced, and half of the ones who stay together will be unhappy," she says. "Even if your husband is looking at the credit-card bills and saying nothing, there will come a day when he says, 'You spent this amount on *that*?' And if you have a Harvard M.B.A., that's like a knife in the back. Maybe things are rosy now, but if he goes sour at any point, or she goes sour, or anything happens that puts stress on the family—if she has no independent source of cash flow, there is no way she can go out and do anything she might need to do without his permission—by that point it's too late to fix it. You not only have no power, but you may have no money, because a husband can tie up a family's complete assets and leave the wife with virtually no cash.

That's something that came as a total revelation to me—me, the sophisticated financial analyst! One spouse can make charitable deductions or put conservation easements or do all kinds of things to tie up the liquidity of up to a hundred percent of marital property. If you think there's community-property protection, that's only if the property is still in community property. If a spouse takes the money he's earned that's in a bank account, he can give it away to anybody. The husband can make a gift of ten million dollars to Harvard without asking the wife how she feels about it, and if she questions him, he can say, 'I've decided I'm going to give everything away.' He can build a new museum, and there go all of the spouse's and children's assets. There's no requirement that both spouses sign off on gifts. In his anger at me, my husband decided to give it all away. I had to force him to agree to set up trusts for our children."

The enormous wealth accrued by Stein's husband is unusual, but the financial conflicts that ruined her marriage are common at every socioeconomic level. When women are satisfied with their marriages, however, such issues are often ignored. The dependent wives I interviewed typically judge the wisdom of their choice in terms of how the husband handles his power, rather than questioning the wisdom of giving him that power in the first place. To justify that sacrifice, such wives often contrast their own husband's generosity with the less forgiving attitudes of other men.

"I have friends whose husbands are torturing them," says Wendy Greenberg, a Manhattan stay-at-home wife who prides herself on being able to buy what she wants without her husband objecting. "The wives feel they don't have as much worth because they don't work, and the husbands don't think they're worth as much either; they think they can treat their wives like shit, because they're bringing in the money, so it's, 'No, you can't buy the boots for two hundred and fifty dollars!' A lot of these women have husbands who make millions of dollars a year, and they still say, 'You can't get the boots.'"

Young women who are unprepared for this loss of power can be shocked by what happens when they become dependent on their husbands. After dropping out of law school, Julia Jamison* held a series of jobs, but she hadn't yet committed herself to an ongoing career when she married a successful Hollywood screenwriter. "We both expected me to work, but he was very clear that I could do whatever I wanted as long as it made me happy," says Jamison, who was thirty-one and unemployed when she wed. "But what he said, and what we agreed to before we got married, didn't turn out to be true at all. The minute we got married, he started being insane. He was so angry with me, and so dismissive of me when I was not working."

Much of their conflict revolved around finances. "He was very controlling about money, and he didn't give me the kind of access to our money that I had expected or that he had said he would," says Jamison, who lives in Los Angeles. "He also gave me an extremely high degree of accountability that made it impossible for me to feel any kind of freedom in the marriage. I would get the third degree when I went to the grocery store. He made so much money that his financial worries were all imaginary, and we were never in any financial trouble. But there was no way I could do any kind of leisure spending, because of the recriminations. He would scream and yell, even when I bought a wedding present for other people. He would throw a temper tantrum when the credit-card bill came every month. When I went to the grocery store, it would be a diatribe: 'How long is this food going to last?' I had never seen any of this behavior before; we lived together before we got married, but this was new."

Although Jamison tried to work out a budget her husband felt comfortable with, their relationship quickly deteriorated. "If he didn't have firsthand experience of spending the money, even if it was for a dinner party he had co-planned with me, it was as if it had been stolen from him," she says. "If he wasn't spending it, it felt like a wound to him every single time. It was horrible. I was incredibly naive; I'm not an idiot, but I had not realized that money is power in a relationship. If I had been economically independent, I wouldn't have taken nearly as much shit from him, but I didn't have the freedom to check in to a hotel when he threw a temper tantrum. I felt so powerless that I had a lot of trouble expressing my anger, because I wasn't in a position to; I didn't have any chips. So I tried to do all this domestic shit to forestall his bad moods. I did the laundry; I cleaned up in the kitchen. These were never things we talked about, but it was just a given that if there was stuff to be done, I was the one who would do it. He was bringing home the money, so I felt compelled to do that stuff."

Within a year, the marriage was over—as was Jamison's willingness to play the role of a dependent wife. "I'm going back to law school to finish my degree, because I'm never going to be in this position again," she vows. "I don't want to be psychologically terrorized because I went to Whole Foods and spent money on something. I want complete financial independence."

Jamison is convinced that her disastrous marriage is "an extreme example," but social scientists believe that this dynamic is actually common, to varying degrees. "The data has suggested that women without their own sources of income have less power in their marriages," says sociologist Barbara Risman, co-chair of the Council on Contemporary Families. "Marriages are more male-dominated when women are not economic partners, which tends to decrease the quality of interaction. If your partner is also your paycheck, you're in a different position to make demands. If the husband controls her standard of living, there's a huge imbalance in power. Power is related to decision making—who gets the final call when you disagree. If you earn no money, or less money, you're going to be less likely to win when you have disagreements, and this decreases the quality of the marriage."

In my interviews with working women, money was almost always mentioned as an important reward, and power was understood to be one of the corollary benefits. "I would be unhappy if I weren't work-ing. I like the intellectual challenge, I like the social contact, I like the recognition I get," says sociologist Louise Roth. "But I also like hav-ing my own money. I was in Singapore recently, and I went out and spent five hundred dollars on clothes. I would have felt guilty doing that if it weren't my money, but I didn't feel guilty at all. If I were a homemaker, I would feel like I needed permission to go out on a spending spree. I'm glad I don't have to do that. Let's face it—it's power you lose in a marriage when you stay home. The person who has the most power in a relationship is the person who has the least to lose by leaving. When you stay at home, you have a lot to lose; you're dependent, so money is a big part of it. I think dependency is the worst part, but there's also a greater tendency to rely on your spouse as a connection with the outside world."

And yet happily married women are often loath to acknowledge the underlying power dynamic in relationships where the husband is the sole breadwinner. Margaret Hein has seen other couples fight about money, but she believes that such conflicts have no relevance to her own situation. "I have friends whose husbands handle all the finances, and they'll sit down and say, 'You went to the ATM and took out two hundred dollars? You went to the grocery store? Where's the receipt?' That's not us," Hein says. "I do all the bill paying; I have the check-book. If my husband needs a check, he'll get it from me. If he was checking up on me or looked at the Visa bill and said, 'What's that charge?' it would drive me berserk. If he was making the money and doling it out to me and saying, 'Here's your allowance for the month,' and I went through it and had to come back to him and say, 'Can I have more money?'—it would be like he was the boss and I worked for him. But this balances it out. I've never felt like it was his money; it's our money. We have a partnership."

When such marriages are working well, wives can easily convince themselves that control isn't even an issue. Ruth F., the contented lifelong homemaker who lives in Michigan, didn't chafe at her husband's financial authority because it was always exercised in a benevolent fashion. "He never lorded it over me; he trusted me, and I trusted him that this would work out fine," she says.

In telling me that financial dependency has never been a problem for her, Ruth is reminded of a purchase she made several decades ago. "I do remember once buying a twenty-six-dollar spring jumper for my daughter. It was so cute, and it was so much more expensive than anything I'd bought before," she recalls. "But my husband didn't get mad; he didn't say, 'You have to take it back.' He said, 'That's okay.' "

Ruth, whose children are now adults, offers this anecdote as proof of her husband's generosity, which she appreciated. A self-supporting woman might instead be struck that Ruth remains grateful because her husband didn't chastise her for spending twenty-six dollars on a dress for their daughter a quarter of a century ago. For women accustomed to financial autonomy, such institutionalized subservience can be tough to take.

"It's really hard to ask for money," says a New Jersey mom who gave up her career as an actress when she and her husband adopted two children. "If I want to stop and get a chai while I wait for the results of my allergy tests at the doctor's office, I feel guilty. The other day, I had to ask my husband for money to go buy some new underwear. He wants to know every little penny I'm spending and what it's spent on."

When this loss of power dawns on dependent wives, it can cause great unease. "My sister is a stay-at-home mom, and her husband is a very successful physician. She didn't need to work, but being financially dependent scares her," says a working mother who lives in New Jersey. "She doesn't want for anything, but her husband keeps all the financial information from her. He has literally awakened her in the middle of the night and told her to sign the tax returns, so she wouldn't review them. She has a master's degree, but she says, 'I don't even know what we have. My husband says I'm taken care of for life, but I have to blindly trust.' He won't tell her. Money is power in a marriage. If a man chooses to exercise that power, you can become totally disenfranchised. Men who are successful tend to be strong and controlling. My sister drives a Lexus, but her husband decides what car to get and when. So what price are you willing to pay for the house in the Hamptons? It's a question of control. When you're a wage earner, it's much more likely you'll exercise an equal vote about buying a house or replacing a sofa. As a working wife, I didn't have to ask permission. I don't think women realize how easy it is to get into the mode of asking as opposed to stating. When the husband says, 'I'll let you know,' you're waiting for permission."

Apprehensive about whether they will get it, wives often resort to subterfuge to purchase the things they want. "In my business, I see the shell game women play with their husbands, particularly where there's this imbalance of economic power," says investment adviser Darcy Howe. "There's a certain amount of economic secrecy with many couples, and women who don't have economic power feel this need to sneak around to do things if their husbands might not approve of the ways they're spending the money. It's a little game they're playing."

Dependent wives frequently rationalize that they're entitled to exert some control over spending even if they have to do so covertly. This is hardly a new phenomenon; many Baby Boomers retain vivid memories of their own mothers behaving this way. "If my mother wanted a new pair of shoes, she went to Filene's and got them, but she said, 'Don't tell Dad,'" recalls a working mother who lives in Connecticut.

"Forty percent of us still admit to lying to our partners about what something costs," Liz Perle wrote in *Money, a Memoir*, which deals with the "voluntary blindness" many women adopt regarding financial affairs.

Such deception is so common that dependent wives often assume all women dissemble to conceal their purchases. Marilena Greig had a high-powered career in finance before she quit to become a stay-at-home mother. Despite her husband's seven-figure income, she never felt free to spend money as she wished. "I kind of had to ask," Greig admits. But those constraints only made her want to rebel against her husband's authority. "He made so much money, and I thought, 'I'm earning this money, too!' So with spending, it was like, 'Let me not show him this, because he'll be upset and get pissed off.' Like every woman does, I had to watch, I had to hide. I thought, 'This is what women do. They buy what they want, and they hide it.'"

Financially independent women are frequently appalled by such self-degradation. "How about the woman who goes out and buys shoes and then hides them—how humiliating is that?" exclaims marketing consultant Tanya Mandor. "The thought of having to ask your husband's permission for anything is unbearable to me—incomprehensible! I cannot imagine having to go to my husband and say, 'I need three hundred dollars,' or having him say, 'What did you do with the three hundred dollars you took out of the bank?' So I need your approval? I don't believe that's what marriage is. I think it's about having a friend, a lover, a spiritual companion, somebody who can share the intellectual and social interests you have, somebody who's a lot of fun to be with. If you don't have those pieces, I don't think you have a marriage that lasts. My husband and I have been married thirty-one years, and we're very much in love. We have always been financial partners, and I think that has been very positive. Money gives you freedom. It's given me the freedom to do whatever I want, whenever I want. My husband and I had the Thousand-Dollar Rule: Spend anything you want, up to a thousand dollars. You didn't have to discuss it; just go and do it. There was never any question or any explanation that was required."

Women who earn their own incomes tend to take such freedom for granted. "I would absolutely hate not having my own money," says

Michelle Young, a thirty-three-year-old high-school counselor in Wichita, Kansas. "I think it would make me feel like a child, almost shameful about my purchases. When I have to say, 'Can you pay my credit-card bill?' I feel like I'm asking my parents for money."

The reluctance to submit to that kind of control has become more common as women have earned more financial power over the last couple of generations. The *Wall Street Journal* recently reported that growing numbers of married women are keeping their money separate from that of their husbands, instead of merging all assets in joint accounts. They can spend what they want, when they want, without having to ask permission. "One day, on a whim, I bought some article of clothing that was horribly expensive, and I said to my husband, 'Don't you want to know how much it cost?'" recalls Miranda Blake, a criminal defense lawyer. "He said, 'No, not particularly.' It wouldn't occur to him to say anything about it, because I can afford to pay for it out of my own money."

MY OWN HUSBAND and I have been together for nearly twenty years, but we have never held a joint account. We co-own our apartment, our financial obligations are divided equitably, and we each take care of different responsibilities. He has never once questioned me about how I spend money, let alone criticized or imposed conditions.

In our parents' generation, we would probably have been regarded as freaks, but these days such arrangements are not unusual—although they continue to distress conservatives who yearn for the good old days when women knew their place and lacked the resources to extricate themselves from it. In an op-ed column in *The New York Times*, David Brooks expressed his dismay about recent reports that the number of couples with separate checking accounts is rising rapidly and that roughly half of all married couples now keep multiple accounts. "We should pause before this becomes the social norm," Brooks warned.

"It's so easy for the powerful force of individualism to wash over and transform institutions—like family, religion and the military—that are supposed to be based on self-sacrifice, loyalty and love."

I can only conclude that Brooks hasn't interviewed many divorced women who based their concept of marriage on self-sacrifice, loyalty, and love, only to find themselves bereft of financial options when their husbands flew the coop. From a female point of view, the problem with the self-sacrifice model of marriage is that it's usually the woman who's being asked to sacrifice.

Unlike dependent wives, women who earn their own money don't have to sacrifice their economic interests in favor of the family unit, and they readily admit how liberating financial independence can be. "If I wanted to buy expensive fabric, I just did it," says Darcy Howe, whose husband is a lawyer. "That's the freedom I get. We've always kept separate accounts. He pays some things, I pay others. Each of us has autonomy. I think it's a healthy thing in our marriage."

As *Money* magazine put it recently, "Who's the boss depends on who brings home more bacon." And women are bringing home a lot more bacon these days. Wives are now the major breadwinners in a third of all married households, a development that is causing significant changes in family dynamics. A *Money* magazine survey revealed that "nearly four in ten women in households where the wife is the primary earner say they take the lead in investing. That's twice as many as in families where wives earn less."

Dan Baker, the founding director of the behavioral medicine department at Canyon Ranch and director of its award-winning Life Enhancement Program, calls this syndrome the Gold Rule. "He who has the gold rules," Baker says sardonically. "I've seen a lot of husbands who have this power thing: 'I'm going to take care of you, honey! You don't need to know about it or worry about it.' But it's a power deal: 'I have the money; you don't.' When the woman asks about finances, he won't tell her, 'I know where it's at, and you don't.

And if you treat me bad, I'll take the money and go!' That's a bad marriage. There are husbands who engender that dependency because of their own power needs, but it's devastating to the woman. She lives in constant fear; she's ready for the hammer to fall at any time. She should be as involved with finances as he is, and if she's not, she's flirting with disaster."

And yet millions of wives not only abdicate responsibility for their family finances—they surrender that control voluntarily. "We're doing it to ourselves," says Darcy Howe. "I don't know whether it's a girl thing, but most women have no idea what kind of risk they're putting themselves in when they make the choice of economic dependency. The emotional issues seem to outweigh the economic issues."

Throughout her career as a financial expert, Howe has been struck by the way married women withdraw from participation in managing their family's money. "When we take on a client relationship, the women say, 'I know I should be more involved,' but it's generally not on their radar screen; the women who want to be at the meeting are the exception," Howe reports. "There certainly is a feeling that the men understand these things better, and women don't educate themselves as much. I don't know if men really are any better at it. Men are good at bravado: 'I'll take that on, little lady!' But women will take the passive route if they're not encouraged by their husbands to do otherwise. Culturally, women think this is related to math, and there is this math phobia among women. When it comes to numbers, a lot of women tuned out long ago. It is insane. Why are we doing this?"

Such attitudes often take hold long before women even marry. Remember *Sex and the City* heroine Carrie Bradshaw, who frittered away her disposable income on Manolo Blahniks and then found she had forty thousand dollars' worth of shoes but no down payment to buy her apartment when the building went co-op? Like Carrie, single women frequently assume they don't have to get serious about money because they'll eventually get married, whereupon their husbands will take care of it.

This attitude endures despite countless efforts to get women to wise up. "A man is not a plan," warned Michelle Singletary, a *Washington Post* financial columnist, in her book *Your Money and Your Man.*

Although this kind of thinking is a dumb mistake, it's not entirely women's fault. "We've been programmed from birth . . . to believe that catching the man means catching the cash," Joni Evans wrote in an article called "Your First Million" for *O, The Oprah Magazine.* "When was the last time you saw a magazine with a coverline: 50 Best Ways to Make a Six-Figure Salary at Home! No, it is: 50 Ways to Have a Hot Body."

Evans, who has enjoyed a powerhouse career as a book editor and literary agent, was forthright about her message. "I'm not talking about marrying it. I'm not talking about inheriting it. I'm talking about earning it. . . . Women should do what men do: Make the money! Success is a choice."

But it's not the choice most women make. "For every woman who earns $100,000 or more, there are four men," Evans noted.

In *Nice Girls Don't Get Rich*, psychotherapist Lois Frankel identifies the leading mistakes that "nice girls" routinely make with money. Among them: "Being a Financial Ostrich" who avoids thinking about money at all; "Trusting the Wrong People," almost always men; and "Delaying the Purchase of a Home"—because, as Frankel puts it, "Too many women wait for Prince Charming."

When nice girls graduate to marriage and motherhood, many simply perpetuate that state of willful ignorance; after all, isn't Prince Charming supposed to handle those tiresome details like savings, taxes, and investments? But turning over the financial reins can have terrible consequences.

Barbara Stanny's father was one of the founders of H&R Block, the tax services company, and she began adult life as a very wealthy young woman thanks to his success. But Stanny's parents never taught her how to manage money, and when she got married, she turned over her assets to her husband.

"My first husband, however, turned out to be a lousy Prince Charming, losing a fortune (of my trust fund) in reckless investments. After our divorce, he left the country, leaving me to deal with colossal tax bills, three small children, and a brain incapable of deciphering financial jargon," Stanny wrote in her book, *Secrets of Six-Figure Women: Surprising Strategies to Up Your Earnings and Change Your Life.*

The characteristically female lack of confidence noted by Howe and Stanny is borne out by research data. In a recent report on family finances, *Money* magazine cited one survey in which 47 percent of the women felt they were not knowledgeable about investing, as compared with 30 percent of the men—a gap that did not necessarily reflect the reality of their performance in financial matters.

"There's little reason to suppose investing is really something men do better," *Money* stated. Convinced of their financial acumen, however, men do tend to be more aggressive, a trait that can be costly. Another study cited by *Money* found that men trade stocks more frequently than women do, thereby lowering their returns by about one percentage point a year in comparison with women's trading patterns.

In *Money*'s own survey of family finances, 84 percent of the husbands and wives reported that money was a source of tension in their marriage. "The gender divide seems to conform to some of our hardest-to-shake stereotypes," the magazine noted, specifying the clichéd model of breadwinner husband and spendthrift wife. "In real life, however, there's nothing funny about the arguments that can flare when financial roles are so divided."

And yet many stay-at-home wives deny that crass economic calculations are a factor in their marriage. They have no trouble perceiving that employees who depend on their job for a paycheck are inhibited from telling the boss exactly what they think of him—but they resist any comparison to their own most intimate relationships. Whether or not women choose to admit it, however, dependency breeds vulnerability, inhibits open communication, and creates an unhealthy balance of power in which the subservient partner must always fear the loss of her meal ticket—unless she's in complete denial, which is often the case.

"I think young women initially see it as a power trip to have a man spending money on them, but this is a real Pyrrhic victory, because it does give him a sense of entitlement," says family historian Stephanie Coontz. "The research is pretty clear that even in marriage there's a male sense that 'I'm the one who earns the money, so I should get the final say.' And women feel like, 'He's the one who earns the money, so I'll give him the final say.'"

When a woman at the wrong end of the power imbalance suddenly acquires economic clout, the results are often a revelation. Wendy Greenberg's mother, Hilda Rothstein, was furious when her husband lost his job and she had to go to work after twenty years as a stay-at-home mother. "I thought it was terrible, but it turned out to be good for me, because it sent me out the door," says Rothstein. "He didn't want me to work, but I was frightened for my future. We had one son in private school, and we had to take him out, which was traumatic for him. I knew I had to do something, so I got a weekend job working in a real-estate office. I was forty-five years old, and I started as a weekend secretary; I didn't even know how to run the phones. The first day on the job, they said, 'Please vacuum the rug.' I had had a cleaning woman myself until then, so that was a blow; I stood there and cried. But when I decided to work full-time, I became the top producer in that office in the first two years."

Despite Rothstein's success, her husband "still expected me to cook and take care of things," she says. "He always resented my job." As she became more successful, however, she was thrilled to be liberated from her husband's financial control. "Having to ask him for money was not easy; he didn't necessarily approve of the things I wanted to buy," Rothstein says. "Everything would be an argument. I stayed home for twenty years and put up with it, but I just felt trapped. I felt I had no power. My husband is a controlling person, and I had to fight for my own power all the time. We've had fifty years of marriage, but we've been fighting the whole time. After I started working, I said, 'I'm paying for everything myself.' Having my own money was wonderful; it was exhilarating. It was so nice to get a check and be able to buy whatever I wanted to buy—to fix the house, to get an air conditioner, all the things my husband didn't think we needed. I tell my daughter all the time, 'It's nice not to have to ask.' Her husband has been very generous; he never gave her a hard time. But the men that have the money are controlling things. A man may give his wife everything she wants, but he still has control."

The more income a woman brings into her household, however, the more leverage she tends to have. In the early years of her marriage, Ellen Warwick* sacrificed her own career several times to follow her husband from one country to another. He was finally transferred home to Washington, D.C., where Warwick eagerly resumed her professional life. A couple of years later, her husband announced that the family had to move abroad again, because he was taking on a new foreign assignment.

But, to his astonishment, Warwick said no. Their relationship had arrived at a critical turning point—one that he hadn't noticed until she pointed it out to him. "My marriage changed forever the day my husband realized I was making more money than he was," Warwick says. "He realized he couldn't order me around like a servant anymore, and he started treating me with much more respect."

At Warwick's insistence, her husband changed jobs so their family could stay in Washington while he traveled intermittently—a move that benefited their children, who were tired of being uprooted, as well as benefiting her career. Because her time was now as valuable as that of her husband, his attitude toward sharing housework also became more cooperative.

In effecting such changes, a wife's growing feeling of self-worth is often as important as her husband's increasing respect for her income. "Now that I make a lot more money than I ever made in my life, my husband gives much more weight to my opinion," says book editor Susan Mercandetti. "He's not an autocrat, but it's a more powerful position to be in. We bought a house in the country, and we're building a pool and fixing up the barn. I said, 'I don't want the pool here, and I don't want the barn fixed that way, so I'm not doing it that way.' I have the power to say, 'I don't want the pool here,' because it's half my money. If it weren't, I would roll over."

Mercandetti knows whereof she speaks; when she first got married, she quit her high-powered career as a television producer. "After a while, economic dependency scared me," she says. "I eventually came to hate the feeling of being economically dependent. It was okay at first, but it's not a situation for the long term, because you give up all your options. I didn't want to answer for myself if I felt like buying a dress. I never had before; I'd had my own money since I was fourteen."

Such issues color a woman's relationships no matter what her socioeconomic class. Jennifer Friedman is a public-interest lawyer at Sanctuary for Families, an organization that provides services to battered women and children in New York City. "I see in my work that control is a big issue in heterosexual relationships, and I don't think it's good for women to be completely financially dependent on men," says Friedman. "If their marriages cease to work for them, they end up trapped, feeling that they can't get divorced because they don't have access to financial resources and wouldn't be able to provide for their children."

As an expert on spousal abuse, Friedman knows that financial control is a critical component in many destructive relationships. "Domestic violence is a pattern of abuse of power and control, and one of the ways you can have power over women is through money," she explains. "One of the classic signs of a domestic-violence situation is economic abuse, where one partner exerts control over the other partner through economic means: 'He refuses to allow me to work.' 'He makes me turn over my paycheck.'"

Many people assume that domestic violence is a problem of the lower classes; popular stereotypes often associate spousal abuse with the kind of disenfranchised poor women who might end up at a shelter, if not homeless. But even privileged women in affluent communities can be victimized by physical abuse as well as by the dark side of economic control.

A stay-at-home mother of two in a wealthy New York suburb, Lucy Peters ceded the management of family finances to her husband after she quit her own job on Wall Street. "My attitude toward money was ignorant bliss," she says. "Nothing was in my name; everything was handled by him. I didn't want to deal with it, and he convinced me that that line of thinking was valid. I had nothing—zero, zip, nada."

The consequences of that default turned out to be catastrophic. "I thought I wasn't vulnerable, because I thought that if he left, everything would be fifty-fifty," says Peters, who was thirty-four when her husband ended their marriage ten years ago. "But he hid a lot of money before he left; I still don't know where. All of a sudden he gets a lawyer and stops supplying us with money. I had to get a lawyer to go to court and make a judge make him support us. I thought I was going to be okay then, since he was earning between half a million and a million dollars a year. But one year his bonus was only three hundred and fifty thousand dollars, which really pissed him off, so he quit his job, went out on his own, crashed, and stopped paying us money."

Peters spent several years fighting her husband in court, but he always found ways to evade his responsibility to their children. She already knew he could behave in a threatening manner, having experienced several episodes of physical abuse. "Before he left, he got a little violent," she admits. "He would throw things at me."

But when she stopped letting him dominate her life, the situation really got ugly. In an effort to establish her financial autonomy, Peters opened an upscale gift shop while preparing to take her husband to court yet again. "Two days before we were supposed to go to court, he lit fires and tried to burn down my store," she says. "He was arrested and charged with arson. It was a control thing; I would say, 'You have no power over me anymore,' and he didn't like the fact that I was exerting control. He was trying to intimidate me not to take him to court over the kid issues, but now he's shot himself in the foot, because he's a felon. The fire was three years ago, and he hasn't paid child support or alimony since then. He claims he looked for a job and couldn't get one."

While arson admittedly represents extreme behavior, men employ a wide range of threatening tactics to maintain financial control of their dependent partners. In contrast, women who are capable of supporting themselves often find they can use that leverage to effect far more positive changes in their relationships.

At the age of forty, Mary Noonan* has a lucrative career in a glamorous media field, as well as two children, who are now one and three years old. After she had her first child, her husband, a lawyer, responded badly to the increased responsibility of parenthood and began drinking to excess. Prodded by Noonan, he eventually brought his drinking under control, but after she got pregnant with their second child, she says, "It got really bad again."

Noonan and her husband's family staged an intervention, and he went into rehab and stopped drinking. He got a new job that made him much happier than his previous one, and their lives improved greatly. "Then he started drinking again," Noonan says. "There was all the stuff that goes with that—the lying, the sneaking, the volatility, the arguments. I finally felt I had to give him an ultimatum. I said, 'You've got to go back to AA—and if this happens again, we're done.' It happened again, and we were done. There were a lot of fights, and my three-year-old was getting old enough to feel the tension. I didn't want him to be this damaged kid who grows up in an alcoholic household. I felt I had no choice."

A successful professional woman, Noonan also has a healthy sense of self-esteem that made her unwilling to tolerate her husband's alcoholism as a permanent condition. "I felt like, 'I don't have to put up with this shit,'" she says. "I felt I deserved better. If he can't do it, I don't have to take it, because I'm not fearful about managing on my own."

But after Noonan and her husband separated, he realized how much he stood to lose, and he entered rehab again. "He wants his family back, and he'll do whatever it takes to get it back," Noonan says. "He wants this to work." Her husband has now been sober for several months, and they are trying to repair their marriage. When she feels confident that he is truly committed to sobriety, she plans to let him move back in with the family. "We're getting along great," she says.

But Noonan would not have been able to insist on such changes if she were financially dependent. "Having a job that pays well, I feel like I can do anything," she says. "I just feel like my future is bright. But I have a friend in Chicago who has three kids and is not working, and she's going through the same thing with her husband. She envies me; she wishes she could force the situation, but she can't afford to do what I did. She says, 'I wish I could put my foot down, but I can't. How am I going to support everyone?'"

So Noonan's friend is stuck with an alcoholic husband, no leverage, and little hope of improving her situation, whereas Noonan herself feels extremely optimistic. "I'm in the catbird seat, professionally, and I feel very empowered," she says. "That's all about a paycheck; that's everything. Not only does my paycheck benefit me and benefit our family, but it benefits my husband, because it's going to force him to get his shit together."

Financial autonomy becomes even more crucial for wives when their marriages fail. Self-supporting women can extricate themselves from bad relationships—and go on to seek out better ones. They don't have to put up with physical or emotional abuse, alcoholism, or addiction in their partners, because they can take care of themselves and their children. No matter what problems they're facing, they enjoy a range of options that dependent women can only dream about.

As a result, the behavior of financially empowered women is very different from that of the economically disenfranchised. An AARP study found that two-thirds of the divorces among people over forty were initiated by women, often as a response to substance abuse or mental, physical, or emotional abuse by the husband. That startling figure reflects both the sense of autonomy and the economic self-sufficiency achieved by many Baby Boom women.

In some cases, as Mary Noonan discovered, a woman's power to leave her husband can actually save their marriage. I personally know half a dozen couples whose marriages were nearly destroyed by the husband's problems, which ranged from alcoholism to drug dependency to serious depression to faltering careers. In every case, the husband refused to deal with his issues until the wife finally got so fed up she told him she wanted to end the marriage. Only then did the men get sober, stop doing drugs, go on antidepressants, get therapy, change jobs, or do whatever else was necessary to earn their way back into the family. All these couples subsequently reconciled and now describe themselves as being happier than they've ever been before. But the changes that saved the family unit were made only at the insistence of a working wife who made it clear that she was ready and able to go it alone if necessary.

Life is very different for stay-at-home wives who lack economic resources and therefore resign themselves to making the best of a bad situation. "I think my mother might have left my father, but she did not have the financial means to do so," says Cyndy Byrnes, a Connecticut working mom. "She always stressed the importance of being self-sufficient and not relying on your husband. I had regrets about not being with my children when they were little, but my mother said, 'Hang on, because as soon as they're in school, what are you going to do all day?' She said, 'Be careful—you don't know where life is going to take you or what's going to happen. You've had great jobs, and I would hate to see you lose that foothold and not be able to go back or not be able to earn your own living.' I think she might have made choices she was not able to make because she wasn't financially self-sufficient."

For other dependent wives, a sudden infusion of money can precipitate a dramatic change in both their attitude and their circumstances. Up until recently, if you had asked me to consider all the wives I know and name the stay-at-home mother who most closely approximates the Stepford ideal, I would have put Ramona Hill* at the top of my list. The wife of a professional colleague, she always seemed preternaturally perky and enthusiastic about her life as a soccer mom, chauffeur, and full-time homemaker. Unlike other married women I know, most of whom complain frequently, if affectionately, about their husbands, Ramona never murmured so much as a word of dissatisfaction about her spouse or her role in life.

Then Ramona's mother died. After learning how much she would inherit, Ramona promptly bought a Lexus and informed her astonished husband that she wanted a divorce.

"But why?" I asked her when I heard the news.

"Because I can," she replied.

It turned out that she'd been unhappy for years, and her husband had long ignored her feelings—but it was only when she acquired the financial means to buy her independence that she finally felt empowered to change her circumstances.

While many dependent wives stay with their husbands out of economic necessity, the marriages of independent wives often serve as a far truer measure of their commitment, rather than simply their lack of alternatives.

Amanda Wagner* met her husband in the fourth grade and dropped out of college to marry him when she was twenty-one years old. But she always understood that she should be prepared to support herself.

"My mother's father ran off and left her mother when she was pregnant with my mother, never to be seen again," says Wagner, who grew up in a small town in West Texas and now lives in Dallas. "Then my grandmother married again, had a baby, and her husband died of influenza. My dad had a drinking problem, and we used to say, 'How can Mom stand it?' But she said, 'What would I do with three children and my mother to support?' She couldn't have made enough money, so she stayed with him. My sister's husband left her with three children, aged two, four, and six. He ran off with another woman who worked in his office, and he gave my sister three hundred dollars a month to live on. I saw all these single women being left with children and no money, and it scared me to death. I didn't want it ever to happen to me."

Over the years, the Wagners had three children, but Amanda always worked—in a library, as a technician in a research lab, and as a real-estate salesperson, among other jobs. Meanwhile her husband, an entrepreneur who bought and sold different companies, was amassing a considerable fortune. "He was always doing deals, but I never had a good idea of our finances, because he didn't want me to know," Wagner says. "He was a very secretive person, and I didn't really know how much money he'd made. He was always in charge of the money, and I trusted him."

That trust was misplaced. "When the baby was three, my husband tells me he's unhappy in the marriage and says he's going to leave," Wagner reports. "I was devastated. I just couldn't believe it. But I was still working, thank God, and I had built up a nice business selling real estate, so I felt secure. I said, 'If you're going to divorce me, fine—I'm going to be okay.'"

Her feisty, self-respecting attitude eventually prompted her husband to reconsider. "He decided he wanted to come back," says Wagner, who has now been married for forty-four years.

Whatever the ups and downs in her marriage, Wagner has always viewed her independence as a lifeline. "Work made me feel so good about myself," she says. "It was a challenge; I learned something new and different, I realized I was good at it, and I met some fabulous people who are still my friends. I am glad I worked when the children were little, because it gave me a separate identity, and it made me think I did have some wherewithal. If my husband divorced me, I would be okay financially. I didn't stay with him for the money, because I had money."

So why has she remained in her marriage? "I have stayed all these years because we do love each other," she says.

For Wagner, autonomy and self-esteem were the most important benefits of working. In families that are less wealthy than the Wagners, economic considerations are more important, and a wife's income can elevate their standard of living to a different level entirely. "Clearly my family has benefited financially from my career," says Darcy Howe. "My husband works for a nonprofit organization, and we couldn't have the lifestyle we have on his income."

And yet working mothers remain vulnerable to conservative scolds who, like Dr. Laura Schlessinger, disparage them as greedy materialists more interested in unnecessary indulgences than in meeting the emotional needs of their children. Although two-income families can afford amenities that would not be possible if they lived on the husband's salary alone, the reality is that a lot of us are struggling to pay for basic necessities rather than splurging on luxury vacations in the Caribbean. In most families, a wife's income ends up empowering everyone. "If you're not working, you've diminished by half what you can offer your children," says Tanya Mandor, who has two daughters.

The benefits of a second paycheck can range from higher-quality medical care to intellectually, culturally, and educationally enriching experiences like travel and study abroad. I've never understood why women are deemed selfish for working to elevate their families' standard of living.

Women's earnings can also help buttress a couple's financial security in old age. When Tilde Sankovitch was a professor of French and comparative literature at Northwestern University, she appreciated her income for many reasons. "Besides liking my work, I always believed that it was a very important thing for a woman to have a little financial security of her own," says Sankovitch, who also made dinner for her three children every night when they were growing up. "It gives you a feeling of independence and of strength, that you could take care of yourself financially, and it gives you a certain sense of protection against emergencies. For me, it was also very important psychologically; it gave me a sense of being my own person. If I wanted to get a present for somebody, or get something for myself or my husband, I could do that."

At the age of seventy-one, Sankovitch is especially grateful for the comfort her earnings have provided as she and her husband grow older. "I feel the financial impact more now that we are retired and we have two retirement incomes coming in," she says. Such couples demonstrate how successfully the partnership model of marriage can work in every stage of life and what an important role a wife's income can play in ensuring both opportunity and long-term security for the entire family. Egalitarian marriages like these also illustrate the truth of Simone de Beauvoir's prescient analysis in her seminal 1949 book on women's lives, *The Second Sex*.

In discussing the importance of financial self-sufficiency, de Beauvoir observed that women's "civil liberties remain theoretical as long as they are unaccompanied by economic freedom. A woman supported by a man—wife or courtesan—is not emancipated from the male

because she has a ballot in her hand. . . . It is through gainful employment that woman has traversed most of the distance that separated her
from the male; and nothing else can guarantee her liberty in practice.
Once she ceases to be a parasite, the system based on her dependence
crumbles."

Today's stay-at-home wives would doubtless recoil at de Beauvoir's
description of them as parasites, but it is hard to argue with the fundamental truth of that characterization. When women don't work, they
must rely on men to support them. Needless to say, parasites are dependent upon their hosts for survival. This fact alone is sufficient to
belie the current vogue among stay-at-home wives for pretending they
have equal power in their marriages.

## CHAPTER TEN

# MEN, MARRIAGE, AND MONEY

## "IT'S A MACHO THING!"

W hen *The New York Times* ran its controversial front-page story about Yale women who were planning to give up their careers, a member of its editorial board wrote an opinion column taking issue with the women's blithe assumption that their future husbands wouldn't mind carrying the full burden of supporting their families.

"Men of my generation were brought up to accept and even embrace equality between the sexes," Nicholas Kulish pointed out. "Well, some of you may want to be Harriets again, but we men may not be prepared to become Ozzies. Returning to the 1950s just doesn't look appealing . . . I beg you to reconsider. I thought we had a deal."

Even in the 1950s, the stereotype of the family breadwinner often featured a Man in a Gray Flannel Suit who was so stressed out that he needed a three-martini lunch and a bottle of ulcer medication just to get through the day. But in today's era of skyrocketing expenses, when many families require two incomes simply to maintain a middle-class standard of living, that responsibility is far more onerous. Even among the affluent, the burden of supporting a family alone can seem down-right crushing.

"The Agriculture Department estimates the cost of raising a child in a middle-income family at $242,070—and that does not include college," Kulish observed. "The estimated cost per child jumps over $350,000 for upper-income families. The Yalies planning their escape from the work force before they've even entered it may be in for a big shock. They may not have enough money."

Money is a vitally important consideration for young men who don't choose high-earning careers, whatever their sexual politics. "I have enough trouble supporting myself on my income," says Dan Nasaw, a twenty-five-year-old newspaper reporter in Little Rock, Arkansas. "With car loans, student loans, and rent, I'm constantly concerned with how I'm going to be able to raise a child. If I'm going to have a partner, I'm not going to be able to support her. She'll have to work, too."

Such views are reflected in a growing body of social-science data. "A woman's earning power, while hardly the first thing that men look for, has become a bigger draw, as shown in surveys of college students over the decades," John Tierney noted in a *New York Times* op-ed column. "In 1996, for the first time, college men rated a potential mate's financial prospects as more important than her skills as a cook or a housekeeper."

The 1950s ideal can hold more appeal for men who don't have to worry about its financial implications. "I very much want a woman who is intelligent but doesn't work," says Robb McGregor, a thirty-four-year-old investment banker. "I make a lot of money, and I could very easily support a family without anybody else contributing to the wages. I have always been the dominant person in a relationship, financially speaking, and I enjoy being able to take care of somebody financially. I'm very much of a traditionalist. I want to be the one who takes care of my family."

McGregor hasn't had any trouble finding women whose views are compatible with his own. "The majority of women I've dated have either had no desire to work or they say, 'If I met the right guy, I'd be willing to quit my job,'" he reports.

Women who feel clear about their desire to marry a high-earning husband and then stay home are presumably prepared for what they get. But too many young women don't seem to recognize the trade-offs that will be involved if they have children with a master-of-the-universe type who must put in long hours to hang on to his megabucks job. And yet there's no doubt that choosing a cooperative partner is critical for any woman who hopes to sustain an independent career after having a family. If you marry a professor instead of a partner at a major law firm, you probably won't be as rich, but you might be more likely to share the domestic workload while maintaining your own career.

Unfortunately, however, many women fail to anticipate the conflicts that inevitably arise after they have children. Like Patsy Wiggins, who was forced to give up her career as a successful lawyer because her husband wasn't around to "help" more on the home front, they find themselves shocked by the sacrifices they have to make in order to take care of their children. It's far better to explore these issues before you marry and get pregnant than to be blindsided by such conflicts after it's too late to do anything about them.

According to many young singles, such issues are indeed at the forefront of their decision making these days. Young women are particularly concerned about whether they will have to give up their careers in order to raise their children. "It's an enormously hot topic in business school, especially in terms of choosing an employer," says Ben Ensminger-Law, a twenty-eight-year-old banker who recently earned his M.B.A. from the University of Virginia. "I knew people who chose not to go into management consulting, where the travel is bad, or investment banking, where the hours are terrible, because they're too difficult to combine with having a family. I know girls from business school who looked into entrepreneurial endeavors that would provide them the flexibility to have a family."

But while young women agonize about such choices, young men generally seem to assume that worrying about domestic responsibilities is not their department. "I want to marry somebody who wants to stay at home and make peanut butter and jelly sandwiches for my children," says McGregor. "I like the way I grew up. We came home from school, and my mother was there to make our snacks. Do I want somebody who works the hours I do, who isn't there for my children? Absolutely not. I want somebody to be there with the children so they know there's this loving family all around them, as opposed to this vacancy where both Mom and Dad are at work. No one's saying, 'Don't go to Harvard and get a degree,' but if you want to have a career, I personally believe your family suffers as a result of your professional desires. I do believe you can go to college and get an M.B.A. and you can still be very fruitful in society without having a job at an investment bank. You can apply those skills to charities or to schools."

Such views demonstrate the enduring influence of traditional gender roles. When Ben Ensminger-Law was working toward his M.B.A., he discovered that conventional expectations predominated among his male peers. "Most of my friends from business school presume that they'll be the sole earner for some portion of this life," he says. "It's a macho thing."

Male attitudes are changing, to be sure; numerous studies have found that younger men are less inclined to sacrifice family time to all-consuming careers. "What is surprising is how many more young men interviewed in 2002 disagreed with the statement that it is 'much better for everyone involved if the man earns the money and the woman takes care of the home and children,' compared with young men interviewed twenty-five years ago," Judith Shulevitz reported in *The New York Times Book Review*.

Traditional values nonetheless remain deeply entrenched in many male-dominated fields. Jim Shaw,* a lawyer who is married to another attorney, attended a big anniversary dinner held by his wife's firm at which the managing partner gave a speech to congratulate all the other partners. "He said, 'I think it is important that we also recognize all those women who stand behind the partners. They're at home taking care of the families and making hot meals. All these women make it possible for us to do the jobs we've done, and I want to thank them for all they've done,'" Shaw recalls. "His whole assumption was that behind every partner is a woman who's cooking and raising children."

As the husband of a female partner, Shaw couldn't resist tweaking his wife's boss. "I stood up and said, 'On behalf of all the spouses, I'd like to thank you,'" he reports with a broad grin.

Shaw and his wife are bringing up their children with very different assumptions. Not surprisingly, young men who were raised in more egalitarian households often view the prospect of a stay-at-home wife with alarm. "I don't think I would like that kind of power dynamics," says Ensminger-Law. "The person who controls the earnings is in an advantaged position, and that's not a power balance I would want. I would want more equitable sharing of responsibility for the financial burden."

The son of Sylvia Law, Ben Ensminger-Law grew up with a father who shared all domestic tasks as well as with a high-achieving mother. "I'm proud of what my mom has accomplished, and I got a lot out of her colleagues and environment," he says. "I can think of times when I had to wait around school because both of my parents were caught up with some unexpected thing, but I kind of liked the independence of it. I and most of my peers with working mothers had enough focus on us; I think it's fine for us occasionally to be reminded that the entire universe doesn't revolve around us."

In contrast, young men who were raised by a stay-at-home mother and a breadwinner father often assume that they, too, will be comfortable with the conventional family model. But when they actually try it, some discover that a woman's dependency creates problems they did not anticipate.

David Graham* is a twenty-nine-year-old equity salesman at a private Wall Street bank and one of Robb McGregor's closest friends, although his views represent a striking contrast with those of McGregor. Graham's last serious girlfriend was a marketing executive at an oil company, and when they started living together in Boston, they shared costs equally, splitting the rent, food, and other expenses. Then Graham was transferred to London, and his girlfriend accompanied him.

"This set me up for the shock of my life," he says. "The suggestion that she contribute was not met well; it was made pretty clear that gender rules are that the male pays for the house, and I was breaking gender rules. But she resented taking money from me, so the times when she wasn't working were very stressful. When someone is dependent on you, it's not an equal partnership; it's more of a paternal relationship than a boyfriend-girlfriend relationship. If someone counts on you for food and housing, what are you to them? You're a parent; you're a patron. It puts more stress than you ever imagined on a relationship, and it drove us apart."

Now living in New York, Graham has become extremely wary about the infantilizing effects of female dependency, although he is trying to keep an open mind about the kind of woman he might marry. "My preference is that she would work," he says. "I could accept a stay-at-home wife, but it's not what I'm looking for. I'm looking for somebody who has new experiences to talk about, not somebody who relates to a child all day."

As Graham's relatively subtle condescension makes clear, many smart, well-educated young men anticipate that living with a stay-at-home wife would be intellectually stultifying. But some are far less diplomatic about that expectation. "I'm not going to marry some idiot," says Dan Nasaw. "My feeling would be, 'Here's a productive woman who's letting her potential go to waste by staying at home, doing

God knows what.' Your brain starts to rot; you lose a lot of energy. I wouldn't want a partner like that. I need dynamism. I need to have a woman who is engaged."

When men speak candidly about women's roles, such disparaging remarks are common. Full-time wives typically claim that their husbands value what they do, but even when their husbands genuinely appreciate the domestic services being provided, women often discover they have sacrificed other kinds of respect.

ANN LEWIS AND her husband, Richard Seltzer, are both lawyers who met on the job as assistant district attorneys in the Manhattan DA's office. Their relationship grew from the mutual respect of a collegial friendship into an enduring marriage that has lasted a quarter of a century. But during Lewis's stint as a stay-at-home mom, her purely domestic role gradually affected her husband's view of her—a shift that was imperceptible to both of them until they had a memorable argument.

"Richard is the most liberated of men, but one night he came home and said, 'How was your little day?' " Lewis reports. "He wasn't being sarcastic or anything; it was just like, 'What did the little woman do at home today?' "

Lewis was devastated by the implications of her husband's casually patronizing remark. "I got hysterical," she admits. "It was awful. We got into a huge fight. He appreciated everything I was doing with the kids and at home, but we had started out as colleagues, and he had a lot of pride in my professional accomplishments. I think his remark reflected some feeling about having seen my world diminish. It indicated to me that his feelings were mixed."

Until that blowup, Seltzer didn't even realize that his wife's role as a stay-at-home mom might have changed the way he related to her. "We met in the same career, in the same position, in the same office,

and we liked that," he explains. "We enjoyed the repartee of being involved in work and in the larger world. If I had thought she was going
to give all that up permanently, in some ways she'd be a different person than the person I fell in love with. I didn't feel that way about her
staying home for a period of time, but if I had thought that was the
end of her career, I would have had a very different attitude. As a practical matter, the household ran better when she was home, but I've always been happy that she decided to go back to her career. When you
stay home for a long time, you lose some of the intellectual sharpness
and interpersonal sharpness as well. You're caught up in your kids'
world, and it's a wonderful world, but it calls on different talents. As
busy as people are at work, they're attuned to what's going on in the
news and in the world, partly because that's what they talk about;
there's a sharpness to discussion and analysis. I do think people who
stay at home for long periods lose some of that."

Seltzer has enormous intellectual admiration for his high-achieving
wife, but other husbands are less respectful of their partners and their
domestic contributions. When I was a newspaper reporter, an editor
who was separated from his wife had a temper tantrum in the newsroom one day after a colleague reminded him to send a wedding present to a staff member. Already beleaguered by the demands of his job,
the editor exploded in anger and frustration at the thought of dealing
with such trivia. "I need a wife to take care of this chickenshit!" he
bellowed.

Many men still view their wives as glorified servants who should
relieve them of all the annoying minutiae of domestic life. Older husbands accustomed to a traditional household are often particularly reliant on the services provided by stay-at-home wives, and they are
accordingly dismayed when deprived of those amenities.

Recently my husband and I went to dinner with another couple, a
seventyish theater producer and his considerably younger second wife,
who raised their three children to late adolescence before growing

restless with her housewifely routine. "Ever since she went back to work, we're spending more money on restaurant meals than she makes," the husband groused. "It's costing me a fortune to have her work!"

His wife rolled her eyes in exasperation. She wasn't able to resume her previous career, so she's just "helping out" in her husband's office—but she is thoroughly enjoying her return to the workplace after two decades of being a homemaker. He would just as soon have her go back home, but she has escaped the domestic ghetto, and she isn't about to return to such a circumscribed life—no matter how much her husband complains.

And yet even when men rely on the services provided by stay-at-home wives, that doesn't necessarily mean they respect the women who take care of them. When my apartment building's exterminator made his bimonthly visit this week, he was still irate about an argument he'd had with his wife. After their fight, she consulted her friends, who all agreed with her. But the exterminator was unswayed by their point of view, however unanimous. "They're all a bunch of dumb Long Island housewives who have never worked a day in their lives," he said contemptuously. The simple fact that these women didn't work rendered them unworthy of respect in his eyes.

Things aren't much different at the other end of the status spectrum, according to many men in the financial world. As a Wall Street hedge-fund manager, Whitney Bronstein* is unusual in having a genuine partnership with a professional wife. But most of the marriages he sees among his male peers involve high-earning husbands and stay-at-home wives.

"Many of the women were compatible at the outset; they met in graduate school, they had M.B.A.'s or whatever. But over time, they grow apart, because they're leading such separate lives," says Bronstein, who is forty-five years old. "The husband has developed his life on his own, and his focus is on his job; the woman has developed her life at home, and the smart ones are bored."

Couples in egalitarian marriages typically have more in common. A recent study by sociologists at Duke University and the University of Arizona found an increase in spouses talking over important subjects, and Dr. Lynn Smith-Lovin, a sociologist at Duke and co-author of the study, believes this may be due to the increasing structural similarity of men's and women's lives. When both spouses are working at jobs they care about and the husbands are participating more in domestic matters, "Spouses literally have more to talk about," she told *The New York Times*.

Baby Boomer men often learned such lessons from their parents' negative example. "As my father's world got bigger, my mother's world got smaller," says Bill Ennis,* a fifty-eight-year-old expert in health-care policy whose father was a successful business executive and whose mother was a stay-at-home mom. "There needs to be equilibrium within the family, in terms of power and life experience, and if there's not, it's very hard to maintain intimacy. My mother did volunteer work and was active in our church, but she just didn't have that much to talk about."

Ennis doesn't believe he benefited from his mother's domestic focus either. "My mother's life revolved around me, and it wasn't good for me," he says. "Because she was too enmeshed with me, it was hard for her to see me make mistakes or take risks; it was hard for her to let go. I think my parents would have had a better marriage, and I would have had a better childhood, if my mother had worked, and I think she would have been happier."

For Mrs. Ennis, the empty nest proved traumatic. "When I went off to college, my father left for a thirteen-week course at Harvard Business School," says Ennis, who grew up in Burbank, California. "What happens when you focus on raising a child and he leaves, and you focus on being a helpmate to your husband and he leaves, even if it's only for thirteen weeks? Years later, my mother said to me, 'You went to Stanford, your father went to Harvard, and I went to bed.' She literally stayed in bed for weeks."

Depression has been recognized as a significant risk for full-time homemakers ever since the 1950s stereotype of unhappy housewives popping pills and swigging cocktails at ever-earlier hours of the afternoon. Last fall *The New York Times* reported that this cliché is currently being updated by stay-at-home mothers who gather regularly for "cocktail play groups," although the story also questioned whether these "modern martini mothers" would tolerate such on-the-job drinking from hired caregivers.

According to many men, the separate-spheres arrangement can also lead to an inordinate amount of male infidelity. "In finance, you have large expense accounts and stay in expensive hotels and eat at expensive restaurants, and that lends itself to extracurricular activities that would be expensive if you had to pay for them on your own," says Whitney Bronstein. "Among very successful white males, there's a frat-boy image. These men show total disrespect toward women; they treat women as pure sex objects, and they get away with saying things that should have them hauled up on sexual-harassment charges."

Although many of these men indulge in extramarital activities that range from one-night stands to serious affairs, their wives rarely protest. "Whether their wives know, I don't know," Bronstein says. "Some are aware but turn a blind eye; they've reached a business understanding. There's another group of wives who are completely submissive. They are definitely happy with the affluence, with the things the money can buy, and with the comfort that comes from having a big bank account. But they seem insecure when they're around their husbands. The guy doesn't go home for three nights a week; he's out on 'work' nights. The wife feels an emotional insecurity. The wives are afraid they might be dumped if they confront the issues. The men don't worry about the consequences of their actions, because their wives are not holding them accountable—and the wives don't want to be confrontational, because of their lack of power. It's clearly not an equal relationship. The husband doesn't treat the wife as a peer, because he doesn't respect what she does at home with the kids enough. These guys get their sense of self-worth through how much money they make; their entire hierarchy is based on money as a measure of how successful you've been in your life. They have no idea what value their wives are providing, other than being home in the abstract. So you see this strange level of formality between husband and wife; it's almost as if the wife has to ask permission to do something."

Men with more egalitarian values may be put off by that kind of power dynamic, but the idea that a wife can still be railroaded into remaining docile and submissive retains a powerful hold over the male imagination. "Guys, a word of advice," business writer and editor Michael Noer wrote on Forbes.com last year. "Whatever you do, don't marry a woman with a career."

Attributing his claims to social-science research, Noer argued that "professional women are more likely to get divorced, more likely to cheat and less likely to have children. And if they do have kids, they are more likely to be unhappy about it." Although he cited various sources for his opinions, Noer's underlying problem seemed to be rooted in the feelings of insecurity that strong women clearly provoke in him. "The more successful she is, the more likely she is to grow dissatisfied with you," he complained. Should you marry one of these harridans, he concluded, "even your house will be dirtier."

Such fears might conjure visions of ruthlessly high-powered female executives earning six-figure incomes, but Noer specifically set the bar much lower. "For our purposes, a 'career girl' has a university-level (or higher) education, works more than 35 hours a week outside the home, and makes more than $30,000 a year," he wrote. "Marrying these women is asking for trouble."

This wasn't Noer's first excursion into the fraught territory of sexual politics; he had already antagonized many women with an earlier column entitled "The Economics of Prostitution," which began, "Wife or whore? The choice is that simple." Drawing on the work of two economists who published a paper called "A Theory of Prostitution," Noer observed that their analysis "considered wives and whores as economic 'goods' that can be substituted for each other. Men buy, women sell."

Although that piece drew some angry responses, Noer had based it on the work of others, casting himself as a journalist who was simply reporting on the economists' views. But the deliberately inflammatory essay advising men not to marry career women seemed deeply personal, and it generated the predictable outcry. "Disgusting Misogynistic *Forbes* Article One Step Away from Stepford" was the headline on a furious response on the Huffington Post, which attacked Noer for his "flawed, presumptuous, lazy, selectively sourced article." Noting that Noer attributed his conclusions to "many social scientists," the Huffington Post added, "He doesn't let us know if many more social scientists have drawn different conclusions from conflicting data, or this data, or more complete data." The verdict? "He's an idiot."

A response on Opinionistas.com came up with a list of "Forbes' Nine Ways to Avoid Becoming a Pathetic Dried-Up Unmarriageable Waste of Humanity," which included Number Three: "After marriage, lock yourself in your white picket fence home and never again interact with another human being in possession of a working penis (with the exception of your husband, of course)," and Number Four: "Within a year after marriage, make absolutely sure that tidy, photogenic offspring are shooting from your womb with superhuman frequency," adding, "Be sure to breed them to look exactly like him; that will assuage any leftover fears from Step #3." Helpful hints were also offered for achieving Number Five: "Make yourself happy by any means necessary. . . . There's nothing that'll dampen a man's spirits more than coming home to a morbid, lifeless wife who spends her days fantasizing about excising his eyeballs with a plastic spatula. Prozac is an option. As is Zoloft. Or Paxil. Or Valium. Alternate days. Add two cups of gin per serving. Works every time."

The flap over Noer's antediluvian views even roiled the waters on the other side of the Atlantic. In London's *Sunday Times*, Sarah Baxter Washington and John Elliott reported Salon.com's suggestion that "the article might just as well have been called, 'If You Are Really Self-Loathing and Weak, Try to Find Someone Who Doesn't Work and Will Consent to Live with You Out of Financial Desperation for the Rest of Her Life.' "

Inspired by the feeding frenzy, some men added their own gleefully derisive commentary. In the *Chicago Tribune*, Rex Huppke wrote a column called "When It Comes to Women, Smart Guys Can Be Real Dumb," which surveyed other responses to the article, like a posting on Gawker.com noting that "Noer 'failed to discuss the advantages of selecting a woman with birthing hips.' Another rattled off additional reasons not to marry career women, including 'Career women talk too much when you bring them to benefit dinners' and 'Career women won't end a financial argument by pressing their breasts against you and cooing, "Oh, well, you're the money man." ' "

Huppke was delighted to provide an alternative male point of view. Noer's column "overlooked us intrinsically lazy men who would love it if our wives made gobs of money, allowing us to stay home and solve important problems like how to arrange five plasma televisions in one room," he wrote. A report on the controversy in *The Week* concluded, "We can only hope that Noer's intemperate attack on wives who bring home lots of bacon hasn't already ruined that dream for the rest of us."

When a wife earns a hefty paycheck, that household contribution will likely be noticed by even the most inattentive husband. But as Whitney Bronstein observed, some men have a more tenuous grasp on the long-term value provided by their wives' domestic services. While their children are young, the husbands of stay-at-home mothers are most likely to appreciate the many tasks their wives take care of, thereby freeing the men to concentrate on their own jobs. But as the kids grow up and the men themselves age, they sometimes discover that they have paid an unexpectedly high price for those amenities.

If men are unhappy with their jobs, they may feel trapped by their financial responsibilities, unable even to consider alternatives that would compromise the family's income. "My husband really feels he chose the wrong career," says one New York wife who is married to a Wall Street investment manager. "He wishes he had become an architect, but he can't change careers now. We couldn't afford for him to stop earning money for all the years it would take for him to start over, so he feels stuck."

That dilemma provides a sharp contrast with the freedom enjoyed by couples in which both partners have significant incomes. "Because each of us earns a salary, the conversation we have with each other has always been, 'Anytime you don't want to do this anymore, you can do something else,' and the other one will step up to the plate," says Jim Shaw. "Either of us could go to a public-service or a nonprofit job, and we could still lead a good life. It takes an emotional load off my mind, because I don't feel like I have to be trapped in a particular job, earning a particular income, with a wife who's saying, 'It's up to you to bring home the bacon.' It's an emotional relief even if I don't exercise it."

Such mutual support can become a lifesaver when disaster strikes. "At one point, my husband's law firm went bankrupt, but he didn't have to worry about feeding his family," says Miranda Blake, Shaw's wife. "We always had an income. I felt great that our family was safe and that I could do that. He said, 'I can't imagine what I'd do if my wife didn't work.'"

My own husband felt the same way when the magazine where he worked was abruptly shut down. "It was a tremendous relief to me that we had another income that would get the family through the crisis," he says. "It allowed me not to have to jump into something that might not be right for me or that I might regret, just for a paycheck."

In response to the *New York Times* story about Yalies who expect to give up their careers, one twenty-eight-year-old woman wrote a letter to the editor noting that her husband's salary would allow her to stay home when they have a baby. "Still, I've fought hard to convince him that I can share the privilege of providing for our family so that he'll have the same freedom I do to pursue alternate career paths and a deep relationship with our children," wrote Sarah Vincent, a marketing executive from Tampa, Florida. The young women who plan on giving up their jobs are "locking men in the provider role just as securely as postwar women were locked into the homemaker role," Vincent added. "Not fair then; not fair now."

The flexibility offered by more egalitarian marriages goes a long way toward preventing either partner from feeling imprisoned, by financial or domestic responsibilities. As Simone de Beauvoir observed in *The Second Sex,* "The self-supporting wife emancipates her husband from the conjugal slavery that was the price of hers."

"Maybe if you're making five million dollars a year, it doesn't feel so hard to be the sole breadwinner, but it's a lot of pressure," says Richard Seltzer, recalling the period when his wife was a full-time mother. "We were able to provide our kids with the education we've given them because Ann worked, too. If I had thought she was never going back to work, I would have felt very pressured. It's scary; it feels like a heavy load. You make a mistake, or something happens with your job, and the whole family collapses."

To the young and affluent, such possibilities often seem remote. Working in the financial sector, Ben Ensminger-Law says he is particularly struck by what he calls "the blind optimism" of many of his peers. "There's a misperception that there will always be a job available, because you're smart and connected and in our experience there always has been," he says. "People think, 'It won't happen to me,' or 'I'll be able to work it out,' but it's unrealistic and shortsighted not to acknowledge that there are a lot of risks in the future."

Some young men, however, are wise beyond their years, often

because a painful personal experience gave them an early lesson in financial vulnerability. When David Graham was growing up in New Hampshire, his father left his mother, a stay-at-home wife, shortly after the birth of their third child. "My mother was unemployed, and we went to the poverty line really quickly," says Graham, who remembers feeling as though he never got enough to eat as a boy because money was so tight. "Her feeling was, 'I let myself depend on a man to support me, and I thought it would be forever, and this person has now left me with nothing.' It was a really big shock."

Graham's mother slowly worked her way out of the abyss. "She went back to school, got a master's degree, and became an accountant while raising three kids," he says.

But to her son, the lesson was clear. "You always have to be prepared for what may come in life," he says.

## CHAPTER ELEVEN

# HOME EQUITY

## "MY HUSBAND AND I ARE PEERS."

A s a reporter, I often travel on assignment. When my children were small, the prospect of my leaving town for a few days typically elicited great alarm from our friends and family.

"Who will take care of the children?" they exclaimed, as if the little darlings had only one parent. When I replied that their father would doubtless make sure they didn't starve to death while I was away, everyone from my women friends to my mother would simper adoringly, "Oh, you're so lucky! Jeremy is sooo wonderful!"

Like my husband and me, our upstairs neighbors during those years, Amy and Nick, were both working journalists with children and a dog. When Amy saw my husband hauling grocery bags into our apartment one day, she asked me what he was doing. Since the bags were crammed with the usual staples of family life, from breakfast cereal to toilet paper, the answer seemed pretty obvious. I nonetheless explained that twice a month Jeremy bought large quantities of household supplies, thereby reducing the number of necessities I have to lug home every day. Duh.

Amy looked as if she were about to swoon. "Oh, you're so lucky!" she moaned. "My husband would never do that! Jeremy is sooo wonderful!"

When the big holidays roll around, I spend days planning and cooking lavish meals for hordes of friends and relatives. I do everything from the flower arranging to the silver polishing to the table setting. After eating themselves into a stupor, one or two people usually make halfhearted offers to help clean up. We tell them not to worry about it; Jeremy does the cleanup.

"Oh, you're so lucky!" they murmur. "Jeremy is sooo wonderful!"

Here's a news flash for you: Jeremy may be wonderful, but it's not as if I'm sitting around with my feet up. He performs a reasonable share of the labor generated by our home and children, which I would argue are as much his responsibility as mine. But I have almost always done more. The sainted Jeremy may look like the Husband of the Year in comparison with a lot of other guys, but that just goes to show how low we set the bar for men in this society.

Granted, the imbalance is considerably worse in many two-career American homes where the female is responsible for the infamous "second shift" described by sociologist Arlie Hochschild. "On average, women perform two or three times as much housework as men," reported Scott Coltrane, a sociology professor at the University of California, Riverside, in his study "Research on Household Labor." "Men tend to perform less housework when they marry and assume a smaller share of the household work after their wives have children. . . . In general, women have felt obligated to perform housework, and men have assumed that domestic work is primarily the responsibility of mothers, wives, daughters and low-paid female housekeepers. In contrast, men's participation in housework has appeared optional."

Even before having children, men seem to view this sorry state of affairs as a preordained privilege of their gender. "According to Phyllis Moen and Patricia Roehling's *Career Mystique*, 'When couples marry, the amount of time that a woman spends doing housework increases by approximately 17 percent while a man's decreases by 33 percent,'" Linda Hirshman reported in her *American Prospect* article "Homeward Bound."

After the kids arrive, a woman's disproportionate burdens are exacerbated by the additional job of masterminding the whole domestic enterprise. Ask your typical American dad what size shoes his children wear and you're likely to draw a blank stare. Try asking him about his children's teachers and playmates. Most moms will be able to describe the social dynamics of the entire third-grade class, but the dad will be lucky to dredge up a name or two, and he is highly unlikely to know who's feuding with whom.

"Our culture assumes that mothers will be responsible for the well-being of children, the upkeep of the home, and the marriage, so men don't need to do a lot to get a lot of credit," says Coltrane. "Women still put in more labor and have more of the burden of taking care of domestic details. But most Americans think the division of labor is fair when the wife does two-thirds and the husband does one-third. When he starts approaching half, they think it's unfair. To assume that men only need to do one-third when their wives are working as many hours as they are is just absurd. I think we have to raise expectations for men, in relationships and as parents. We should not assume that men are incompetent or can't do it."

My own husband claims that any inequity in our household contributions derives solely from the fact that he goes to an office while I work at home, which permits me to take care of many domestic tasks during my workday. This disparity may explain why I make dinner every night—because I'm home to stir the pot on the stove—but it does not explain why I'm the one who always knows when the next orthodontist appointment is, what the cross-country meet schedule is, or on which dates the guitar teacher is coming an hour earlier.

And yet everyone acts as if Jeremy is a hero for making a run to the supermarket or washing the dishes. In fact, however, the reason Jeremy "helps" as much as he does (an offensive terminology that tells you who's really being held responsible) is simple: He doesn't have a choice.

From the beginning of our relationship, I made it clear that I wasn't going to be any husband's unpaid servant. If Jeremy wanted to be married to me, he couldn't stick me with all the boring, mundane stuff nobody wants to do. And if we were going to raise children together, we had to share the work—or he could forget the whole deal. That was eighteen years ago, and while we haven't exactly achieved parity, we've come closer to it than many other couples, judging by all the dreary surveys proving that men are slugs and their wives are superwomen.

Maintaining some semblance of equity in your marriage can force you to deploy all those nasty tactics you swore you would never stoop to as a parent but nonetheless found yourself using the minute you actually had a kid. Bribery and punishment work; so do yelling and complaining. Threats are also effective, as long as everyone knows you mean business. With husbands, tender blandishments are particularly useful. These strategies admittedly take a lot of energy, but not as much as performing all the functions necessary to maintain home and family by yourself. When I'm feeling overwhelmed, I hand my husband a list and say, "This is what I need you to do today." He may groan, but the jobs get done. I still have to supervise everybody—somehow he is never the one who remembers that our son needs new mosquito netting, baseball cleats, and basketball shoes for sleepaway camp—but I'm not the only one schlepping around town checking items off the packing list.

What I don't understand is why my insistence on a rough semblance of equality is unusual. I live in Manhattan, which is full of smart, educated, successful women who are juggling the responsibilites of family and career with extraordinary competence. And yet most of them will readily admit that their husbands don't do half of anything remotely domestic, whether it's child care or grocery shopping or bed making or birthday-party planning.

Go to any school event for parents and you find it crowded with working women who have taken time out of their busy professional schedules to sit in on Class Day or attend the fourth-grade play. My children's school sponsors a regular forum where parents meet to discuss such pressing issues as curfews, homework, and the social mores of hormone-addled teenagers. With a daughter and a son in different grades, I have attended countless such events. At every single one, the room is full of women—doctors, lawyers, and CEOs as well as stay-at-home moms. Even when the wives are the primary breadwinners, they show up at such events far more often than the husbands do.

Women are now the major breadwinners in a third of all American married-couple households, and the average working wife contributes more than a third of her family's income. But women remain much more likely to take time off from work when their children are sick, even when they earn more than their partners. Needless to say, one survey after another shows that men also have more leisure time. Ask most working mothers what they do with their leisure time and you're lucky if they don't hit you.

But despite women's increasing economic clout, most wives are not demanding the husband perform a fair share of the housework. "Whatever men do is considered such a gift that instead of asking for equality, women feel they have to be appreciative for any 'help,'" observes sociologist Kathleen Gerson. Indeed, many men are actually making matters worse instead of helping to relieve the burden, according to a study by the Center for Work-Life Policy. Forty percent of the women surveyed said that their husbands create more work around the house than they perform.

It's hardly surprising that women are not happy about this arrangement. "When women shoulder a disproportionate share of responsibility for housework, their perceptions of fairness and marital satisfaction decline, and . . . marital conflict and women's depression increase," Coltrane reported in "Research on Household Labor."

The association between doing household chores—what social scientists call low-schedule-control tasks like making dinner, which can't be postponed until next week—and unhappiness is so pronounced that even when women reduce their hours to work part-time, they don't get any happier. In fact, their marriages may even suffer, because women working part-time end up doing far more of the household chores. A study by the Community, Family and Work Program at Brandeis University's Women's Studies Research Center found that full-time women doctors actually had better relationships with their husbands than did women who worked part-time, because the full-time doctors were performing a smaller share of household tasks. "Reducing work hours does not necessarily have a positive impact on the quality of life," the study's authors concluded.

The stress inflicted on women by their unjust share of domestic burdens can harm their physical as well as mental health. "In one extraordinarily revealing study, researchers periodically measured the blood pressure and norepinephrine levels of managers during the day. (They chose norepinephrine because this hormone responds rapidly to changes in stress.) They found that the male managers' blood pressure and stress-hormone levels dropped dramatically at five P.M., but the women managers' levels actually jacked up as they turned their attention from their 'first-shift' jobs to their 'second-shift' responsibilities as wives and mothers," reported Linda Babcock and Sara Laschever in *Women Don't Ask: Negotiation and the Gender Divide.* "Another researcher, who looked at the levels of stress hormones in employed mothers and childless women, found that the women with children at home excreted higher levels of the stress hormone cortisol and reported more stress around home responsibilities. The amount of stress they experienced around their work responsibilities did not differ from the stress experienced by childless women."

The consequences of this physiological toll can even be life-threatening. According to Babcock and Laschever, "These higher levels of both norephinephrine and cortisol represent a genuine threat to women's health. As Linda Austin reports in *What's Holding You Back?* 'Chronic elevation of blood pressure caused by norephinephrine secretion . . . is a significant risk factor for heart disease, the number one killer of women.' Dr. Bruce S. McEwen, director of the neuroendocrinology laboratory at Rockefeller University, confirms that 'prolonged or severe stress has been shown to weaken the immune system, strain the heart, damage memory cells in the brain and deposit fat at the waist rather than the hips or buttocks (a risk factor for heart disease, cancer and other illnesses). In addition to these threats, stress can contribute to aging, depression, rheumatoid arthritis, diabetes and other illnesses."

To make matters worse, the strains imposed by women's disproportionate domestic burdens are often the reason they finally give up in disgust and quit their jobs. Patsy Wiggins never intended to become a full-time mom. "I planned to go to law school since I was in second grade," she says. She did so, becoming a commercial litigator who regarded stay-at-home wives with disdain. "My husband worked for a big firm, and none of the spouses of the big partners worked. I thought it was pathetic," she says. "I was very critical. I couldn't understand why anyone would do that. I thought, 'Don't any of them have any self-value?'"

But when Wiggins had children, she says, "I found out why none of the partners' wives had jobs. My husband worked crazy hours, and he worked through the night a lot of the time; he was sent to live in different places; he would be away for weeks at a time. If I ever needed him to cover for me at home, he never could—not once."

Wiggins continued working until she became pregnant with her second child. "I thought I was doing well, but in my boss's eyes I wasn't there for the one minute he needed me at eight o'clock on a Wednesday night," she says bitterly. "It was always a problem. I felt like I wasn't doing the best job I could do at home or at work. For me, it was horrible. My husband understood my stress level, and he wanted me to leave work, because he didn't feel he could help me out in any way. It used to drive me crazy that he couldn't do anything, and it really upset me that he didn't feel the same responsibility I did to make sure things were happening correctly at home. His answer was, 'Then you leave work.' It was my problem. His job was more important to him than mine."

So Wiggins quit her job, knowing full well how unfair the choice was. "Why do men always feel they are 'helping' as opposed to raising their children?" she says. "That's a question I ask all the time. I tell my husband, 'You're parenting—not baby-sitting!' I find with most of my friends that raising children, purchasing their clothes, scheduling activities, making sure they have food—it's all the mother's job, whether or not they have a full-time job."

Unlike many stay-at-home mothers, Wiggins understood the economic risks she was taking on by surrendering her financial self-sufficiency. "Yes, I'm vulnerable," she says, "but I feel like there's nothing I could do about it." That will doubtless remain true as long as women permit their partners to get away with acting as if they have no joint responsibility for taking care of their own children. When wives allow their spouses to dismiss all the domestic responsibilities as a woman's problem, even as they themselves make the career sacrifices necessary to pick up the slack, they ensure the maintenance of a grossly unfair status quo.

It doesn't have to be this way. Like my husband and me, most of our friends are Baby Boomers who came of age during the exhilarating heyday of the modern women's movement. We entered adult life determined to avoid the gender-stereotyped roles played by our parents, many of whom were absent fathers and frustrated, depressed mothers.

In the years since, most of my friends have forged fascinating careers as well as raised wonderful children. Many of their husbands cook (some considerably better than their wives), and almost all share the household tasks in addition to being active, engaged fathers.

As a devoted dad, my husband really was exceptional. When I had our first child, Jeremy put together the vacation days and overtime compensation he had earned and took seven weeks off from work to help care for the new baby. While I recovered from my C-section, he was the one who stayed up with our colicky infant as she screamed through every night. From the outset, he was determined to be an equal partner in parenting. That kind of paternity leave is unusual, and many men don't even take advantage of the time they could get. But most of the husbands I know have made many accommodations to the work schedules of their wives and the needs of their children. "I can pretty much count on my husband to do whatever needs to be done," says Darcy Howe.

And the more men contribute, the happier their partners tend to be. Cyndy Byrnes, a forty-nine-year-old mother of two, runs her own business dealing in art and interiors from her home in Westport, Connecticut. "Working at home is absolutely the answer," says Byrnes. But a reasonable division of labor with her husband, a Wall Street bond trader, is also key to her contentment. "My husband and I are peers," she says. "I always made myself a valuable part of the equation; at certain junctures I was making more money than he was. We've been married for eighteen years, but we're colleagues in this adventure. We both work, and we consider the kids both of our responsibility. We have a division of labor: He takes care of certain things, and I take care of certain things. We each earn half of the family income. It's very equitable."

This kind of fairness is increasingly common in so-called peer marriages. "In general, wives who make more money enjoy more equal divisions of labor," Coltrane wrote in "Research on Household Labor." "When relative earnings between husbands and wives are more equal, the relative distribution of household tasks is more balanced."

A host of social-science data demonstrates how far our society has come in recent decades. "In the last twenty years, men have doubled their contributions to child care, and if you look at the weekends, the change is even greater," Coltrane reports. "There's a lot of change here; women are demanding more of their husbands, and men are doing more."

Coltrane cites the work of Joseph Pleck at the University of Illinois, among others who have quantified such changes. "In two-parent families in the 1960s to the early '80s, men did one-third as much interacting and caretaking as mothers, and they were available to their children half as much as the women were," Coltrane reports. "From the '80s to the early '90s, men interacted two-fifths as much as the mother and were available two-thirds as much. From the early '90s to the present, men interacted two-thirds as much as the moms on weekdays and were three-quarters as available, in terms of being in the house. On the ground level, men and women are negotiating more things, and more things are on the table. There's not the assumption that the wife will do it all. The fact that we're even expecting men to do one-third or one-half is remarkable."

Some studies actually suggest that if you compute each spouse's contributions differently, parity may already have been reached. "Women still do twice as much housework as men" in two-parent families, according to Suzanne Bianchi, chairwoman of the department of sociology at the University of Maryland and co-author of *Changing Rhythms of American Family Life*, whose findings were based on thousands of personal time-use diaries chronicling parents' activities.

But Bianchi and her fellow researchers "said that total hours of work by mothers and fathers were roughly equal when they counted paid and unpaid work," *The New York Times* reported. "Using this measure, the researchers found 'remarkable gender equality in total workloads,' averaging nearly 65 hours a week."

Among younger men, the trend toward egalitarian relationships is even more pronounced. "Fathers born between 1965 and 1979 spend almost the same number of hours a day with their children as working mothers—about 3.5 hours," Celinda Lake and Kellyanne Conway reported in *What Women Really Want.* "According to a recent study, 70 percent of men would take a pay cut to spend more time with their families."

Even more notable is the increase in genuine role reversal among married couples. "The numbers are still small, but the percentage of stay-at-home dads has doubled in the last decade, and it's now around five percent," says sociologist Kathleen Gerson. "The number of women supporting men has also increased."

Such trends would be hard to deduce from much of the current media coverage. "Men are changing more than we're led to believe," says family historian Stephanie Coontz. "I think men's expectations have changed a lot. Most men expect to do work around the house, and they also expect to share breadwinning. The younger men are, the more likely they are to expect an egalitarian marriage. And the longer a woman has been at work, the more housework her husband starts to do."

In other words, while we have hardly achieved gender equity, many of us have come a long way from the Paleolithic Era represented by our parents' marriages. My mother commuted to an office every day, just like my father, but she spent the evening making dinner, cleaning up, doing laundry, baking cookies for whatever child-related event required them the next day, and helping my brother and me with our homework. My father put up his feet, snoozed in front of the television set, and then went to bed early while she stayed up until some ungodly hour, finishing her labors.

The fact that guys, when left to their own devices, rarely rush to offer more toilet scrubbing and diaper changing is not in itself surprising. As Martin Luther King Jr. once observed, "We know through painful experience that freedom is never voluntarily given by the oppressor; it must be demanded by the oppressed." These days it's not fashionable to talk about oppression, at least in so-called sophisticated circles. It's so passé. It's so earnest and humorless. It reminds people of those early feminists with frizzy hair and no makeup, wearing overalls and Birkenstocks.

But the thing that baffles me is women's complicity, which has far-reaching consequences. If wives permit their husbands to shirk the responsibilities of homemaking and parenting, they are likely to sentence their children to a similar fate. When you have children, everything you do teaches them how to live their own lives after they grow up. Unfortunately, what all too many mothers are demonstrating for their children is that "woman is the nigger of the world," as John Lennon and Yoko Ono put it so memorably in a song lyric in 1972. What too many fathers show their sons and daughters is that men can get away with dumping the scut work on their wives—and that women will grit their teeth and put up with it, even if they're contributing more to the family income than their husbands do.

This does not bode well for these children's futures, according to Coltrane's research. "From the interviews I've done with young families, women who expect to be taken care of and men who expect women to take care of them emotionally are less likely to be happy in their own marriages," Coltrane says. "Young adults raised in families where the women were employed and the men helped have more realistic expectations. We've been in a conservative swing for the last ten to fifteen years, but we live in a world where gender equality is so much a part of our culture that we're not going back. Young men who expect not to have to do any parenting or change any diapers—their marriages are going to be in trouble, because their wives are not going to put up with it."

Contrary to the dire predictions offered by many conservative commentators, a growing body of research demonstrates that egalitarian marriages not only have significant benefits for children but are also viewed more favorably by them. Kathleen Gerson, the author of several books on marriage and gender, has been conducting studies for her next book, *Children of the Gender Revolution*. "I'm interviewing young adults, and children who grew up in relatively egalitarian homes are overwhelmingly supportive of that arrangement, whereas children who grew up in traditional homes are much more ambivalent and divided," she reports. "You hear all these stories about children suffering from having working mothers, but we're not really listening to what the children are saying."

Not only are their views positive, but so are the concrete benefits. "The Victorian ideology of separate spheres was a nineteenth-century ideal that assumes that women are the most fulfilled when they're taking care of men and children and that men's rightful place is as the head of the family and breadwinner," Coltrane explains. "In the separate-spheres family, there is less co-parenting. But when fathers share more of the parenting and the domestic duties, the kids are more cooperative. If parents work together as a team in raising their kids, setting limits, and talking through issues, the children do better emotionally, socially, and academically."

Sharing domestic duties can also be helpful to children's overall well-being. Stay-at-home moms place great emphasis on the services they provide for their children, most of which are necessary in the early years of childhood. But as kids get older, many full-time mothers continue to service them in ways that not only deplete their own time and energy but also fail to teach their children skills and self-sufficiency. When children are given defined responsibilities within the home, however, the results can be surprising.

Coltrane's research found that children who did housework with their fathers were more likely to get along with their peers and to have more friends. They were also less likely than other kids to disobey teachers or make trouble at school, less depressed, and less withdrawn. "When men perform domestic services for others, it teaches their children cooperation and democratic family values," Coltrane reports.

Of course, democratic family values are anathema to right-wing ideologues who are working overtime to discredit the idea that cooperative, equity-based families might actually be successful and desirable. Last year, the media gave prominent and uncritical coverage to a study by two University of Virginia sociologists who claimed to demonstrate that women are actually happier in traditional marriages where they are confined to conventional gender roles while men support the family. W. Bradford Wilcox and Steven L. Nock analyzed data from a University of Wisconsin survey of families conducted in the early 1990s and found that 52 percent of the wives who didn't work outside the home were "very happy" with their marriages, compared with only 41 percent of the working wives.

Many academic experts found the media's unwarranted credulousness as appalling as the study's flawed methodology, exaggerated conclusions, and apparent political bias. "The way it's being spun is that you'll be happier if you tamp down your expectations and don't expect equality, but that conclusion is fallacious; it was spun in a way that was completely unjustified by the findings," says Stephanie Coontz.

The much-ballyhooed conclusion was also contradicted by a large body of other research, as Caryl Rivers and Rosalind Chait Barnett have pointed out. "Over the past fifteen years, some twenty studies have looked at the association between women's employment and earnings and their marital happiness," they reported on Women's eNews. "They all tell the same story: Employed women are as happy (and perhaps happier) in their marriages as non-employed women, and having an income generally improves a woman's marital happiness."

Although the Virginia study claimed that wives were happier if their husbands were the breadwinners, Barnett and Rivers added, "Other research disagrees. Some 42 percent of today's married women outearn their husbands. Are these marriages falling apart? Not according to the divorce data. These marriages are as stable as those in which husbands earn more.... In a 2001 analysis of data from our own study of 300 dual-earner couples, funded by the National Institutes of Mental Health, wives' earnings—whether higher, lower or the same as their husbands'—had no effect on their marital happiness. (And, for the most part, men's marital happiness was unrelated to how much their wives earned.)"

The media reports on Wilcox and Nock's conclusions generally failed to note such contradictory facts. Much of the coverage also managed to ignore their study's real findings—that a crucial determinant of a wife's happiness was the amount of "emotion work" done by her husband, a term used to describe his efforts to be attentive, supportive, and appreciative.

"Wilcox is on the speakers' board of the Institute for American Values, a very well-funded right-wing think tank, and these right-wing institutes spin stories in a way that makes them news that has to be covered," explains Barbara Risman, co-chair of the Council on Contemporary Families. "The agenda, in my view, is to support traditional gendered marriages; they think traditional marriage is the backbone of America. But their own data show that what really predicts wives' marital happiness is the amount of emotional work men do in the marriage. The big story was that what makes women happy is being married to Alan Alda rather than John Wayne, but that's not what the headlines said, because the press release was terribly misleading."

"Conservative social scientists think the world works better when fathers are breadwinners and wives expect to do all the family work," Coltrane observes. "It's about men being in charge. Conservative evangelicals invoke Biblical references to show that the husband is the God-given leader, and sharing decision making with his wife is abdicating his God-given role. They want to promote the idea that egalitarian marriages are passé, that women are expecting too much of men, and that women are happier in traditional marriages. It's just bad social science. The data show that egalitarian women are just as happy as traditional women."

And the more their husbands do, the happier the women are, according to another Coltrane article, "Elite Careers and Family Commitment." "When men perform more of the routine housework, employed women feel that the division of labor is fairer, are less depressed, and enjoy higher levels of marital satisfaction," Coltrane reported.

Rarely acknowledged by those advocating traditional gender roles, the not-so-startling truth is that housework doesn't make either men or women happy. Although "research has consistently shown that working mothers experience more stress and depression than working fathers do, . . . as Linda Austin writes, 'the cause of the stress is frequently misattributed. It is often implied that employment is causing women stress and depression and that the remedy is staying home,'" reported Babcock and Laschever in *Women Don't Ask*. "In fact, the opposite is the case: A study of 3,800 men and women concluded that paid employment is associated with reduced depression among both husbands and wives, while time spent on housework is associated with increased depression for both genders, regardless of other roles."

Conservatives also like to portray nontraditional families as a freakish anomaly confined to a handful of radical feminists and wimpy men—an impression that belies the facts. "They're defending a form of marriage that is statistically the minority," Coltrane points out. As he reported in "Elite Careers," there were more than twice as many traditional families with a breadwinner father and a homemaker mother as there were dual-earner families in 1960. But by 2000, there were more than twice as many dual-earner families as traditional single-breadwinner ones—a striking reversal that appears to have prompted a panicky backlash from those determined to enforce traditional gender roles. "The separate-spheres idea is waning in reality," Coltrane says. "I think much of what we see is a reactionary response to wanting things to be the way they were before—but you can't put the genie back in the bottle."

"There's a strong minority arguing to restore traditional gender roles, but I don't think they're the voice of the future," adds Stephanie Coontz. "This is all a transition, and it's a long transition. We're not headed for equality right now, but the trend is toward more convergence in male and female work and family roles. This is not to say that there aren't huge obstacles that will continue to re-create wishful thinking, but I don't see a reversal in the cards at all."

Indeed, those who bemoan the lingering double standards that afflict so many marriages sometimes lose sight of how rapidly things have evolved in a relatively short span of time. As Coontz told *The New York Times* recently, "Marriage has changed more in the past thirty years than in the previous 3,000." Citing the shifts in women's economic, legal, and political independence as well as gender roles within marriage, Coontz added, "Taken together, this is as dramatic a change in human history as the Industrial Revolution."

While most husbands still aren't dying to scrub more toilets, Coltrane has also found that nontraditional marriages confer significant advantages on men as well as women. "As men get more involved in egalitarian relationships, they grow emotionally," he says. "They parent better. The intimacy with their wives increases. There's an emotional enrichment to partnership marriages, and the benefits for men are profound, as they assume more of the caregiving."

There's no question in my mind that my husband is a better father because I leave town every once in a while. When I'm not around, he has to make the kids' breakfasts and take them to their doctors' appointments and supervise their homework. He is the one they turn to with their troubles, and he is closer to them as a result. Is it an exaggeration to suggest that they actually love him more than they might have if he hadn't been such a participatory father? I suspect that this is true. My own father was a nice man, but he thought his job was done when he came home from the office. It was my mother who listened eagerly to what had happened to my brother and me every day. As a result, we grew up feeling intimately connected to her while having a far more remote relationship with our father. I don't think I ever really knew him; I know he didn't really know me. My children will never have to admit such a thing about their own dad, who has been at their sides for every triumph and every challenge.

In families structured around traditional gender roles, absentee fathers often pay a high price for the long work hours required of a sole breadwinner. "You work in a completely macho environment: I can fly more miles, work more hours, take on more cases, do bigger deals; I can multitask while moving hundreds of millions of dollars around," says the former managing partner of a New York law firm. "But it's all focused on the business side of the ledger, and the implicit assumption is that the woman is going to cover the home side of the ledger. Women are the losers to the extent that they cannot remain involved as productive members on the business side, but men are the grand losers, because we don't have the opportunity to enjoy as much of our kids growing up and of our home life. So everyone loses. I know powerful lawyers whose children are saying, 'We are going to choose a different lifestyle. We don't want to spend three thousand hours a year working and missing out on the rest of life; it's not worth it.' I think that's a direct reaction to having had a parent who wasn't around enough. These very successful fathers think their sons are blowing it because they're going off to live in Washington State and become agrofarmers or do community service in California for forty thousand dollars a year. They say, 'Look what they're not going to be able to afford! On the other hand, they seem to be happy. I have golden handcuffs on, and they're coming home at six o'clock!' "

The choices are far less stark in egalitarian households where both partners earn an income and share the professional compromises necessary to take care of their families. Children in nontraditional families also absorb lessons about fairness that can't possibly be taught in homes characterized by gender-segregated roles. "I hate to cook, and my husband has done all the cooking," says Kathleen Gerson. "When my husband was away, my daughter would say, 'Yay! Daddy's leaving town—now we can have takeout!' She assumes that men should be able to cook, and she sees that housekeeping is not gendered. Why should our egos or our self-worth be tied up with this stuff?"

The ultimate benefits of greater equity will benefit the larger society as well. As men handle a growing share of domestic responsibilities, they have increasing incentives to join with women in taking on the institutional forces that tyrannize both genders. "Men don't want to be working this way either," Gerson says. "When you ask men as well as women who are working more than fifty hours a week what their ideal situation would be, they routinely say thirty-five to forty hours a week. But until men have to pay the same price for parenthood as women do, you're not going to get a collective political force to bring about change, in the workplace or in the government."

I'll admit that it's not easy to convince men to accept the challenge; when I've asked my husband five times to take the dog to the vet and he still hasn't done it, fairness on the home front still feels like a struggle, and it is often the source of friction. "Gender equality is messy," Coltrane acknowledges. "If you just assume the man is the breadwinner and the wife does everything else, people know what's expected of them. Equal-partnership marriages are more fulfilling for both partners, but they take more work—and because negotiation is difficult, they look like there's more conflict; there's the risk of more butting heads, more foot-dragging. It's not fun to demand change. If women bring it up, they're nags; if they don't, they have to do it all themselves. But conflict helps you work through difficulties; people learn and grow. It enriches children's lives, because they see how to negotiate, and they see how to live together as equals."

In general, however, women are the prime movers in effecting such changes. "The thing I find in my studies is that it's the wife who takes the initiative," Coltrane says.

When I started working at home, I felt depressed every morning after my husband left for the office. There were beds to be made and breakfast dishes to be cleared up; domestic drudgery seemed to loom like a mountain I had to climb before I could even get to my desk to start my own work. So I asked my husband to make our bed before leaving the house. That was eighteen years ago, and he's done so ever since—far better than I would have, I might add. Every morning, I feel a surge of pleasure as I pass our bedroom and see our neatly made bed, pillows arranged perfectly at the head, comforter folded at the foot. It may seem like a small thing, but to me it has great symbolic importance in terms of my husband's willingness to accept responsibility for a given task and relieve me of it entirely—forever.

The power of such a role model can be startling. From the moment our son got his first grown-up bed, he has made it carefully every morning before leaving for school, without even having to be asked. While my daughter has many stellar qualities, reliably making her own bed is not one of them. I often wonder whether this is merely a coincidence.

Many couples assume that the only issue in such negotiations is who makes the bed. But the stakes are far greater. It seems obvious that if women weren't so overwhelmed on the home front, they could perform better at work and derive more satisfaction from it. The ultimate solution to the stress level felt by working women is not for them to give up their jobs in despair; it's for men to relieve them of their disproportionate share of domestic tasks, thereby freeing women to maintain their careers, their incomes, and their financial autonomy.

So all I can say to my fellow wives and mothers is, rise up—you have nothing to lose but a lot of boring drudge work.

In the process, you'll also get rid of a lot of your anger. Too many working women live in a state of suppressed rage while trying to manage the inordinate load our social roles have saddled us with, but seething in silence is not a healthy long-term solution. Okay, I know what you're thinking now: "I've tried to get him to help out more, but he just won't listen! What am I supposed to do?"

You're supposed to insist, that's what you're supposed to do. It's not as if women don't have leverage these days; despite the stereotype of the middle-aged guy running off with the secretary half his age, two-thirds of all divorces among Americans over forty are initiated by women, not men. What does this tell us about their relative levels of satisfaction within marriage?

Whether in the labor force or in the home, the role of men is crucial to the prospects for systemic change. "Our society is not structured to accommodate caretaking, and our workplaces are not structured to allow the dually responsible worker to exist," says Martha Fineman, a law professor at Emory University. "It is only when men start demanding changes that change will happen, but the current system exacts no costs on men for continuing to allocate the costs of dependency to their wives. Men lose nothing."

It's high time for that to change. In my own experience, husbands will get away with whatever you let them get away with when it comes to sharing housework. But when you put your foot down and make it clear that you won't take no for an answer, somehow the groceries get purchased, the laundry folded.

You don't have to trust me on that.

Just try it.

CHAPTER TWELVE

# BUT WHAT ABOUT
# THE CHILDREN?

## "YOU KNOW WHAT? I THINK MY
## KIDS REALLY BENEFITED!"

W hen Diane Miller went back to work part-time after several years as a stay-at-home mother in Pennsylvania, the
moms she had gotten to know on children's play dates
acted as if she were performing some distasteful but nonetheless superhuman feat. "I felt as if there was some judgment or criticism:
'How long are you working?' 'Where are your kids going to be?'"
Miller says. "I'm only working two days a week, but they all say, 'I
don't know how you do it!' They look at me like I'm an alien."

Most working mothers know exactly what she's talking about.
While interviewing full-time moms for this book, I heard a lot of passionate speeches about how they had to stay home in order to make
sure their families were fed dinner every night. Although some of
these women don't even cook, they insisted they couldn't possibly
provide adequately for their families' needs if they worked outside the
home.

Trying to manage a noncommittal smile, I would nod politely to
acknowledge their point of view, although what I really wanted to do

was to burst into a resounding chorus of that down-and-dirty old blues song: "I can bring home the bacon, fry it up in a pan / Never let you forget you're a man / Cuz I'm a wooooooooman—Doubleyew-O-M-A-N!" So far the stay-at-home mothers of America have been spared that outburst, but if I hear too many more lectures about how working women can't feed their children, I'm not promising to restrain myself forever.

Such frictions are inescapable reminders of the so-called Mommy Wars, which have been chronicled ad nauseam in recent years. Although commentators offer different reasons for the tensions between working mothers and stay-at-home moms, the one that makes the most sense to me was described by psychologist Daphne de Marneffe, the author of *Maternal Desire,* in an interview on Salon.com. Because women on both sides of the fence feel defensive and guilty about their choices, she explained, "people 'solve' their ambivalence by idealizing a choice or an approach to being a mother, and it becomes this rigidified: 'This is the way to do it; I'm better because I do it this way.'"

That conviction may offer some consolation to women who feel conflicted about the choices they've made, but as far as I'm concerned, the entire debate over the Mommy Wars misses the real point, since my argument against stay-at-home motherhood is ultimately an economic one rather than a judgment about different values.

I certainly don't mean to minimize the larger issues involved in meeting children's needs, which are real and urgent. How dinner gets on the table is merely a logistical question, but making sure that children are properly cared for, emotionally nurtured, and intellectually stimulated is critical, both when they're with their parents and when they're with others.

And yet the prevailing wisdom on how best to achieve such goals is stunningly ill-informed. Stay-at-home mothers typically believe that their kids turn out better than those of working mothers, and many use this cherished myth as a weapon. But their prejudice is unsupported by the facts, according to social scientists. "The research on the impact of working mothers on kids shows that there isn't any," says sociologist Pamela Stone. "Since the 1940s, this has been researched every which way. People have always looked to working mothers as the cause of problems, but it always came out a wash. What's more important is other things, like the quality of child care."

An even more crucial determinant of children's well-being is the emotional and mental health of the mother. "All the research shows that what matters most in a child's life is whether the mother is happy with her situation, whether she's working or not—but the culture is constantly hitting women over the head with this notion that if they don't stay home with their children, they're bad mothers," says Kathleen Gerson.

Some analysts caution that the impact of maternal employment is different for infants than for older children. "Children do fare better on average if their mothers do not work full-time in the first year of life, although . . . the effects vary by context," reported Jane Waldfogel, a Columbia University professor of social work and public affairs, in her book *What Children Need*. "But this finding is pretty specific to the first year, and to full-time work in that year. Part-time work in the first year does not have adverse effects on most outcomes, and work after the first year has neutral or positive effects."

And yet no matter how much social-science research proves that children don't have to be glued to their mothers 24/7 until they leave for college in order to thrive, the whole discussion seems somehow impervious to actual data. The issue of children's welfare, which generally ignores the economic aspects of the situation, also provides a curious parallel with the debate over working moms versus stay-at-homes. "Many studies suggest that one of the most powerful determinants of a child's future success is its family's wealth," Chrystia Freeland pointed out in the *Financial Times* last year.

Undeterred, conservative ideologues continue to promote gender-segregated roles as the time-honored way of structuring families. In fact, however, the whole idea of the "full-time mother" is a recent invention, as Carol Sarler noted in a recent essay in the *London Times*. Sarler wrote that Waldfogel's book suggests that "at least part-time work is actually positive for mother and child. But no matter. The guilt-inducing damage to parents is already done by the implicit perpetuation of the most tenacious of contemporary myths: that young children historically, traditionally and therefore properly have grown up under the constant, vigilant, hands-on care of their mothers. The truth is that this has never been the case. Further: it is not the part-time mother who has been fashioned by and for modern woman; it is the full-time mother who is recent—a construct, actually, of only the past three or four decades. Before that, women had neither the time, the luxury nor, in many cases, the inclination to devote their waking hours to the raising of their children."

Noting that rich women traditionally employed wet nurses, nannies, and governesses to attend the needs of their children, Sarler observed that "poor women worked in fields and factories, often with babies strapped to them until they had given birth to enough of them that the older cared for the younger in a haphazard daisy chain of comfort." In her mother's time, Sarler added, "The practice of childcare (a word as yet not invented) involved a kindly but determined shooing 'outside to play.' "

As far as work outside the home is concerned, Sarler scoffed at "the accusation that the daily excursions by women to places of earning are robbing their children of the dedicated childraising selflessly exemplified by their mothers and grandmothers before them. To them, one can only say this: beware, for propaganda has sapped accuracy from your memory."

Indeed, despite the guilt felt by most working mothers about not spending enough time with their kids, it seems that they're actually doing better than their more traditional predecessors. Antifeminists who idealize the good old days have long delighted in portraying working women as neglecting their children, but this stereotype is entirely false, according to the latest social-science data. "Despite the surge of women into the work force, mothers are spending at least as much time with their children today as they did 40 years ago," *The New York Times* reported in its story on the book *Changing Rhythms of American Family Life*. "With more mothers in paid jobs, many policy makers have assumed that parents must have less time to interact with their children. But, the researchers say, the conventional wisdom is not borne out by the data they collected from families asked to account for their time. The researchers found, to their surprise, that married and single parents spent more time teaching, playing with and caring for their children than parents did 40 years ago. For married mothers, the time spent on child care activities increased to an average of 12.9 hours a week in 2000, from 10.6 hours in 1965. For married fathers, the time spent on child care more than doubled, to 6.5 hours a week, from 2.6 hours. Single mothers reported spending 11.8 hours a week on child care, up from 7.5 hours in 1965."

What today's working women are really neglecting is housework, not their kids. "As the hours of paid work went up for mothers, their hours of housework declined. . . . It was almost a one-for-one trade," said Suzanne Bianchi, who co-authored *Changing Rhythms of American Family Life* with her fellow University of Maryland sociologists John Robinson and Melissa Milkie.

Having failed to prove that working mothers are bad for kids, social scientists have also failed to prove that full-time moms are superior. "There's absolutely no long-term data that says motherhood as a career is good for kids," reports sociologist Barbara Risman, co-chair of the Council on Contemporary Families. "There is some data that children who are in full-time child-care under the age of one have some detrimental effects; the boys have a little more acting out at six or eight. Beyond that, there's no data that suggest in any way, shape, or form that kids whose mothers choose motherhood as a career do better."

Moreover, that particular study focused on children in group day care, not the experience of children with baby-sitters or nannies. Those of us fortunate enough to have had caregivers who functioned as consistent, reliable surrogate mothers are often delighted with the results. "With my kids, it was clear to me that everything was working out fine, and good child care was a very important part of it," says Pamela Stone. "When my kids were younger, we had full-time care, usually au pairs that lived in. My husband did not have a flexible job, and he traveled a lot. But when he's home, he's an engaged parent; he stepped in quite seamlessly. He set up play dates; he cooks. My husband was very much a part of the equation."

In the endless debates about working mothers, what rarely gets mentioned is the fact that a combination of good child care and an egalitarian marriage enables many of us to manage these challenges without undue difficulty. "I didn't have much trouble with the juggling act," says economist Heidi Hartmann. "We had dinner together as a family most nights. We always had baby-sitters who came to our house, and I had a very supportive husband who has not only been involved in child care but who has done at least his fair share of the housework. I think having a supportive partner is key. We covered for each other very well. I think that's a great model, and it's been very rewarding for my husband, who is closer to our kids than he would have been otherwise."

And yet the loudest voices in our society continue to insist that the logistics of working motherhood are unbearably stressful. Because of this overwhelming cultural bias, I have always felt secretly embarrassed by the relative ease of my own life, in which I managed to sustain a demanding and lucrative career while working at home and sharing many of the domestic burdens with my husband and with the world's best baby-sitter, Norma Mohabir Ingram.

When I was eight months pregnant, my husband and I moved into an apartment building where we knew a couple with a three-year-old son. They were planning to move to Paris the same month I was due to deliver my daughter, so their beloved baby-sitter was looking for a new job.

At first, Norma sounded too good to be true. After Gioia, the boy's mom, rhapsodized at length about her, I finally asked, "So what's the bad news? What are Norma's flaws?"

Gioia looked puzzled. She thought for a moment, then replied calmly, "Norma has no discernible flaws."

*Yeah, right,* I thought, ever the skeptical reporter. But that was nearly eighteen years ago, and I still haven't found Norma's flaws. To my kids, she was a second mother, someone who loved them with unflagging patience and good humor, even when their own mom had temporarily misplaced those qualities. To me, Norma was an intelligent, competent surrogate with impeccable judgment, someone I trusted completely to handle any situation as well as I would have (including the inevitable medical emergencies when one child or the other falls off a balance beam at the playground and breaks an arm). We have similar values and the same general approach to child rearing, and she always respected my wishes in dealing with my kids when I wasn't around, even when my views made life more difficult for her (as did my insistence that my kids not watch television, play video games, or eat junk food).

And because Norma grew up in a Third World country, my own children's lives were enriched and their horizons expanded by their intimacy with someone who was raised in such a different culture. My daughter still remembers the day she was going to some middle-school party when she was, as she puts it, "obnoxiously complaining about how I couldn't decide which dress to wear. Norma told me, 'When I was growing up in communist Guyana, I only had one dress. It was simple that way, because I never had to worry about what to wear.'" As my daughter recalls, somewhat sheepishly, "That put things in perspective."

So when I hear stay-at-home mothers talk about how impossible it would be to find satisfactory child care if they went back to work, I always feel torn. Because my own child-care experience was such a blessing for everyone in my family, for a long time I thought I had simply been the beneficiary of freakish good luck. But part of me also feels indignant at what seems like the elitist bias of women who dismiss the possibility of quality child care. Why do these people think that no one working as a baby-sitter could ever be an adequate caregiver, let alone a wonderful one? Why do they believe that their children's lives could only be harmed, not enhanced, by other influences? Why are they so convinced that different perspectives must necessarily be inferior?

"If an infant is with another caregiver on a regular basis, that caregiver could become as good as the mother at knowing the child and reading the child's cues," Waldfogel pointed out in *What Children Need*.

It turns out that the horror stories about negligent or malignant baby-sitters do not reflect the reality of quality child care as those with reasonable means typically experience it. "Here's a refreshing truth that no one ever talks about in the media: Many working moms love their day-care providers!" Carol Evans wrote in her book *This Is How We Do It*.

As the CEO and president of *Working Mother* magazine, Evans commissioned a survey of working mothers entitled "What Moms Want." The study found that "a whopping 89 percent of mothers were happy with their day-care choice: 56 percent were 'very satisfied' with their child-care solutions, and 33 percent were 'somewhat satisfied,'"

Evans reported. "Many of us are better able to shake off some of our guilt and doubt when we see how great caregivers help our children thrive."

Because day care has been demonized for so long, the fact that quality day care is available can come as a big surprise to mothers who believed they had to stay home in order to meet their children's needs. Sophie Curtis, a New Jersey mom who works at a day-care preschool, wishes she had considered such alternatives when her children were young instead of staying home for so long. "Had I known there were places like this that provided this much love, care, and teaching, I would have been willing to go back to work earlier," she says.

Indeed, the benefits of quality care can be striking, Evans reported in *This Is How We Do It*. She wrote:

> Kids in accredited day care were more than twice as likely to be rated school-ready when they started kindergarten compared to kids who hadn't been in day care, according to a 2005 study by the state of Minnesota.
>
> Kids who spent a lot of time in child care before age one showed *no difference* from children who stayed home with mom in terms of attachment and bonding to their mother, according to a 1997 report from a long-running study by the National Institute of Child Health and Human Development.
>
> In 2002, the same ongoing study showed that children in child care had better cognitive and linguistic abilities than those who weren't in day care.
>
> As far back as 1995, a study of 401 child-care centers showed children in day care had better cognitive and social development.

To be sure, the quality of group child care can vary dramatically, depending on the ratio of caregivers to children, the competence and personality of the caregivers, the safety as well as the level of stimulation offered by a particular facility, and numerous other factors. For many parents, institutional care is also supplemented by other arrangements. As Evans pointed out, women often use a patchwork of child-care providers that may include child-care centers, family child-care homes, nannies, baby-sitters, au pairs, and assorted relatives, as well as fathers and domestic partners. As a result, it's impossible to generalize about the cost of child care, although it is often higher in expensive urban centers than it may be in other areas.

But one point worth making is the shortsightedness of the common view that a woman shouldn't bother to work if most of her salary will be eaten up by child care. Even when this is literally true at a given moment, that argument fails to consider the long-term growth of a woman's earnings as well as the finite nature of child-care needs. If she remains in the paid workforce, her earnings are likely to increase over time. Meanwhile the need for child care decreases—and its cost therefore declines—as her children get older. Within a few years, the differential is apt to be quite significant, clearly demonstrating the financial value of remaining on the job. In contrast, a woman who quits work to stay home will find her future earnings potential severely curtailed by her time out of the labor force, and she is unlikely ever to make up that difference.

Despite the obvious benefits of a growing paycheck, working mothers rarely speak up in defense of the sensible accommodations they have made in order to meet their children's needs as well as the demands of their jobs. In this culture, full-time mothers have bragging rights; working mothers don't, no matter how remarkable their children are. One of the hardest-working professionals I know has twins who were both school leaders and outstanding citizens as well as academic superstars. When they were accepted early decision to Harvard, their mother was gratified by the high praise of their admiring teachers. "Whatever you're doing in your family, you'd make a fortune if you could bottle it and sell it," commented one. No matter how busy they were, the twins' mother and father were always emotionally available to them; their kids were their highest priority, which was far more important, in the end, than whether one or both parents worked.

While the biases against working moms never seem to change, women sometimes switch sides and make unexpected discoveries. "I used to be very critical of people who put their kids in day care, but I've changed my view," says Diane Miller, whose children are now five and seven. "My kids are at a great day-care facility, and I think it's great *for* them. At this point, I regret not doing more of it. A lot of the kids I have gotten to know who started in day care at very young ages are really great kids."

Miller's reassessment is based on professional as well as personal experience. "In the work I do as a social worker, I see that children today spend so much of their time isolated from other human beings, due to the changes in our society like the demise of the extended family and so on," she explains. "The schools have cut back on recesses, and everything is so academically focused that the kids really miss out on opportunities to develop social skills. I think kids need to have relationships with other people, to learn about other people's styles, to learn about socialization with their peers; I think it makes for healthier human beings. In day care, you have to learn how to get along. You have to learn how to be more patient, because your needs are not always being fulfilled right away. You have to learn to cooperate with other people. With kids who are staying at home, it's more difficult to teach them these social skills, and there's a tendency to spoil them. There's a sense of entitlement, a kind of demanding, self-absorbed attitude: 'You need to take care of my needs right now! I don't want to wait! I don't have to wait!' In the counseling work I do, I see a big difference between the kids whose parents both work and the ones whose mothers don't. They're so sensitive; everything's catastrophic. Every little thing that goes wrong feels huge to them, and seems insurmountable. They're less resilient."

If a mother works, her children necessarily learn how to do many things for themselves. "A lot of mothers at home feel like they have to do everything for their kids," observes Darcy Howe. "As my kids got older, it became clear to them that some of these other kids couldn't do a damn thing for themselves. Our job as parents is to make them self-sufficient, and I think my children felt that kids whose mothers work have more self-reliance."

Ann Lewis, an attorney who has been a full-time worker, a part-time worker, and a stay-at-home mom, saw the benefits for her children as soon as she went back to work. "They're better off being independent than having you at their beck and call," she says. "The first time they forget something and Mommy isn't home anymore to bring it to them, that's a good thing."

As the years pass, working moms who once fretted about harming their kids are frequently surprised by how well things turned out. Howe's children are sixteen and eighteen, and she has stopped worrying that they were cheated by their mother's high-powered financial career. "I look back on it now and say, 'You know what? I think my kids really benefited,'" she observes. "There are not a lot of relationships that are better than the ones I have with my kids. The type of job I chose had enough flexibility for me to be able to do some things with them; I missed out on other things, and they didn't suffer. My children would tell me that so-and-so's mom did some fantastic project I could never do, but when I asked them if they would prefer that I stayed home, the kids at every step of the way said, 'We're glad you work.' There's certainly a pride factor for them that their mother had her own life."

Even when a mother's job requires travel, she may be able to figure out ways to use her trips to enrich her children's lives. According to a recent report in *The New York Times*, "The Travel Industry Association of America reported that of 163 million business trips taken in 2003—the last year it tracked the statistic—10 percent included children.

This figure has grown steadily over the last decade, said Cathy Keefe, an association spokeswoman, in large part because more women hold high-profile jobs that require travel."

Women are taking their children on business trips to increase their quality time together, or even to accommodate their nursing schedules with infants. And the travel industry is responding to their needs. "Many hotels, even in remote locations, offer babysitting services or have concierges who can help parents find nannies," *The Times* reported. "Some even customize camps or services for visiting conventions. At the Hotel del Coronado in San Diego, 'group children's programs are becoming as commonplace as spouse programs' at corporate conventions, said Victor Woo, the director of sales and marketing at the hotel."

As children get older, their perspectives evolve. "My children often thought I worked too hard, and I missed a certain number of dinners, but especially after they went off to college, they realized that I really made an effort to be there at the times that were important to them," says economist Heidi Hartmann.

As they age, the children of working moms often reconsider the idealized view of full-time motherhood they had when they were young. "I think my kids saw the other mothers as not having their lives and not being very interesting people—and also as being abnormally focused on their kids," Howe says. "My daughter personally doesn't have as much respect for women who have made their lives about being mothers. She wants to be a lawyer. I don't think it would ever occur to her to look for a man to support her."

During this transition, working mothers often find that their achievements earn new admiration from their children's friends or their friends' children. "Some of these schlepper mothers are not respected by their daughters," Howe reports. "A friend went to Yale, Stanford, and Wharton, but for most of her life she hasn't worked. My daughter told me that her daughter named me as one of her role models for some who-do-you-admire kind of thing."

"My son is very contemptuous of women who don't do anything but micromanage their children's lives," says Geraldine Cochran, a Chicago mother of a teenager. "I've heard him make disparaging remarks about these professional-momdom moms who bring home-baked goods to the soccer match: 'She doesn't have anything else to do!' "

When young people enter the workforce, this shift can become even more apparent. "The kids of stay-at-home mothers are coming to me for advice," reports marketing consultant Tanya Mandor. "They're saying, 'I don't know what career I want,' or 'I'm going to interview with this company—can you help me?' Their mothers are not a resource for them. You want advice from somebody who's been successful."

Mandor has little patience for stay-at-home mothers who suggest that professional women are negligent parents. "The nanny schlepping— that's not raising your children, that's managing their time," she says. "There are career women who do not raise their children; I will not condone that. I believe that if you're going to have children, it's your responsibility to raise them. But if you want to tell me that I didn't raise my children, I beg to differ, and my children would also differ. Does it make a father a bad father because he went to work every day? No, but the stay-at-home moms will tell me I'm a bad mother because I missed the pearls that came out of the children's mouths at three o'clock in the afternoon. My daughters felt they got the benefit of everything. I'm a role model for them. They don't remember me not being there because I had to go to a sales meeting in Arizona. That was Daddy time. They don't feel I gave them up in any way, shape, or form."

A competent mother who manages multiple roles effectively can also help teach her children a strong work ethic. "Family comes first, but as long as you don't take it to the extreme, working is good," Ann Lewis says. "It's not a bad thing for high-school kids to see a parent doing work after dinner, as they're doing their own homework. And it's also not a bad thing that working parents don't have the time to do their kids' homework for them!"

Stay-at-home mothers are sometimes shocked to learn that their purely domestic roles imparted some unfortunate lessons. "If the mom doesn't do anything, it sets a bad example for the kids," says Cochran, a writer who works at home. "The kids can end up identifying with the unachieving parent. Instead of identifying with the high-achieving father, I've seen boys identify with the mother who doesn't achieve, especially if there's hostility toward the father. It's really important for the psychological health of children to see how important it is to have a passionate interest and make your mark."

When Donna Chatsworth gave up her career to care for her family, it never occurred to her that her children might emulate their mother instead of their superachieving father. But her kids—now twenty-four and thirty-two—are chronically unemployed and living on financial subsidies from their wealthy father, despite their anger toward him for having divorced their mother. Although Chatsworth has encouraged both of them to make a commitment to work, they dismiss her as a dilettante who didn't do so herself and who therefore has no credibility. "My son has utter contempt for me; he has totally absorbed his father's attitude that I have no value in the world, because I don't make money," Chatsworth says. "At this point, he sees me as pathetic and useless."

In contrast, the accomplishments of working mothers can be very meaningful to their children. After Vicki Gault became a stay-at-home mom, she was startled by the change in her kids' attitude. "My older daughter really felt a lot of pride in me being an executive, and my younger children would say, 'Wow, Mom, you get to fly on a private jet!' They do have the attitude that this is cool stuff," Gault says. "Now it's, 'What did you and the dog do all day?' It's not, 'Oh, Mom, thank you so much, I love that you're home!'"

Working mothers often feel so much guilt that they are astonished to discover that their children don't feel slighted. "One day a few years ago, I had a really bad day at work, and I came home and said to my husband, 'I don't think it's worth it,'" recalls Vicki Gordon. "My kids heard me and said, 'Mom, we like your job! We don't think you should quit. Let's figure it out.' I said, 'Don't you want me home all day with you?' They said, 'No! We like coming to your office!' I've discovered that my daughters don't have much regard for women who stay home. They don't see them doing very much that's valuable with their time. Even when they're not working, a lot of these moms don't seem to be with their kids that much. You're a role model for your kids no matter what you do, and I want my kids to be out in the world, to be productive."

Experts attest that children can derive important benefits from such examples. "Girls who are daughters of employed mothers have higher aspirations for getting good jobs and having career mobility; their expectations go up," says sociologist Scott Coltrane. "For boys, the expectations for sharing with a partner are greater if they have a working mother. Even menial working-class jobs give women a feeling of self-efficacy that makes them better mothers."

"Having a working mother gives girls a sense of self-confidence, and it gives boys a much greater sense of empathy and makes them much more respectful of women," adds family historian Stephanie Coontz.

Contrary to popular mythology, many children also feel that their working mothers are just as emotionally available as their friends' full-time moms, many of whom maintain busy schedules of volunteer work and other activities. "The question isn't whether the mothers work or not, the question is whether they're involved and participating with their children," says Kris Myers, a school administrator who lives in Indianapolis. "Sometimes the working mothers are putting in more time at school than the mothers who are home all day. With some of these stay-at-home moms, I really don't know what they do with their time. They crowd up their lives, but I see a lot of kids whose mothers are unavailable. I know one mother who has an excuse every time you turn around."

When my children were younger, I felt guilty each time an assignment took me out of town, although they were well cared for during my infrequent absences. Recently I asked my kids, now fourteen and seventeen, whether they felt shortchanged by the fact that I worked. They both rolled their eyes and said no. "But what about when I went away?" I asked.

"I don't remember feeling bad about that," my daughter replied.

"But what about when I missed seeing you in the fourth-grade play?" I persisted, feeling my umpteenth surge of shame about this horrible dereliction of maternal duty nearly a decade ago.

My daughter, who had a handful of speaking lines as one of five different girls playing the part of Lucy in *You're a Good Man, Charlie Brown*, looked blank. "Did you miss the fourth-grade play?" she asked. "I don't remember that. The only thing I remember is that I didn't like when you went to the theater with Daddy at night." My son nodded.

So it turns out that all my guilt about work-related travel was wasted energy, and the one thing my kids minded was the occasional evening out with my husband—something I would have done even if I had been a stay-at-home mother! What can you do but file this away in the you-can't-win section of your maternal memory bank?

For many of us, the bottom line is that meaningful work is an important component of who we are—and therefore a significant part of what makes us good mothers. "Working gives you the opportunity to be happy with your own choices," says executive recruiter Maxine Martens. "I was happy working; it's given me independence, and my children have seen that I like what I do. One of the best things anyone ever said to me was years ago, when I worried about going back to work. My children's pediatrician told me, 'I have taken care of thousands of children from all sorts of backgrounds, and the one consistent thing in raising well-adjusted children was parents who were happy with their choices.' "

We'll just have to keep working on the guilt part of the equation.

## CHAPTER THIRTEEN

# BACKWARD PROGRESS

## "YOU'RE TAKING THE SAFE ROAD!"

Whenever I look at *Real Simple* magazine on a newsstand, I see the appeal of the spare, clutter-free environments featured in its glossy photo layouts. Who wouldn't want to have such an exquisitely well-organized life?

And yet another part of me finds these homes sterile and stultifying. The most creative people I know tend to live amid a certain amount of cheerful chaos: the electrician who brings home found objects and creates astonishingly original artworks from the jumbles of junk he squirrels away; the hard-driving magazine editor who likes to sew and keeps piles of fabric remnants and other odds and ends in the spare room where she whips up beautiful children's clothes and elaborate costumes; the professor whose real passion is painting watercolors in an attic crammed with postcards, photographs, handmade pottery, sculptures, and an eclectic assortment of other objects that inspire her. My own teenage daughter loves to create spectacular cards and other craft projects, using bits and pieces of stuff from the overflowing boxes of paper, ribbons, buttons, feathers, lace, paints, colored pencils, glitter, sequins, embroidery appliqués, and innumerable other items we have saved for such a purpose. Much of this stuff spends more time on her floor than neatly stashed in the boxes, and occasionally I harbor dark thoughts about throwing away all the mess. But then I think about the gorgeous card she made me for Mother's Day, and about her interest in a career as a graphic designer, and I decide that it's better to be messy and creative than neat and uninspired.

There's a lot to be said for simplifying our lives and clearing out the unnecessary detritus that piles up in every household, but many women seem to have absorbed the message that simpler is better on deeper levels as well. When confronted with the stresses that come along with juggling work and family, they think that the best solution is to sacrifice their careers. In doing so, however, a lot of them will stifle the exploration of their own potential far more definitively than I might squelch my daughter's imagination by ransacking her room.

Restricting our scope can make life feel more manageable, and clearly defined roles are very seductive. It's easier to feel good about completing a small task successfully than it may be to take pleasure in tackling a more challenging project with less definitive results—but that doesn't mean that circumscribing your aspirations is necessarily a good idea.

Bonnie Fuller has enjoyed a remarkably successful career as an editor at a succession of women's magazines and celebrity tabloids, and she recently explained her philosophy of life in a book called *The Joys of Much Too Much: Go for the Big Life—the Great Career, the Perfect Guy, and Everything Else You've Ever Wanted (Even If You're Afraid You Don't Have What It Takes)*.

In an article for *The New York Times Magazine*, interviewer Deborah Solomon described Fuller's book as arguing that "greed is good"—a typically sexist way of implying that women who refuse to accept the limitations imposed by conventional gender roles are demanding too much.

Fuller was blessedly unfazed. "I think it is good to be greedy in terms of your dreams and in terms of trying to have everything you want out of life," she replied. "The road to the richest life is one in which you partake of careerhood, lovehood, mommyhood—all of those things."

"But we can't have everything. It's impossible to do everything well all the time," Solomon protested, parroting the usual line on why women should give up trying.

"I'm not suggesting that you do," Fuller retorted. "In fact, I say it's O.K.—your house doesn't have to be clean. You don't have to have clean floors. Your drawers don't have to be perfect, and dishes can pile up in the sink. That's part of my philosophy."

"What philosophy is this? The philosophy of Dishevelism?" Solomon asked.

"It's certainly a philosophy of non-perfectionism," Fuller said. "It's O.K. to let newspapers and magazines and the mail pile up."

At the time of this interview, Fuller—who has four children, two of whom have survived life-threatening illnesses—was reportedly receiving $1.5 million a year as the editorial director of American Media, Inc., and that's without counting her bonus. Let's see—which would you rather have in addition to your precious children: a salary of a million and a half dollars a year for being happily successful in your chosen career—or tidy drawers? I know what my answer is, and I'm not afraid to admit that my drawers reflect it.

"A jam-packed, maxed-out, full-to-the-very-top existence is the secret to an insanely happy life, no matter what those odes to 'simplicity' say," Fuller wrote in *The Joys of Much Too Much*.

Working at something you love is an immeasurable blessing, but it's one that continues to elude many women. Purely as a result of trial and error, I was lucky enough to stumble into the perfect job at the age of twenty-three. I had already tried out book publishing, advertising, theater, radio, and television and found that I wasn't happy in any of those fields. Coming upon journalism was like finding the key that fit the lock, so precisely did the demands of the profession dovetail with my abilities. *So this is what I'm supposed to do with my life!* I thought, as thunderstruck as I might have been by the appearance of a celestial choir singing the "Hallelujah Chorus" in my living room. This revelation filled me with a feeling of euphoria that has never left me in all the years since.

Many people take longer to identify their own passion, while others—like Wendy Greenberg, who wanted so badly to become an actress—know what they love but lack the courage to commit themselves to making it into a career. For too many women, marriage and motherhood represent the default position, one they can fall back on when other things don't pan out. Unable to decide what they want to do with their lives as readily as they had anticipated, they give up and have children instead of grappling with the difficult task of developing an independent identity. For females, that choice is still considered socially acceptable; no one questions a young wife's decision to start a family instead of figuring out her life's work, whereas many eyebrows would be raised if her husband or brother did the same thing.

Other women commence their careers and then, over time, grow frustrated with the inevitable setbacks and disappointments of advancing in any profession. When this happens to men, most of them persevere, because they feel they have no choice; they figure out how to triumph over obstacles, and they progress toward greater success. But for women, the fallback option of dependency continues to hover in the background, singing its siren song: "You can always bag it and go home." Those who succumb to it give up their careers, proclaim the necessity of caring for their children around the clock, and retire to a domestic life.

"There's a lot of dissatisfaction and weariness among male and female associates in law firms about slogging their way through the work," says the former managing partner of a major firm. "The guy says, 'I'm going to keep on slogging through this,' but the woman thinks, 'There's an option to get out of this, and maybe I'll take it.' "

Such women typically consider that decision only in terms of what they perceive to be best for themselves and their families at a specific point in time, rather than evaluating their long-term interests. That choice is risky enough for the individuals involved, but it also has broader social implications that are profoundly worrisome.

After several decades of increasing possibilities for women, the current fashion for repudiating careers and retreating to the home has alarmed many analysts who fear that existing opportunities are being eroded and further progress will be derailed. "What's really pernicious is, 'See—we gave you all these chances, and you don't even want to take advantage of them, so why should we open our law schools and medical schools to you gals!' " says sociologist Kathleen Gerson. "It's a way of justifying not opening doors to women."

While representatives of major institutions won't admit such incriminating things for the record, ominous portents are everywhere. A woman who earned an M.B.A. from one of the nation's most prestigious universities told me about a passionate argument she had with its president at a recent cocktail party. "Fifteen to twenty-five years out from the M.B.A., overwhelming numbers of women have left the workforce, and they view that as a failure," she says. "This particular university is now rethinking whether they should have so many women in the business school if they're going to leave the workforce."

Similar questions are being raised at other professional schools. "If the dental school has fifty percent women but the dental community has ten percent, the assumption is that they graduate, they marry, they stay home, and he goes to work. The fields where there are limited positions are saying, 'Why should I give it to a woman who's not going to contribute to society?' " says the wife of a dentist who has been privy to such discussions.

But debates over professional-school admissions are only a prelude to the ongoing issues of the workplace. "Will firms invest in women by hiring and training and making the accommodations needed to make them productive leaders, if they think these women are going to drop out?" says Harvard law professor Elizabeth Warren. "You can get a Catch-22. Young women are anticipating with genuine alarm what faces them after they graduate. They are concerned that law practice at the highest levels has become incompatible with a private life, for both men and women—but women are more focused on the problem. The firms say that because law practice is so lousy, we should assume that young women will leave us and we won't get a return on our investment, and therefore we have less interest in helping them to flourish."

Such views are causing considerable apprehension among professional women who once struggled to break down workplace barriers and are loath to see their hard-won gains slip away. "I think the most serious effect is the effect it has on employers and people in power," says Sylvia Law. "It says to them, 'You get a free pass. If a woman wants to have kids, you get to just write her off; you don't have to make accommodations.'"

Others recognize the practical logic behind such responses even as they fear for the consequences. "I think there's a huge risk the barriers will go back up," says Miranda Blake, a fifty-five-year-old criminal-defense attorney. "When I was a young pup, I was horrified at the questions women were asked in hiring interviews: 'Do you plan to have kids?' 'What form of birth control do you use?' 'When do you plan to get married?' The judge I worked for said, 'People with children eat into my time.' But it's different when you're the employer. If I were a managing partner at a large firm, and I was putting money into hiring somebody, I wouldn't want to lose that money by having them leave. If you're a law firm hiring fifty-fifty male and female, you're not going to come out with the numbers you need if the majority of your women are dropping out in the third or fourth year."

And when women relinquish their jobs instead of staying to fight for change, that choice inevitably relieves the pressure on those institutions to adapt to the needs of the females in its workforce. "If the best and brightest of these women now drop out, there will be fewer women making partner, which means that there will be an even smaller pool of women making their way into the executive committee and chairmanship positions—which means that the law firms and investment banks don't change culturally," explains a male partner at a large international law firm. "Once people are in power, they change the culture of a place, but you only get that change when the institution feels it needs to change. When women first started to enter law, you did see changes, but if women are now dropping out instead of taking it to the next level, the real consequence is going to be for the generation that follows them. The further momentum is stalling out and won't get going again until women are in positions of power."

Having fought for the opportunities that young women now take for granted, many older women are deeply dismayed that the most privileged simply walk away from the challenge of addressing the remaining problems that still need to be corrected. In "The Opt-Out Revolution," Lisa Belkin quoted a Princeton graduate with a Duke University law degree who had given up her career to become a stay-at-home mother. "I've had people tell me that it's women like me that are ruining the workplace because it makes employers suspicious," she said. "I don't want to take on the mantle of all womanhood and fight a fight for some sister who isn't really my sister because I don't even know her."

Such attitudes appall many Baby Boomers, who are shocked by the failure of younger generations to understand that the majority of women, whether they know each other or not, share common needs. According to the U.S. Census Bureau, 81 percent of all American women become mothers by the time they are forty-four years old. And yet the opt-out generation continues to act as if it's every woman for herself. Passively accepting the status quo, they seem to lack any recognition that their choices have implications far broader than the personal consequences.

"There's no sense of social responsibility," says Vicki Gault, the New Jersey mom and former corporate executive now struggling to reenter the workplace. "If the best and the brightest continue to opt out, what about the rest of us poor slobs who don't have the most well-educated, best-connected to join with us? How do the poor working stiffs try to reenter into a fifty-five-thousand-dollar-a-year job if everyone they interview with is a male? Show me a man who has any inkling about the needs of women in the workplace and I'll show you a man who has a working wife. As long as men in power positions have stay-at-home wives, they will be totally unable to understand what working women's issues are, because they just don't have a clue."

It's not as if the needs aren't clear. "Policies can support families with working parents in three main ways: by ensuring parents have the right to take time off to care for their children at particular times or when certain events occur; by providing, or supporting, nonparental care for children while parents work; and by providing financial assistance with the costs of raising children," Jane Waldfogel wrote in *What Children Need*. "In each of these three areas, . . . the role of government policy in the United States is fairly minimal, compared with what is typically the case in other developed nations."

And yet women's failure to demand collective action permits our government to continue to ignore those needs, even as the exodus of mothers from the workplace deprives its institutions of potential leadership on family issues. "It percolates downward, because it removes those women who have nurturing responsibilities from the elite decision-making roles in society," says sociologist Barbara Risman. "The women who break the glass ceiling have to compete with men who have wives at home, so they have to opt out of motherhood. If you look at the few women who reach the boardroom, they mostly live male lives. They don't have children, or they have one child. You don't have people at the top who are struggling with this, so therefore things don't have to change. When these women leave instead of demanding organizational change, what they do is reify this either/or choice that women have to make. The men in the labor force are not change agents, because they have wives to do everything. If women made the same demands as men and said, 'It's our right to have children as well as work,' things would change."

The pressures of caregiving are further exacerbated when workers must manage the needs of aging parents as well as young children. When Sylvia Ann Hewlett studied women who dropped out of the workforce, she found that children were not the only reason they did so. "Twenty-four percent off-ramped because of an elder-care crisis," reported Hewlett, president of the Center for Work-Life Policy in New York.

Thus far, however, such needs are typically addressed in terms of gender stereotypes. "It's all about the way you organize the labor force; the whole modern workforce in the industrial era was designed for men who have wives," Risman explains. "When you organize jobs so that people have to be out of the home for ten hours a day, fifty weeks a year, and have no flexibility in their lives, there's no room there for nurturing work. The presumption in corporate America was that workers who would be high achievers would have wives. Underlying the premise of such a structure is that people in the workforce have no moral, ethical, or practical responsibility to the care of anybody but themselves, because historically we had a divided world where men were in the workforce and women took care of social reproduction. Flash forward to the twenty-first century, and you have a world where women who also want to be mothers are in these jobs. When people have to take care of somebody other than themselves, either sick children or parents, you've got a real social problem with this disconnect between work and family. So mothers—and men who take their nurturing responsibilities seriously—are in trouble. As more and more men are married to women who don't want to do everything, there's real social angst out there. This is a serious social issue that people are struggling with in their daily lives."

The incendiary potential of this issue was amply demonstrated by the fierce controversy that erupted in 2005 after Dr. Lawrence Summers, then the president of Harvard University, speculated that the shortage of women in the sciences and engineering might be the result of innate differences between men and women. "He implied that the eighty-hour workweek demanded of many high-achieving professionals is simply a matter of personal choice: for some reason more men are 'prepared to make' that 'commitment,'" Rachel B. Tiven wrote in a letter to the editor in *The New York Times*. "By framing the choice in a vacuum, Dr. Summers utterly missed the point. It is not simply that more men want to devote themselves to their work; it is that more men can because they have wives."

In another letter to *The Times*, Anne D. Yoder, an associate professor of ecology and evolutionary biology at Yale University, also noted the main reason most men don't worry about work-life balance as much as women do. "They assume (and many women do not bother to overturn this assumption) that their wives will handle the bulk of the family end, leaving them to climb the ladder of professional success, unfettered by petty concerns like diapers, groceries, pediatrician appointments and so on," Yoder observed.

As a result of such assumptions, women continue to struggle with these problems largely alone, trying to find individual solutions rather than understanding the work-family conundrum as a systemic problem whose remedy would benefit men as well as women. "I hear these young women say, 'I don't want to have to work twenty-two hundred billable hours a year in order to make partner,' and I totally agree with them," says Marna Tucker, who became a leading expert on matrimonial law while raising a family. "It's very hard to bill more than five or six hours in an eight- or nine-hour day, because of all the other things you have to do. And yet some of the large law firms in New York require twenty-two hundred billable hours a year for their associates. It's the greed of the legal profession that's taken over, and that's wrong. But you don't need to do that. I never wanted to work for those twenty-two hundred billable hours a year, and I didn't. I went into a firm that had four people in it, and I started doing sex-discrimination cases, which at the time were brand-new, and then I did a couple of divorces. It was a time when divorce law was changing to value the interests of women, and I said, 'I'm going to build the biggest, best firm in Washington.' What if women lawyers all got together and said, 'Screw you—we're not going to buy into the greed of the profession! We'd like to work for these firms for reasonable hours at a reasonable salary, but we're not going to work for these firms for those kinds of hours.' The legal profession has to change, and they can change it. Men don't want to work those horrible hours now either."

Some men readily admit that their own interests are also at stake. "Here's the deal: this isn't a 'women's problem'; it's a human problem," wrote Matt Miller, a senior fellow at the Center for American Progress, in a *New York Times* op-ed column. "Yet for thirty years women have tried to crack this largely on their own, and one thing is clear: if the fight isn't joined by men (like me) who want a life, too, any solutions become 'women's' solutions. A broader drive to redesign work will take a union-style consciousness that makes it safe for men who secretly want balance to say so."

But too many of today's young women show little inclination to join forces in working to help restructure the workplace, or even in figuring out creative solutions to their own scheduling problems. "It's a question of expectations; so much of it has to do with wanting everything *now*," Tucker says. "When I went to school, I knew it would take time. We didn't need to be making huge amounts of money. We've become so financially driven it makes people want to have everything faster.

The idea of working for anything, of going to boot camp and putting in the time—they just don't think that way. When you have it now, you have to give up some other things, including the sanity that occurs with building a career slowly and not having to make a fortune quickly."

This lack of perspective is the source of constant amazement to Baby Boom women who spent decades working their way toward the professional success they now enjoy. "With my students, I find that they assume it was always easy for me," says sociologist Kathleen Gerson. "They don't understand that we started out where they're starting out. This generation is more likely to assume that what we've accomplished was somehow preordained, rather than something we fought for. One of the things our generation did was that we postponed childbearing until we had gotten a toehold at work, so by the time our children were born, they saw the people we had become, rather than the process of becoming. Maybe we haven't talked enough, not only about the joys and pleasures of our careers but also about the hard work involved. It wasn't something that was just given to us. These were choices we had to make."

As I interviewed professional women in a wide range of occupations for this book, many deplored the sense of entitlement they discern among today's younger women. "I think they're whiners," says one attorney. "They say, 'It's so hard; we can't do this.' But there are women senior partners all over the place. They can do it, but they're spoiled; they want everything now. There are lots of ways to change things, but I haven't seen the young Gloria Steinems."

Another prominent professional woman says, "Where are the leaders, not to mention the troops? These young women could be the cutting edge, but what they're doing right now is sort of like being a blunt knife and complaining. Maybe they're too comfortable. In my generation, we all knew there was something wrong with the fact that as women we couldn't go to certain places. These young women will hit the glass ceiling way down the road, but we all knew it was there from day one. There are no easy paths. There are always stumbling blocks, but they have to realize that nobody's going to pave the way for them. They're captains of their own path. We've educated them with all the capabilities, but life throws out lemons as well as orchids, and you have to be able to grab onto either."

As Tucker suggests, the overwhelming materialism of contemporary American culture is another factor. Some young women seem more interested in ensuring an affluent lifestyle than they are in individual achievement or social progress, and those values are also damaging women's potential opportunities. "When I started working on Wall Street, women generally wanted to have careers; they wanted to work and prove themselves," says Rhoda Mason,* a forty-four-year-old financial-research analyst. "Now I think there's been a generational shift. The older generations have already been the trailblazers, so the younger generations don't feel they have as much to prove, and they don't want to work as hard. With young women, I sense that they're looking for easy money; they're not that motivated. They see it as a job, not as a career."

And even the job is viewed only as a means to an end; all too often, the ultimate goal is marriage to a high-earning man. "I see them looking for the good life through the husband," Mason reports. "This one woman at my firm hasn't produced at all. She just got married and came to work with this enormous rock on her finger. The boss said, 'She's done her Wall Street thing; she's found her sugar daddy.' "

Such attitudes have soured Mason on helping women to advance. "In the past, I always wanted to hire more women and promote more women; I really wanted to train them and bring them up," she says. "But now I feel like the men are more motivated. The women are just there temporarily. I can't see the commitment and the drive. It's really sad. These are young people from good colleges, but they're dilettantes. It's really upsetting to me. They have an appalling inability to deal with basic tasks. I think they want to be rich wives who don't do a lot of work, because they're so lazy."

Such observations are obviously broad generalizations, and some women report far more positive experiences with younger female subordinates. But even among those committed to hard work, many young women seem to lack an understanding of how much compromise and negotiation are necessary to make your way in the world. "No matter what they do, they're not going to make an A-plus in life; you just can't," observes Marna Tucker. "I was a B-plus. I told my kids, 'I can't do it all well; I'm just doing the best I can. If you don't like it, complain to the Parental Complaint Authorities!' And we'd all laugh—but it would make me feel better. I think I was saying, 'I'm not a perfect mother. I'm not pretending to be, and you love me anyway, the way I am.' It reaffirmed my own fallibility, but it was okay. It worked because we didn't have these crazy expectations. We just did what we wanted to do to get where we wanted to get. If you hit a block, you figured out a way to go around it. You may fall down and bruise your knee and put a Band-Aid on it—but get up and go on, and quit whining about it."

Many Baby Boomers are puzzled by the passive acquiescence of younger women who accept an unsatisfactory status quo instead of working to generate new possibilities. "They say, 'There aren't any public-interest jobs,' but we went out and found the problems and figured out how to solve them," Tucker says. "We created organizations and got the money to do it. You create your own jobs."

She sighs. "I tell them this—and they look at me like I'm nuts."

Some analysts see the current failure to conceptualize work and family within a larger social context as consistent with our national character and its historic emphasis on the individual. "We believe we can overcome obstacles; it's a very American way of approaching things, rather than saying, 'We really need to make a collective effort to rethink the way work and family are organized in our society,'" observes Kathleen Gerson. "Because it's left as an individual problem, rather than a larger social one, it leaves women isolated, whether they decide to stay home or to juggle work and family. It's so easy to fall into women being pitted against each other. Rather than making moralistic judgments about women's choices, we need to keep our focus on the institutions that are making it more or less difficult for women to survive. We live in a society where there is no organized universal child care and no reasonable parental-leave policies, all of which are routinely available in European countries. Why aren't we fighting for these larger institutional supports that other rich industrial countries take for granted?"

While collective action is badly needed, individuals can also have a surprising impact in bringing about institutional change. Having both failed and succeeded at doing so, I am the first to admit that institutions can be highly resistant. During my ten years as a reporter for *The New York Times*, I was among the many women who lobbied for issues that ranged from equal pay for women to abolishing sexist honorifics like "Miss" and "Mrs." in favor of "Ms." Our arguments fell on deaf ears, although some of those reforms did occur years later, and my own frustration eventually helped to drive me out the door.

But no institution is immutable, and an experience at the very beginning of my career taught me how much impact one determined individual could have when her boss was more responsive. At the age of twenty-three, I landed my first job as a newspaper reporter. *The Philadelphia Bulletin*, then the nation's largest afternoon daily, was a fusty institution mired in old-fashioned practices that no one seemed to question. I was appalled by a regular feature called "Today's Joke," whose ostensible humor often involved tired old groaners about my-wife-the-ball-and-chain or my-mother-in-law-the-battle-ax.

As a fervent young feminist, I was equally perturbed by the sexist conventions of the paper's news coverage. If a woman was named to an important position, the resulting story would describe her physical attributes, her husband, her children, and her favorite recipe. If a man was named to the same position, he was described solely in terms of his credentials and experience; in those days, when hard news rarely contained the kind of personal material reserved for feature stories, no one ever wrote about an important man as a bubbly brunette with four grandchildren and a great recipe for banana bread.

One day I got fed up, marched into the executive editor's office, and sounded off about how sexist the paper's coverage was—arguably a rash move, since I was a lowly novice. But he listened carefully, and when I finished my feminist rant, there was a short silence while I stood there wondering whether I was about to be fired for my impertinence. Then he told me he thought there was a lot of merit in what I said and asked me to develop a set of guidelines for nonsexist coverage in the newspaper. I went back to my desk and typed out a new code of rules. The chauvinist males who dominated the newsroom didn't reform overnight, but the guidelines were officially implemented, and the paper's coverage gradually began to evolve under the watchful eye of the executive editor. In the first couple of months of my career, I had helped to move an entire institution, to my own astonishment. You never know what you can achieve until you try.

After all, it's not as if corporate America has failed to notice what a lousy job it's doing of keeping the best and the brightest women in the workforce. Although three decades have passed since a woman first became chief executive of a Fortune 500 company, "fewer than 2 percent of the biggest corporations are run by women," *The New York Times* reported recently. "Deborah Merrill-Sands, dean of the all-women Simmons School for Management in Boston, said that despite years of work, 'the majority of corporations don't have a sense of how to retain high-potential women.'"

But according to *The Times,* "Big companies are starting to respond. Industrial powerhouses like General Electric, Procter & Gamble and IBM, as well as partnership firms like Booz Allen Hamilton,

Ernst & Young, and Deloitte & Touche, have all begun programs aimed at keeping women professionally engaged."

The least we could do is help them address our problems by letting them know, in no uncertain terms, what our needs are. As the American abolitionist Frederick Douglass once said, "Power concedes nothing without a demand." And yet understanding how to strategize to achieve reasonable gains seems to be a perennial challenge for women in particular.

One executive at a large institution realized that she wanted to complete the Ph.D. she had never finished, and she spent several months considering whether to quit her job in order to go back to school without shortchanging her family. Ultimately, however, she decided to try to negotiate a compromise with her employer instead. To her own surprise, she found that her boss was so anxious to keep her that she was given an alternative set of responsibilities along with a flexible work schedule that allowed her to pursue her academic interests. She even got a promotion to go along with her new arrangement.

"Women need to learn that it's okay to negotiate and that it doesn't harm relationships if you do it as a skilled negotiator," she said afterward. "You need to figure out what you want, and you need to have a strategy, and you need to learn the skills to negotiate effectively. It's not up to someone else to offer us the way it needs to work for us. We need to go get it."

So here's one message a lot of successful women would like to pass on to those who think that opting out is the answer: If you don't like the way things are set up, work to change them. If you have problems with the way your job is structured, figure out some creative alternatives. If you just walk away from paid employment, you will not only have cheated yourself of the opportunities that might have come your way but you will also have forfeited your chance to have an impact for the better. As Mahatma Gandhi put it, "We must be the change we wish to see in the world."

The current rhetoric of "choice feminism" rationalizes women's abandonment of careers as a personal right, but this explanation entirely fails to place that choice in an appropriate social context. Although the concept of choice was indeed a hallmark of the women's movement, many of the toughest challenges faced by women today are not our choice at all; they have been imposed on us by a larger society that continues to shortchange the needs of women and children. These problems can be addressed only with individual and collective action.

"If this generation is not willing to push the envelope, we'll be losing some of the things we've already gained," says Paulanne Mancuso, who spent twenty years as a Calvin Klein executive before retiring from her job as CEO of Unilever Cosmetics International. "What I would like to tell young women is, don't just throw your hands up and say, 'This is too hard.' Then you're caving to the system and saying, 'Fine—we'll go, and we'll go quietly.' They need to make their voices heard in order to make industry understand that there are ways they can continue to contribute, continue to be an earner, and at the same time get some balance at home. There has to be some way to keep our best and brightest women out there contributing, without saying, 'You have to choose one or the other.' This is wrong for everyone—wrong for them and wrong for our children."

There is little question that gains for women have flagged in many areas. "Much of that progress slowed almost to a standstill in the 1990s," reported Babcock and Laschever in *Women Don't Ask.* "For full-time workers, the ratio of women's to men's annual earnings increased from 60.2 percent in 1980 to 71.6 percent in 1990, but between 1990 and 2000 that ratio increased only 1.6 percentage points, from 71.6 percent to 73.2. Women's progress into positions of leadership in professions that were previously closed to them has also been far from complete. In . . . economics, the percentage of female full professors doubled between 1981 and 1991 (from 3 percent to 6 percent) but still remains shockingly low and has remained flat ever since. . . . This is true even though 25 percent of all Ph.D.'s in economics for the past two decades were awarded to women, meaning that there have been plenty of women in the 'pipeline' who were not allowed to advance. The number of women hired as college presidents has also slowed. From the mid-1980s to the mid-1990s, the percentage of college presidents who were women more than doubled, from 9.5 percent to 21.1 percent. But between 1998 and 2001, this percentage increased by only 1.8 percentage points. These stagnating figures suggest that we may have gotten as much mileage as possible out of the changes we've already made—and that new solutions need to be found if women's progress is to continue."

But if women themselves fail to demand improvements, the prospects seem grim indeed. Some prominent women are hopeful that the younger generations will eventually recognize their potential political power. "As women realize that there hasn't been enough change in societal institutions, I certainly hope they are going to organize and make some changes," says Heidi Hartmann. "I'd like to see greater activism around women's issues, and I think we will." Citing a group of young women who "were very concerned that there didn't seem to be an organization for young women," Hartmann adds, "they formed the Younger Women's Task Force under the aegis of the National Council of Women's Organizations." The task force, a nationwide grassroots movement, is dedicated to organizing young women to take action on relevant issues.

Some activists are specifically targeting the needs of working mothers. In *The Motherhood Manifesto: What America's Moms Want—and What to Do About It,* Joan Blades, the co-founder of MoveOn.org, and Kristin Rowe-Finkbeiner propose a sweeping social agenda that includes paid maternity and paternity leaves, flexible work schedules, subsidized after-school programs for children, health care for all children, fair wages, and high-quality child care, among other measures.

None of these ideas is novel; the family needs of American parents have long been clear. But the determined individuals willing to fight for them seem to be few and far between. Occasionally a lone voice speaks out. After *Newsweek* ran a cover story about the stresses on mothers that Judith Warner described in her book *Perfect Madness,* Hollywood actor and director Rob Reiner wrote the magazine about his own initiative. "The difficult—and rewarding—work of raising children should not be our burden to bear alone," said Reiner, noting that the United States is the only industrialized country in the world without a nationwide system of child care for working parents. "That is why I recently launched an organization called Parents' Action for Children, whose primary mission is to . . . demand a complete overhaul of this country's approach to dealing with children and families."

Others are creating local organizations to address particular goals. Marketing consultant Tanya Mandor became so concerned about the lack of direction she sees among younger females that she founded a group called Young Working Women to help them develop personalized career plans and encourage realistic self-assessment.

"Young women are at a loss," Mandor explains. "We want to get them thinking about careers versus jobs. At our organizational meeting, I said to them, 'Some of you might be thinking, "I just want to find a man, have babies, and stay home." But how are you going to finance your lifestyle?' You get this deer-in-the-headlights look. There's a big difference between what they've been *letting* happen to them and what they've been *making* happen for themselves. My older daughter is twenty-two; she's working for a media-buying company, and she says, 'Maybe I'll just see what happens.' I tell her, 'Don't just see what happens! Decide what you want to do.' I'm big on objectives and strategies. I believe if you don't have an objective in life, you just kind of flow through it, and you may not reach your potential. A lot of these young women haven't even thought about a purpose. They graduate from college, and they are so sure of themselves—and then they start the interview process, and they lose some confidence. Those who do decide they want a career think, 'Okay, I'm going to become the beauty editor of this magazine'—and they get turned down by one after another. They start to doubt that they have anything to offer. The best thing I could wish for my daughters is early success, because that gives you the confidence to believe you can have the career you want. But there are other young women who are not getting feedback that they're doing a good job, so then the thought becomes, 'I'd better get married and find a husband to take care of me, because I'm not sure I can take care of myself.' How many mothers spend a lot of time talking to their daughters about their careers and their lives, as opposed to which boyfriend they're going to marry or what wedding dress they're going to wear? I think a lot of mothers, especially if they're not working mothers, just say, 'Marry a rich guy and have kids.' Our sons are raised to be aggressive, to be successful; they know you have to go out and get a job. But people are raising their daughters to get married. They're not pushing a career; it's, 'You need a husband.' "

As a result, a dismaying number of young women seem to spend more time imagining what their weddings are going to look like than they do on preparing for their life's work.

Having seen too many young women enter the labor force and become discouraged, Mandor is now writing a guide called *On the Way Up* about effective career planning. "We have never bridged education and work," she says. "What happens when you get out there? How do you sort through the maze of the business world? How do you find something you're passionate about? Most people don't discover what they're passionate about at an early age. I tell them that life is not about finding yourself; it's about creating yourself. The beauty of life today is that you have the opportunity to create whoever you want to be. There are no limitations on who you want to be, but creating yourself takes a lot of thought as well as a lot of work. How much time have you spent thinking about who you really want to be?"

A glimpse into one of Young Working Women's meetings shows the accuracy of Mandor's assessment. In a Manhattan town house, more than thirty pretty, well-mannered young women in their early twenties have arrayed themselves around the living room where the group has gathered. Mandor asks them to consider whether they are "knows"— the kind of people who know what they want to do professionally and have been focused on that clearly defined goal since an early age—or "don't knows," who haven't yet figured out what their career direction should be. When she calls for a show of hands, a couple of women raise their hands to signal that they are "knows." When Mandor asks how many are "don't knows," more than two dozen women tentatively raise their hands, looking sheepish.

As they ponder the challenges of creating their own best selves, women today might take heart in the words of Raphael Friedan, one of Betty Friedan's nine grandchildren, in the eulogy he delivered at her memorial service in February 2006. "I don't expect to change the world," said the twenty-three-year-old Raphael. "That doesn't mean I'm not going to try, but I don't expect to change the world. I do know now that I can change *my* world. All it takes is courage and determination. That can be a scary thing, to change your world, but that's what courage is."

His grandmother would have been proud of him as he looked out at the audience, an overflow crowd of middle-aged and older women who had come to honor the immeasurable impact her work had on American life. "If you're not scared, you're not pushing hard enough," Raphael concluded. "You're taking the safe road."

CHAPTER FOURTEEN

# THE ANXIETY OF LIBERTY

## "WHAT AM I GOING TO DO
## WITH MY LIFE?"

Recently a successful Washington journalist told me about a conversation she had with her mother many years ago, when her own career was just starting to blossom. "After I got my first big job as a columnist, I got a call from my mother, who was then in her late fifties," said the journalist, a Baby Boomer. "She asked me, 'Can you get me a job?' Her kids were grown and gone, and she didn't know what to do with herself. She had nothing left. That was heartbreaking to me."

The answer to her mother's question, sadly, was no; although her mother was intelligent, she had no skills or credentials for a meaningful job. Her husband died shortly thereafter, and she spent the next thirty-five years as a bored, if well-to-do, widow with little to anchor her days except lunch dates with other unhappy, restless women.

No matter how many children they have, that moment of reckoning will eventually arrive for every woman who has defined her life in terms of her family. Children keep you busy for a while, but they grow up. A mother can justify her existence in terms of their needs for a decade or even two, but if she hasn't answered the central question of who she is and what she wants to do with her life, she's just postponing the inevitable. In the end, full-time motherhood is a temp job, as legal scholar Sylvia Law put it so memorably—and when the empty nest looms, the need to define your identity jumps out and ambushes you all over again.

Who am I, besides a mother and a wife? When the children are gone, what am I supposed to do with myself? When no one needs me anymore, where can I find meaning in my life? These questions are a lot harder to answer at forty-five than at twenty-five, in part because the opportunities to explore them through challenging employment will have shrunk so dramatically.

And even in middle age, the road ahead looks long indeed, as my friend's mother—who lived well into her nineties—discovered. A hundred years ago, the average American woman's life span was fifty-one years. But women's life expectancy has now reached eighty years, and many of us will live considerably longer than that. As we contemplate the possibility of surviving for up to a century or even beyond, the idea of ceasing to be useful when our children are grown is far more depressing than it was in earlier eras. One working mother tells me how worried she is about her sibling, a stay-at-home mom with no professional prospects. "My sister is forty-six, and her children are seventeen and twenty. Now what?" the professional woman wonders. "What does she do for the next thirty years?" Or forty years, or even fifty?

In trumpeting the virtues of a return to the home, few full-time mothers are willing to acknowledge that this choice represents a fundamental abdication of responsibility for their own lives. The modern women's movement was supposed to have changed such childish thinking. After all, the world was a very different place in 1949, when Simone de Beauvoir scandalized the world with *The Second Sex* and its rallying cry for women to become independent individuals rather than living through men. In analyzing the reasons for their plight, she placed much of the blame on the ways women are culturally conditioned to embrace dependency.

"Society in general—beginning with her respected parents—lies to her by praising the lofty values of love, devotion, the gift of herself, and then concealing from her the fact that neither lover nor husband nor yet her children will be inclined to accept the burdensome charge of all that," de Beauvoir wrote. "She cheerfully believes these lies because they invite her to follow the easy slope: in this others commit their worst crime against her; throughout her life from childhood on, they damage and corrupt her by designating as her true vocation this submission, which is the temptation of every existent in the anxiety of liberty. . . . This is how woman is brought up, without ever being impressed with the necessity of taking charge of her own existence."

"The anxiety of liberty": what a haunting phrase. Nearly sixty years after de Beauvoir's groundbreaking work, and more than forty years after Betty Friedan galvanized America with her own book, the feminine mystique still exerts a powerful hold on our cultural imagination, offering women a dangerously seductive escape hatch from the necessary business of taking charge of their own existence.

But even as women cling to this outmoded ideal, the world continues to change at a pace as rapid as it is inexorable. "The demographic shifts are as powerful as the economic ones, and because of those two factors, we're living much longer, having far fewer children, and having children closer together," says sociologist Kathleen Gerson. "Even if a woman does opt out of the workforce for five or ten years, it's such a tiny percentage of her life that you still have to ask yourself, 'What am I going to do with my life?' "

This is, for many, a scary question. "Most people do not really want freedom, because freedom involves responsibility, and most people are frightened of responsibility," said Sigmund Freud.

Responsibility may be frightening, but so is dependency, if you allow yourself to think about its potential consequences. And in the end, grappling with that anxiety is the ultimate challenge of adulthood. It's hard to figure out who you are and how to make your own unique contribution to the world—not as a daughter or a wife or a mother but as an individual. We can try to avoid this task or pretend it doesn't exist, but it will always be waiting for us around the next bend in the road. Deferring that challenge through marriage or motherhood is a temporary solution at best, and one that exposes us to myriad risks. Whether in our twenties or our forties or our sixties, whether as young woman or divorcée or widow, each of us must eventually confront the question of who we are and how to give our lives meaning.

RECENTLY, I went to my neighborhood Greenmarket to buy vegetables and ran into an enormously accomplished professional colleague who has won many honors in her long, distinguished career. For the first time, both of her children are away from home, one at college and one in a high-school semester abroad. She misses them terribly.

"It's just awful," she said, looking forlornly at the tables of broccoli and tomatoes. Her husband was out of town on a business trip, and there was no one to cook for but herself.

But in the meantime, she had to go to the office—where she is working on an exciting project, where she is surrounded by friends and valued colleagues, where she won't feel lonely all day, where she has a purpose and an identity and a structure that gives meaning to her life, even when she's alone and no one in her family needs her to do anything at all.

"How do women survive without work?" she said, shaking her head at the desolation they must feel when their children grow up.

My heart aches for all the other wives who don't have such protections to fortify them against an unknown future. No one has prepared them for many of the challenges they are likely to face, and some will be devastated by unexpected events. And yet in most of the public debate, these issues are still being framed in terms of the stale formulas of previous eras. Yes, women are entitled to make their own choices; yes, raising children is an essential, deeply meaningful, and socially valuable occupation.

But those arguments entirely miss the larger point, as does the current debate over "choice feminism." In the end, the real question isn't about feminism at all; it's about survival. When women rely on blind faith to safeguard their financial security, they put their own futures and those of their children at risk. If your husband divorces you or drops dead, was it really such a great idea to stay home if you can't afford to buy groceries to feed your kids?

Questions like these tend to provoke a stubborn defensiveness in women who have made that choice. When Linda Hirshman published *Get to Work,* her polemic against voluntary domestic servitude and in favor of paid work predictably offended many full-time moms. Responding to Hirshman's diatribe against the "repetitious, socially invisible, physical tasks" required in taking care of home and family, an Illinois-based organization called Mothers and More held an Internet dialogue with Hirshman to defend stay-at-home motherhood.

"Economically, it is not a good choice," admitted Debra Levy, who spearheaded the discussion. "Yet the majority of us believe strongly in the value of caring for others—even if we were to wind up like Terry Hekker, we'd do it all again."

The first thing that struck me about this comment was the implied dig at working mothers. Does Levy really think that women who work outside the home don't believe in the value of caring for others, or does she simply feel so defensive about her choice that she has to put down that of working women with the worst insult she can think of—the tired old canard that we (unlike stay-at-home moms) don't consider it important to take care of our children?

Equally noteworthy was Levy's reference to Terry Martin Hekker, who was dumped by her husband after forty years of marriage, only to find herself so impoverished that she qualified for food stamps. Hekker's experience clearly struck a nerve among full-time mothers, judging by Levy's insistence that her choice was valid no matter how terrible the consequences.

But if Levy would do it all again, Hekker herself apparently wouldn't. As a self-appointed spokesperson for stay-at-home motherhood, Hekker originally made her name with her 1980 book, *Ever Since Adam and Eve*. Her divorce inspired her to start writing a follow-up volume. Its title is *Disregard First Book*.

Although Hekker still defends her decision to remain home with her children until they were of school age, she admits that it was a big mistake not to maintain some income-producing capability. "We live in a society where there is no job security anymore, so just on that level, women have to be prepared to support themselves," she told Women's eNews recently. "And with the divorce rate at fifty percent, you have got to keep in your field for security."

It's a lesson that women ignore at their peril. All my life, I have been haunted by the hardships that economic dependency inflicted on my mother and grandmother, as well as many friends, and I fear for the futures of the trusting young women who buy into the narrow domestic roles that our society has prescribed for them. I have been a reporter for more than three decades, during which time I've interviewed thousands of people. Throughout those years, with stunning consistency, women of all ages have told me the same story: They counted on a man to take care of them, and they were betrayed, whether by the man himself or by a cruel fate that decreed his untimely death, the loss of his job, or any number of other misfortunes. Endlessly repeated by one grief-stricken wife after another, the refrains are hauntingly similar:

*"I never expected . . ."*
*"I was completely shocked . . ."*
*"It came out of the blue . . ."*
*"I would never have dreamed . . ."*

For women whose husbands had left them, the grief was immeasurably compounded by the anger that accompanied their sense of betrayal. Many years after the fact, they remained incredulous about the simple sentences that shattered their lives:

*"He just told me he wasn't happy."*
*"One day he said he didn't love me anymore."*
*"How could he have changed so much?"*

How indeed. But even as I empathize with their pain, I also find myself wondering why they didn't protect themselves better. For some reason, women continue to marry and build lives predicated on the assumption that their partners will always feel the same as they did on their wedding day. So many wives seem to cling ferociously to the belief that their own marriages will remain impervious to the toll of aging, boredom, stress, depression, financial woes, sexual temptation, and all the other factors so familiar they have long since become cultural clichés. But staying married over the long haul is tough, and those who succeed have usually weathered difficult periods. Among the couples I know whom I would consider to be "happily married," most have been in counseling at one time or another, working on the areas where their relationships have frayed from the inevitable wear and tear of normal life.

And yet so many women are completely shocked when confronted by a divorce—and by the accompanying realization that their own interests and those of their partners have diverged at some point along the way, usually without the women noticing it. I couldn't possibly count the number of men who have told me that they believed women should stay home with their children and that they were delighted their own wives were doing so—only to leave those wives when the kids got older. Having stay-at-home wives worked out very well for the men; their partners provided innumerable services that enabled the husbands to concentrate on their careers. Needless to say, this arrangement didn't work out so well for the wives whose marriages received an unwelcome termination notice.

Even at the height of the 1950s infatuation with the Ozzie-and-Harriet lifestyle, subversive voices could be heard registering doubt. "Honestly, don't you think marriage is just the most important thing in the world? I mean, a woman isn't really a woman at all until she's been married and had children, and why? Because she's fulfilled," said Debbie Reynolds as the ingenue in the classic 1955 movie *The Tender Trap.* Although Reynolds's character was an actress who had just landed her first big Broadway role, she viewed this accomplishment only as a temporary stopping-off point on the road to marriage.

Dissatisfied with his own marriage, one of the movie's male characters tried to tell this earnest young woman that her ode to domestic bliss didn't necessarily reflect the male point of view. "In order to be fulfilled, you have to have a man—but it might just be possible that what fulfills you might not fulfill him," he pointed out.

More than half a century later, many women still haven't gotten the message. "You can never know the truth of anyone's marriage, including your own," as Nora Ephron put it in "Twenty-Five Things People Have a Shocking Capacity to Be Surprised By Over and Over."

And yet women continue to be blindsided when their marriages blow up and life as they know it is destroyed, as definitively as if a sudden earthquake had turned the solid ground beneath them into a pile of rubble. Such upheavals are a frequent occurrence in American life, so the larger question is why women so often find themselves unprepared for the commonplace challenges of adult life. They know what the divorce rate is, but they all thought they would be immune; they know men lose their jobs, but they never dreamed such an embarrassing thing could happen to their own husbands; they understand that spouses can fall ill and even die, but tragedies like that only afflict other people.

Even as I write this, the phone rings with a friend's news about yet another thirty-something stay-at-home mother who has just discovered that her husband is having an affair with their baby-sitter and has been planning to end his marriage.

And yet the promise of the fairy tale—that Prince Charming marries you and takes care of you forever—usually remains far more powerful than the realities these women see all around them. No matter what catastrophes befall their friends or their sisters or their neighbors, the lure of dependency keeps them mesmerized by a mythology so potent that no dose of reality could break its hold on true believers—at least until such shocks are visited upon them personally.

In the long run, that fairy-tale belief system seems destined to be seen as an anachronistic relic that's about as practical for today's world as pantaloons, corsets, and bustles. Larger social and economic forces are driving the changes that are sweeping the globe, as Chrystia Freeland pointed out in the *Financial Times* last year. "Working women are one of the most important engines of the great burst of economic growth in the postwar era," she wrote. "*The Economist* magazine has dubbed this feminization of global gross domestic product 'womenomics' and, in a striking analysis, found that over the past decade or so increased female participation in the paid labour force has contributed more to the growth of the world economy than either booming China or new technology."

Many analysts are therefore convinced that the retrograde trends heralding the current back-to-the-home movement will ultimately be seen as a temporary setback in the ongoing march of progress toward women's full participation in the real world. Over the last three decades, the increase in women receiving bachelor's degrees in the sciences has been stunning, as W. Michael Cox, chief economist of the Federal Reserve Bank of Dallas, and Richard Alm, an economics writer with the bank, pointed out recently in a *New York Times* essay challenging the idea that women are not intellectually equipped for careers in the sciences.

"Today women earn about two-thirds of the degrees in veterinary medicine and pharmacy," wrote Cox and Alm. "They're approaching 50 percent in law, and they've topped 40 percent in medicine. More than a third of new dentists are women. Likewise, women's share of master's degrees from business schools rose from 3.6 percent in 1970 to 41.1 percent in 2002. Women have also greatly expanded their presence in the social sciences. . . . Overall, women earned 46.3 percent of the doctorates awarded in 2002, up from 13.3 percent in 1970."

As economist Heidi Hartmann describes such changes, "Starting in the 1960s, women have been voting with their feet. They have been voting to go into the labor force, they have had fewer kids, they have married later, they have divorced more, and they have reduced the time spent in families. That helps women to achieve more and helps them increase their economic equality and power within marriage. More education, later marriage, fewer children, more employment, greater wherewithal, greater political power, greater power within the family—all of those things go together. Because of the commitment women are making to education, I don't really think we're going to go backward, because the impact of education is to draw women out of the home and into the larger society."

The larger society is admittedly a complex place to live, and there are times when most of us are tempted to withdraw to a cozy suburban Colonial where all we have to worry about is what to make for

dinner. But the seeming security of such domestic havens is a dangerous illusion, and if women retreat to that comforting cocoon, the path
ahead of them is likely to become a minefield.

So the main thing I want to say to other women is this: Protect
yourself. Given the likelihood that you will have to fend for yourself
at some point in the future, protect yourself against economic hardship by maintaining the capacity to support yourself. Protect your
children by making sure you can take care of them financially should
anything happen to their father. Protect your future happiness against
the nagging doubts harbored by frustrated stay-at-home mothers who
can't shake the guilt and regret they feel about failing to explore their
full potential. Protect yourself against the desolation of the empty
nest, which inflicts the deepest sense of loss on full-time mothers with
no other identity or outlets to sustain them. Protect your older self
against the feelings of uselessness and isolation experienced by so
many women who didn't cultivate meaningful work that would nour-
ish them in their later years.

None of this is intended as a condemnation of their choice, only as an
urgent warning to others considering that lifestyle about the pitfalls that
may lie ahead. The persistence of the Mommy Wars provides eloquent
testimony to the defensiveness so many women feel, no matter what
choices they have made—but as far as I'm concerned, it's time for all of
us to stop channeling our doubt, our guilt, and our ambivalence into
anger that's used as a weapon against other women. In my opinion, such
passion is misplaced; women should spend a lot less time worrying
about what other mothers are doing and more about whether their own
choices will truly make them happy in the long run. If you really feel secure about the choices you've made, there's no reason to attack those of
anyone else. And even if you don't feel all that secure, just think of how
many more productive ways women could use that energy.

I'm not pretending that it's easy to take full responsibility for your
own life, nor do I claim the ability to tell you how you should do it.

Every woman has to find her own way. I can tell you how I did it, I can tell you how scores of other women did it, but in the end our magic formulas generally boil down to simple common sense.

"You just sort of make it up as you go along," says Vicki Gordon.

But don't tell us it can't be done, because we know it can.

Martha Fineman is a genuine pioneer, in many ways. A "working-class housewife" who was the first person in her family to graduate from high school, she had her first child when she was eighteen years old. While raising four kids, she became an internationally recognized authority on family law and feminist jurisprudence who taught at the University of Wisconsin, Cornell University, and Columbia University before becoming the Robert W. Woodruff Professor of Law at Emory University in Atlanta.

So how did she do it? "I didn't know any better," Fineman says. "Once you're in the middle of something, you just kind of get through it. There are lots of costs, but you don't quit. You just go one day at a time."

All too often, however, the blanket solutions offered by those addressing these issues just seem silly. In *Perfect Madness*, Judith Warner talks about how much easier it is to combine work and motherhood in France, where she used to live, than in the United States, with its far less enlightened social and governmental policies. This may be true, but most of us can't move to France, so that doesn't help us much. In *Get to Work*, Linda Hirshman advises women to marry much younger or much older men and to have only one child—an equally impractical set of instructions for the majority of women. Although I agree with Hirshman's basic premise about the central importance of work in women's lives, I worry that such flippant advice could become part of the problem instead of the solution. If you tell women that they'll have to give up having a second child in order to sustain a career, many of them will give up the career instead. In any case, it's also manifestly untrue; my husband and I were born less than three years apart, and we have two kids. Virtually all of my friends are married to peers, have two or three children, and have challenging careers as well. Why should any of us voluntarily accept the kind of restrictions imposed on people in Communist China, where women are allowed to have only one child?

Hirshman also tells women not to study art. Again, this advice is facetious at best, but potentially destructive at worst. She wants women to plan and to use their educations as preparation for a career— a laudable goal, to be sure. But what about women who have a true passion for art? Telling them to steer clear of what they love is ridiculous. There's no surefire path to finding meaningful work, but "follow your bliss" is as good a piece of advice as any I've heard. "Don't study art" is about as helpful as "Don't be an English major," which is the admittedly impractical choice of many young women who like to read and haven't thought much beyond that in terms of career planning. I'm all for career planning, but I was an English major who never took a course in journalism, and I've made a good living as a writer throughout my adult life. More important is the fact that I've loved every minute of it. In rising to the challenge of remaining engaged by your career for five decades or more, there's no substitute for genuine passion.

"Why are these women shortchanging themselves?" Fineman wonders about those who forsake their careers. "Life is so exciting! I can't understand how anybody would want to cut off some major area of exploration and excitement. I always want to do more."

"But the system is rigged against us!" young women complain. Yes, it is, and it's certainly true that systemic social change would be a big help in supporting women as they tackle these problems. In order to achieve such change, it will be necessary for at least some of these dubious young women to recognize the importance of working collectively to transform the institutional structures that make it so hard for mothers to balance their lives. Persuading—and, when that fails, forcing—men to join with us in this task is another critical component of progress.

And yet even under the decidedly unsatisfactory conditions that prevail at present, millions of women have managed to do meaningful work while raising wonderful children. While doing so, some of us even worked to change the system so it was a little less rigged against the women who followed us. Is it asking too much that the generations coming along behind us should contribute to further progress, instead of setting it back?

I am proud and grateful to count myself among the working women who have struggled so hard to build complete, self-sufficient adult lives. The juggling act may be out of fashion now, but there hasn't been a single moment when I didn't feel unbelievably lucky to have engaged in all the battles necessary to maintain that ostensibly discredited goal.

Did I do everything as well as I could have? Of course not.

The resulting life may have been imperfect; it surely was hectic, and obviously I didn't achieve the level of professional success that I might have if I'd devoted all my energy to my career. Instead I've had a patchwork life—but it was patched together from the most sumptuous pieces of fabric imaginable, and the result has been an indescribably rich experience that I wouldn't have traded for anything in the world. It wasn't simple, but neither is anything else worth accomplishing—and over time the benefits have greatly outweighed the difficulties.

So if younger generations don't think that Baby Boom mothers with thriving careers are good role models, maybe they're using the wrong criteria to make that judgment. We may not be invincible, and we're certainly not perfect, but we are strong, we are self-sufficient, and we are prepared to handle whatever challenges the future might bring. Are you?

"Here we are—we did it," says Kathleen Gerson, who raised her daughter and sustained a satisfying marriage while writing influential books as a prominent sociologist. "It's a miracle what we managed to pull off. This is a generation that has shown that men and women can integrate these things, and there's a good amount of research that shows that juggling is actually good for people. Psychologically and emotionally, people who do a lot of things are actually better off. Yes, you can have a full work life and a full family life, too."

As far as we're concerned, this is as good as it gets. And it's really great.

You deserve nothing less. So don't jeopardize your future by settling for half a life. The whole world is out there waiting for you to engage with it. If you do, you will earn not only money and acclaim but the truest components of success: the freedom to make whatever choices you need to make, the security that comes with self-sufficiency, the self-knowledge you gain by exploring every facet of your own potential, the intense joy that results from using your gifts fully.

The rewards are priceless.

All you have to do is help yourself.

# NOTES

*Prologue*

Page

xxii    *Terry Martin Hekker:* Terry Martin Hekker, "Paradise Lost (Domestic Division)," *The New York Times*, January 1, 2006.


*Chapter One*

3    *Caitlin Flanagan:* Caitlin Flanagan, *To Hell with All That: Loving and Loathing Our Inner Housewife* (New York: Little, Brown & Company, 2006).

4    *"When a mother works":* As Laurie Abraham reported in her profile of Caitlin Flanagan, which was published in the April 2006 issue of *Elle* magazine, there was a curious omission in *To Hell with All That: Loving and Loathing Our Inner Housewife*. Flanagan wrote one of her most infamous lines in her essay "How Serfdom Saved the Women's Movement," which attacked professional women for hiring poor immigrant nannies and argued that the children of working women love their baby-sitters more than they do their own mothers. "What few will admit—because it is painful, because it reveals the unpleasant truth that life presents a series of choices, each of

which precludes a host of other attractive possibilities—is that when a mother works, something is lost," Flanagan wrote. But when her essays were collected in *To Hell with All That*, this statement had been deleted. "So, I ask her, do you stand by that line?" wrote Abraham, who learned that her own child's gerbil had just died while she was interviewing Flanagan. " 'Yeah,' Flanagan says, her voice now soft, serious. 'The gerbil's dead, and you're here.' "

4–5   *Psychology Today:* A poll cited by *Psychology Today*, January/February 2006, The Washington Post/Kaiser Family Foundation/Harvard University, "Survey of Americans on Gender," November 20–23, 1997, based on two questions: Considering everything, do you think it would be better or worse for the country if men and women went back to the traditional roles they had in the 1950s? Or don't you think it would make a difference? Forty-two percent of all women in the nationally representative survey said it would be better.

5   *According to the U.S. Census Bureau:* "Fertility of American Women: June 2000," U.S. Census Bureau, issued in October 2001, part of a series called Current Population Reports, P20-543RV by Amara Bachu and Martin O'Connell; and "Fertility of American Women: June 2004," U.S. Census Bureau, issued in December 2005, part of Current Population Reports, series P20-555 by Jane Lawler Dye.

5   *Among married mothers* and *The father was the sole breadwinner:* U.S. Department of Labor, Bureau of Labor Statistics, Unpublished Data from the Current Population Survey and the March Supplements of 1997 and 2004.

5   *mothers stayed home:* U.S. Census Bureau, Population Division, Fertility & Family Statistics Branch, Families and Living Arrangements, Historical Time Series Tables, Table SHP-1, www.census.gov/population/www/socdemo/hh-fam.html.

5   *"Gen-X mothers":* Ann Hurlbert, "Look Who's Parenting," *The New York Times*, July 4, 2004. Research data in article came from Reach Advisors' 2003 survey of 3,020 parents entitled *Generation X Parents: From Grunge to Grown Up*.

5   *"home-schooled":* Celinda Lake and Kellyanne Conway, *What Women Really Want* (New York: Free Press, 2005), page 80.

5   *"Seven in 10":* Ibid.

6    *"Half the wealthiest":* Linda R. Hirshman, "Homeward Bound," *The American Prospect*, December 2005, page 20.

6    *brides:* Linda R. Hirshman, *Get to Work* (New York: Viking, 2006), page 7.

6    *Center for Work-Life Policy:* From a report on a study conducted by the Center for Work-Life Policy, using a nationally representative sample of 2,443 women, entitled "The Hidden Brain Drain: Off-Ramps and On-Ramps in Women's Careers," published by the *Harvard Business Review*, March 2005 by Sylvia Ann Hewlett, Carolyn Buck Luce, Peggy Shiller, and Sandra Southwell. This report appeared in a *Harvard Business Review* article, "Off-Ramps and On-Ramps: Keeping Talented Women on the Road to Success," by Sylvia Ann Hewlett and Carolyn Buck Luce, March 2005.

6    *Catalyst:* Catalyst, "Women and the MBA: Gateway to Opportunity: Executive Summary" (New York: Catalyst, 2000), page 9.

6    *Stanford University class of 1981:* Lisa Belkin, "The Opt-Out Revolution," *The New York Times*, October 26, 2003. This figure was taken from a 1994 study conducted by Stanford University Professor Herant K. Katchadourian, as reported by Theresa Johnston in "The Mommy Maze," in *Stanford Magazine*, 1997: "In his book, *Cream of the Crop*, Professor Herant Katchadourian noted that 57 percent of mothers in his Class of '81 sample had spent at least a year at home caring for their infant children in the first decade after graduation and one out of four had stayed home three or more years. The percentages of full-time homemakers and part-time workers were expected to increase, he said, as more children arrived and spousal incomes grew." However, some studies suggest lower figures. In another Stanford University survey of female graduates from the class of 1981, 12 percent were full-time homemakers, according to Stanford University business professor Myra H. Strober and Agnes M. K. Chan, based on a May 1990 survey published in *The Road Winds Uphill All the Way: Gender, Work, and Family in the United States and Japan* (Cambridge: MIT Press, 1999).

6    *Myra Hart:* Myra Hart, Informal Survey, 2001, Harvard Business School.

6    *half the* Times *brides:* Linda R. Hirshman, "Homeward Bound," *The American Prospect*, December 2005, page 23.

7    *more than two-thirds:* U.S. Department of Labor, Bureau of Labor Statistics, Current Population Survey, Unpublished Data, and "Employment

Characteristics of Families," 2005 (Table 5, http://www.bls.gov/news.
release/pdf/famee.pdf).

7    *Boushey:* Eduardo Porter, "Mothers' Flight from Job Force Questioned,"
     *The New York Times,* December 2, 2005. Information comes from
     Heather Boushey's briefing paper, "Are Women Opting Out? Debunk-
     ing the Myth," November 2005, Washington, D.C.'s Center for Eco-
     nomic and Policy Research.

9    *Barash:* Susan Shapiro Barash, "The Wedding Planners: The Top Job for
     21st Century Gals: Finding—and Keeping—a Husband," *The New York
     Post,* January 11, 2004.

10   Tango's *Web site:* Tango Online, reader's response to an article by Leslie
     Bennetts, "She's Gotta Have It All," April 2006.

11   *David Brooks:* David Brooks, "The Year of Domesticity," *The New York
     Times,* January 1, 2006.

11   *Linden:* Corina Linden, "Careers and Kids, Hand in Hand," *The New
     York Times,* January 4, 2006.

12   *"women at all income levels":* Sue Shellenbarger, "More New Mothers
     Are Staying Home Even When It Causes Financial Pain," *The Wall Street
     Journal,* November 30, 2006.

15   *Wasserstein's novel:* Janet Maslin, "Dizzy or Smart? What's a Girl to Be?,"
     *The New York Times,* April 28, 2006.

18   *"Fast-Track Women":* Pamela Stone and Meg Lovejoy, "Fast-Track Women
     and the 'Choice' to Stay Home," ANNALS, *AAPSS,* 596, November 2004.

20   *In October 2006,* USA Today: John Waggoner, "Growing Family on One
     Income?," *USA Today,* October 20, 2006.

23   *poll of nearly five hundred:* Sylvia Ann Hewlett and Norma Vite-Leon,
     High-Achieving Women, 2001 (New York: Center for Work-Life Policy/
     National Parenting Association, 2002).

30   *Ivy League women:* Louise Story, "Many Women at Elite Colleges Set
     Career Path to Motherhood," *The New York Times,* September 20, 2005.

## Chapter Two

33   *"Opt-Out Revolution":* Lisa Belkin, "The Opt-Out Revolution," *The
     New York Times Magazine,* October 26, 2003.

34    *study of Yale University students:* Louise Story, "Many Women at Elite Colleges Set Career Path to Motherhood," *The New York Times*, September 20, 2005.

34    *Massachusetts man:* David English, Editorial/Letters, "A Revived Debate: Babies, Careers, 'Having It All,'" *The New York Times*, September 22, 2005.

37    *Disney introduced its Cinderella line:* Alle C. Hall, Editorial/Letters, "Another Cinderella Tale," *The New York Times*, November 4, 2005.

40    *Schlessinger . . . dinner:* Leslie Bennetts, "Diagnosing Dr. Laura," *Vanity Fair*, September 1998.

40    *"Flanagan confesses":* Jennifer Graham, Bookshelf, "The Ordeal of Domesticity," *The Wall Street Journal*, April 25, 2006.

41    *Nelson wrote:* Leslie Morgan Steiner, *Mommy Wars* (New York: Random House, 2006), page 196.

42    *Total 180!:* Holly Yeager, "Is This Really Feminism?," *Financial Times*, June 9, 2006.

42    Tango: Tango Online, anonymous readers' responses to an article by Leslie Bennetts, "She's Gotta Have It All," April 2006.

45    *"Fast-Track Women":* Pamela Stone and Meg Lovejoy, "Fast-Track Women and the 'Choice' to Stay Home," ANNALS, *AAPSS*, 596, November 2004.

50    *Ellen Bravo:* Ellen Bravo, Editorial/Letters, "Why Should It All Be Up to Women?," *The New York Times*, January 18, 2006.

50    *Schlachet:* Barbara Cohn Schlachet, Editorial/Letters, "Why Should It All Be Up to Women?," *The New York Times*, January 18, 2006.

*Chapter Four*

77    *Wall Street Journal:* Anne Marie Chaker and Hilary Stout, "After Years Off, Women Struggle to Revive Careers," *The Wall Street Journal*, May 6, 2004.

77    *Hewlett:* Lisa Belkin, "The Opt-Out Revolution," *The New York Times Magazine*, October 26, 2003.

77    *"Among women who take off-ramps":* Sylvia Ann Hewlett and Carolyn Buck Luce, "Off-Ramps and On-Ramps: Keeping Talented Women on the Road to Success," *Harvard Business Review*, March 2005, page 45.

78    *"Unfortunately, only 74%":* Ibid., page 46.

78    *Ehrenreich:* Hillary Chura, "Some Signs of Easier Re-entry After Breaks to Rear Children," *The New York Times*, November 20, 2005.

79    *Farrell:* Essay by Warren Farrell, "Exploiting the Gender Gap," *The New York Times*, September 5, 2005.

79    *Hewlett's study:* Sylvia Ann Hewlett and Carolyn Buck Luce, "Off-Ramps and On-Ramps: Keeping Talented Women on the Road to Success," *Harvard Business Review*, March 2005, page 46.

80    *Hewlett bemoaned:* Lisa Belkin, "The Opt-Out Revolution," *The New York Times Magazine*, October 26, 2003.

80    *AARP-funded study:* Patricia Barry, "The New Math," *AARP Bulletin* cover story, January 2006, page 19.

80    *Carol Evans:* Hillary Chura, "Some Signs of Easier Re-entry After Breaks to Rear Children," *The New York Times*, November 20, 2005.

81    *Tory Johnson:* Anne Marie Chaker and Hilary Stout, "After Years Off, Women Struggle to Revive Careers," *The Wall Street Journal*, May 6, 2004.

81    *"six months":* Hillary Chura, "Some Signs of Easier Re-entry After Breaks to Rear Children," *The New York Times*, November 20, 2005.

84    *Dr. Shelley Correll:* Joan Blades and Kristin Rowe-Finkbeiner, *The Motherhood Manifesto* (New York: Nation Books, 2006), page 13.

85    *In another study:* "When Motherhood Is a Liability," *Daily News*, January 12, 2005.

*Chapter Five*

100   *Anna Fels:* Anna Fels, *Necessary Dreams: Ambition in Women's Changing Lives* (New York: Pantheon Books, 2004), page 244.

102   Money *magazine: Money*, June 1992.

103   *"financial collapse":* Elizabeth Warren and Amelia Warren Tyagi, *The Two-Income Trap: Why Middle-Class Parents Are Going Broke* (New York: Basic Books, 2003), page 6.

103   *earnings penalty:* Jane Waldfogel, "Understanding the 'Family Gap' in Pay for Women with Children," *Journal of Economic Perspectives*, vol. 12, no. 1, Winter 1998, pages 137–156.

103   *"wage gap":* Joan Blades and Kristin Rowe-Finkbeiner, *The Motherhood Manifesto* (New York: Nation Books, 2006), page 7.

104 *"mommy tax":* Ann Crittenden, *The Price of Motherhood* (New York: Henry Holt and Company, 2001), page 88.

104 *"two-parent families":* Joan Blades and Kristin Rowe-Finkbeiner, *The Motherhood Manifesto* (New York: Nation Books, 2006), page 3.

104 *"bait-and-switch":* Anna Fels, *Necessary Dreams: Ambition in Women's Changing Lives* (New York: Pantheon Books, 2004), page 244.

105 *"Prince Charming":* Liz Perle, *Money, a Memoir: Women, Emotions, and Cash* (Henry Holt and Company, 2006).

105 *Bumpass:* Dan Hurley, "Divorce Rate: It's Not as High as You Think," *The New York Times*, April 19, 2005.

106 *"working women's marriages":* Caryl Rivers, Rosalind Chait Barnett, "Women Happier as Homemakers? Time to Recheck Data," Women's eNews, March 22, 2006.

107 *Women's standard of living:* Suzanne M. Bianchi, Lekha Subaiya, and Joan R. Kahn, "The Gender Gap in the Economic Well Being of Non-Resident Fathers and Custodial Mothers," 1999.

108 *no husband present:* U.S. Census Bureau, Current Population Survey, (March) and Annual Social and Economic Supplements, 2005 and earlier. www.census.gov/population/socdemo/hh-fam/hh1.pdf.

108 *child-support payments:* U.S. Census Bureau, Current Population Survey, Alimony and Child Support Supplement of April 2004. Current Population Reports by Timothy S. Grall, Census Bureau Analyst.

108 *repay bills:* Jonathan Fisher (Bureau of Labor Statistics), Angela Lyons (University of Illinois at Urbana-Champaign), "The Ability of Women to Repay Debt after Divorce," a study presented at the Institute for Women's Policy Research's (IWPR) Seventh International Women's Policy Research Conference, June 2003.

110 *child-support payments:* U.S. Department of Health and Human Services, Office of Child Support Enforcement, Annual Reports and Statistics, 2005 and 1999.

111 *compensation experts:* Salary.com. May 3, 2006. For explanation of calculations go to http://mom.salary.com.

112 *"Edelman":* Jennifer Steinhauer, "The Economic Unit Called Supermom," *The New York Times*, May 8, 2005.

117 *pension system:* Roger Lowenstein, "The End of Pensions?," *The New York Times*, October 30, 2005.

117    *Women aged sixty-five:* Joint Economic Committee Democrats, Economic Policy Brief, "The Effects of the President's Social Security Proposal on Women," March 2006.

118    *"401(k)":* Thomas N. Bethell, "The Gender Gyp," *AARP Bulletin,* July–August 2005.

118    *retirement income:* Joint Economic Committee Democrats, Economic Policy Brief, "The Effects of the President's Social Security Proposal on Women," March 2006.

118    *source of income:* Sara E. Rix and Laurel Beedon, "Social Security and Women: Some Facts," AARP Public Policy Institute, October 2003. Based on a report from the Social Security Administration, "Income of the Population 55 or Older, 2002," Washington, D.C., USGPO, 2005 Table #6 B2.

119    *"I looked at men and women":* Heidi I. Hartman and Stephen J. Rose, "Still a Man's Labor Market: The Long-Term Earnings Gap," published by the Institute for Women's Policy Research, May 2004.

119    *women outlive men:* D. L. Hoyert and M. P. Heron, S. L. Murphy, H. Kung, "Deaths: Final Data for 2003," National Vital Statistics Report, vol. 54, no. 13, Hyattsville, Maryland: National Center for Health Statistics, Centers for Disease Control and Prevention, 2006.

119    *Women also tend to marry older men:* National Center for Health Statistics, Centers for Disease Control and Prevention, Monthly Vital Statistics Report, vol. 43, no. 12, Supplement, 1995.

119    *outlive their husbands:* U.S. Administration on Aging, based on 2000 data.

119    *sixty-five-year-old women:* This figure was calculated by a demographer at the National Center for Health Statistics, Division of Vital Statistics, (301) 458-4800.

119    *aged seventy-five and older:* U.S. Census Bureau, Current Population Survey, 2006 Annual Social and Economic Supplement.

119    *"women are poor":* Testimony of Jane L. Ross, Deputy Commissioner for Policy, Social Security Administration, before the Senate Special Committee on Aging, Little Rock, Arkansas, June 1, 1999, http://www.ssa.gov/legislation/testimony_060199.html.

120    *Paul Hodge:* The Harvard Generations Policy Program and the Global Generations Policy Institute, a Collaborative Study, "Baby Boomer Women: Secure Futures or Not?," 2006, genpolicy@genpolicy.com.

120   *Ted Mathas:* Ted Mathas, Keynote Address at AARP's launch of the Women's
      Leadership Circle, April 6, 2006.

120   *43 percent:* Joint Economic Committee Democrats, Economic Policy Brief, "The
      Effects of the President's Social Security Proposal on Women," March 2006.

120   *"aged widows":* Testimony of Jane L. Ross, Deputy Commissioner for Pol-
      icy, Social Security Administration, before the Senate Special Committee on
      Aging, Little Rock, Arkansas, June 1, 1999, http://www.ssa.gov/legislation/
      testimony_060199.html.


### Chapter Six

132   *Joyce Purnick:* Joyce Purnick, Barnard Commencement Speech, May 19, 1998.

132   *London newspaper:* Joanna Coles, "U.S. Editor Turns Clock Back in Work-
      ing Mother Debate," *The Guardian* (London), May 22, 1998.

133   *advertising executive:* Julie Bosman, "WPP Executive Resigns Over Remarks
      on Women," *The New York Times*, October 21, 2005.

138   *"Nearly half of all businesses":* Deborah Geigis Berry, "Bank on Your
      Bliss," *Country Living*, March 2006.

140   *front-loaded professions:* Anna Fels, *Necessary Dreams: Ambition in Women's
      Changing Lives* (New York: Pantheon Books, 2004), pages 207, 208.


### Chapter Seven

154   *Cynthia Liu:* Louise Story, "Many Women at Elite Colleges Set Career Path
      to Motherhood," *The New York Times*, September 20, 2005.

156   *Kate White:* Maureen Dowd, "What's a Modern Girl to Do?," *The New
      York Times*, October 30, 2005.

164   *"being a maid":* Maureen Dowd, *Are Men Necessary?* (New York: Putnam,
      2005), page 48.

165   *"flaky research":* Caryl Rivers and Rosalind Chait Barnett, "Why Dowd
      Doesn't Know What Men Really Want," Women's eNews, November 2,
      2005. http://womensenews.org/article.cfm/dyn/aid/2512/. Research cited:
      Stephanie L. Brown and Brian P. Lewis, "Relational Dominance and Mate-
      Selection Criteria: Evidence That Males Attend to Female Dominance,"
      *Evolution and Human Behavior*, vol. 25, no. 6, November 2004. Michelle D.

Taylor et al., "Childhood IQ and Marriage by Mid-life: The Scottish Mental Survey 1932 and the Midspan Studies," *Personality and Individual Differences*, vol. 38, no. 7, May 2005. Heather Boushey, "Do Career Women Trade Away Motherhood?" Economic Policy Institute's *Economic Snapshots*, June 12, 2002.

165   *New York Post:* Susan Edelman, "Dowd's a Ditz, Say N.Y. Brainy Women," *New York Post*, November 13, 2005.

165   *African-Americans have the lowest marriage rate:* "Marital History for People 15 Years and Over, by Age, Sex, Race and Hispanic Origin: 2001," U.S. Census Bureau, Population Division, Fertility and Family Statistics Branch, http://www.census.gov/population/www/socdemo/marr-div/p70-97-tab01 .html. "Marital Status," 2005 American Community Survey, U.S. Census Bureau, http://factfinder.census.gov/servlet/STTable?_bm=y&-geo_id=01000 US&-qr_name=ACS_2005_EST_G00_S1201&-ds_name=ACS_2005 _EST_G00_.

169   *Warner wrote in* Newsweek: Judith Warner, "Mommy Madness," *Newsweek*, February 21, 2005.

## Chapter Eight

174   *"bunch of cowbirds":* Reader's response to "She's Gotta Have It All," by Leslie Bennetts, *Tango*, April 14, 2006. http://www.tangomag.com/tabid/ 89/articleType/ArticleView/articleId/50/Shes-Gotta-Have-It-All.aspx.

174   *female cowbirds:* http://www.enature.com/flashcard/show_flash_card.asp? recordNumber=BD0336.

177   *Frankel:* Alison Frankel, "The Silence of the Moms," *The New York Times*, April 9, 2006.

178   *"IWBF":* Anna Fels, *Necessary Dreams: Ambition in Women's Changing Lives* (New York: Pantheon Books, 2004), page 3.

178   *" 'bragging' ":* Ibid., page 38.

180   *"gifted women":* Ibid., page 206.

184   *"working mothers may be most immune":* Jennifer Senior, "Can't Get No Satisfaction," *New York* magazine, December 4, 2006, page 2.

189   *Bushnell's latest novel:* Lola Ogunnaike, "Trading a Pursuit of Mr. Right for the Chance to Be Ms. Big," *The New York Times*, September 12, 2005.

193   *"My child's life":* Susan Chira, *A Mother's Place: Choosing Work and Family Without Guilt or Blame* (New York: HarperCollins, 1998), pages 287–288.

194 *"spousal help"*: Scott Coltrane, "Research on Household Labor: Modeling and Measuring the Social Embeddedness of Routine Family Work," *Journal of Marriage and the Family*, November 2000, page 1224.

195 *Eaker:* Elaine Eaker et al., "Marital Status, Marital Strain and the Risk of Coronary Heart Disease or Total Mortality: The Framingham Offspring Study," Second International Conference on Women, Heart Disease, and Stroke in Orlando, Abstract #4, February 16–19, 2005. Rita Delfiner, "It's Healthy to Give Hubby Some Lip," *New York Post*, February 19, 2005.

195 *"Employed women"*: Anna Fels, *Necessary Dreams: Ambition in Women's Changing Lives* (New York: Pantheon Books, 2004), page 206.

195 *British study:* Anne McMunn, Mel Bartley, Rebecca Hardy, Diana Kuh, "Life Course Social Roles and Women's Health in Mid-life: Causation or Selection?" *Journal of Epidemiology and Community Health*, June 2006. Paul Rowland, "Combining Work with Family Life Is Actually Good for Women's Health," *Western Mail*, May 15, 2006.

196 *"good health"*: Nicholas Bakalar, "Exploring Women's Health and Double Duty," *The New York Times*, May 23, 2006.

196 *"Wethington . . . Kessler"*: Caryl Rivers and Rosalind Chait Barnett, "Women Happier as Homemakers? Time to Recheck Data," Women's eNews, March 22, 2006. Elaine Wethington and Ronald C. Kessler, "Employment, Parental Responsibility, and Psychological Distress," *Journal of Family Issues*, vol. 10, no. 4, 1989.

197 *"twelve qualities"*: Dan Baker, *What Happy People Know: How the New Science of Happiness Can Change Your Life for the Better* (Pennsylvania: Rodale Books, 2003), pages 19, 257.

197 *Ohio State University:* Janice Kiecolt-Glaser et al., various studies including "Love, Marriage, and Divorce: Newlyweds' Stress Hormones Foreshadow Relationship Changes," *Journal of Consulting and Clinical Psychology*, vol. 71, no. 1, 2003. Full Kiecolt-Glaser publications list at http://pni.psychiatry.ohio-state.edu/jkg/publications.html. Howard Cohen, "What's Love Got to Do with It?," *The Miami Herald*, February 8, 2005.

198 *Seligman:* Dan Baker, *What Happy People Know: How the New Science of Happiness Can Change Your Life for the Better* (Pennsylvania: Rodale Books, 2003), page 121.

198 *Sheldon:* Ibid., page 129.

199   *Gilman:* Charlotte Perkins Gilman, "Why I Wrote the Yellow Wallpaper," *The Forerunner*, 1913, http://etext.virginia.edu/railton/enam312/cpghp.html.


                                *Chapter Nine*

210   *Perle:* Liz Perle, *Money, a Memoir: Women, Emotions, and Cash* (New York: Henry Holt & Company, 2006), page 57. Original statistic from *Smart-Money* survey: Jena McGregor, "Love & Money," *SmartMoney* magazine, February 9, 2004.

212   *money separate:* Sue Shellenbarger, "For Richer or for Poorer, but Only If We Have Separate Checking Accounts," *The Wall Street Journal*, February 24, 2005.

212   *Brooks:* David Brooks, "To Have and to Hold, for Richer for Poorer," *The New York Times*, March 1, 2005.

213   *"Who's the boss":* Pat Regnier and Amanda Gengler, "Men, Women and Money," *Money*, April 2006, pages 93–94.

215   *"A man is not":* Michelle Singletary, *Your Money and Your Man: How You and Prince Charming Can Spend Well and Live Rich* (New York: Random House, 2006), page 3.

215   *"Your First Million":* Joni Evans, "Your First Million," *O, The Oprah Magazine*, September 2005.

215   *"nice girls":* Lois Frankel, *Nice Girls Don't Get Rich: 75 Avoidable Mistakes Women Make with Money* (New York: Warner Books, 2005), pages 59, 68, 159. Lore Croghan, "Get Smart About Money," *Daily News*, May 19, 2005.

216   *"My first husband":* Barbara Stanny, *Secrets of Six-Figure Women: Surprising Strategies to Up Your Earnings and Change Your Life* (New York: HarperCollins, 2002), page 5.

216   *"investing":* Pat Regnier and Amanda Gengler, "Men, Women and Money," *Money*, April 2006, page 94. Original statistic from "Merrill Lynch Investment Managers Survey Finds: When It Comes to Investing, Gender a Strong Influence on Behavior," press release, April 2005.

216   *trade stocks:* Pat Regnier and Amanda Gengler, "Men, Women and Money," *Money*, April 2006, page 98. Original statistic from Brad Barber and Terrance Odean, "Boys Will Be Boys: Gender, Overconfidence, and Common Stock Investment," *Quarterly Journal of Economics*, vol. 116, no. 1, February 2001.

216 *family finances:* Pat Regnier and Amanda Gengler, "Men, Women and Money," *Money*, April 2006, page 93.

223 *AARP study:* Xenia P. Montenegro, "The Divorce Experience: A Study of Divorce at Midlife and Beyond," AARP report, May 2004, page 14.

227 *"economic freedom":* Simone de Beauvoir, *The Second Sex* (New York: Alfred A. Knopf, 1952), page 679.

### Chapter Ten

229 *"Men of my generation":* Nicholas Kulish, "Changing the Rules for the Team Sport of Bread-Winning," *The New York Times*, September 23, 2005.

230 *"Agriculture Department":* Ibid. Original statistic from Mark Lino, "Expenditures on Children by Families, 2004," U.S. Department of Agriculture, Center for Nutrition Policy and Promotion, April 2005.

230 *"A woman's earning power":* John Tierney, "Male Pride and Female Prejudice," *The New York Times*, January 3, 2006. Original statistic from David M. Buss, Todd K. Shackelford, Lee A. Kirkpatrick, Randy J. Larsen, "A Half Century of Mate Preferences: The Cultural Evolution of Values," *Journal of Marriage and Family*, vol. 63, no. 2, May 2001.

232 *Shulevitz:* Judith Shulevitz, "The Mommy Trap," *The New York Times*, February 20, 2005. Original statistic from the Families and Work Institute's "Generation & Gender in the Workplace," published by the American Business Collaboration, October 2004.

238 *Duke University:* Miller McPherson, Lynn Smith-Lovin, Matthew E. Brashears, "Social Isolation in America: Changes in Core Discussion Networks over Two Decades," *American Sociological Review*, vol. 71, June 2006. Henry Fountain, "The Lonely American Just Got a Bit Lonelier," *The New York Times*, July 2, 2006.

239 *"cocktail play groups":* Stacy Lu, "Cosmopolitan Moms," *The New York Times*, November 9, 2006.

240 *"Guys, a word of advice":* Michael Noer, "Don't Marry Career Women," Forbes.com, August 22, 2006. http://www.forbes.com/2006/08/23/Marriage-Careers-Divorce_cx_mn_land.html.

240 *"Prostitution":* Michael Noer, "The Economics of Prostitution," Forbes.com, February 14, 2006. http://www.forbes.com/2006/02/11/economics-prostitution-marriage_cx_mn_money06_0214prostitution.html.

241   *"Disgusting Misogynistic":* "Disgusting Misogynistic *Forbes* Article One
      Step Away from Stepford," The Huffington Post, August 23, 2006. http://
      www.huffingtonpost.com/eat-the-press/2006/08/23/disgusting-
      misogynistic-_e_27864.html.

241   *"Nine Ways":* Melissa Lafsky, "Forbes' Nine Ways to Avoid Becoming a
      Pathetic Dried-Up Unmarriageable Waste of Humanity," Opinionistas,
      August 23, 2006. http://opinionistas.com/2006/08/23/forbes-nine-ways-to-
      avoid-becoming-a-pathetic-dried-up-unmarriageable-waste-of-humanity/.

242   Sunday Times: Sarah Baxter Washington and John Elliott, "Guy Talk Hits
      Career Women Where It Hurts," *Sunday Times* (London), August 27, 2006.

242   Chicago Tribune: Rex Huppke, "When It Comes to Women, Smart Guys
      Can Be Real Dumb," *The Chicago Tribune*, September 3, 2006.

242   The Week: "Marriage: Should Men Avoid Career Women?" *The Week*,
      September 15, 2006.

244   *letter to the editor:* Sarah Vincent, "A Revived Debate: Babies, Careers,
      'Having It All,'" Letter to the Editor, *The New York Times*, September
      22, 2005.

244   *"conjugal slavery":* Simone de Beauvoir, *The Second Sex* (New York:
      Alfred A. Knopf, 1952), page 694.


                          *Chapter Eleven*

247   *"women perform . . . housework":* Scott Coltrane, "Research on House-
      hold Labor: Modeling and Measuring the Social Embeddedness of
      Routine Family Work," *Journal of Marriage and the Family*, November
      2000, pages 1208–1209.

247–8 *"When couples marry":* Linda Hirshman, "Homeward Bound," *The
      American Prospect*, December 2005. Statistic cited from Phyllis Moen and
      Patricia Roehling, *The Career Mystique: Cracks in the American Dream*
      (Maryland: Rowman and Littlefield, 2005).

250   *Women are now the major breadwinners:* Annual Social and Economic
      Supplement, Current Population Survey, U.S. Department of Labor,
      Bureau of Labor Statistics, 2004.

250   *the average working wife:* 1988–2005 Annual Social and Economic
      (March) Supplement, Current Population Survey, U.S. Department of
      Labor, Bureau of Labor Statistics.

250 *husbands create more work:* Linda Hirshman, "Homeward Bound," *The American Prospect*, December 2005. Original statistic from Sylvia Ann Hewlett, Carolyn Buck Luce, Peggy Shiller, Sandra Southwell, "High-Achieving Women," The Center for Work-Life Policy, 2001.

250 *"disproportionate share":* Scott Coltrane, "Research on Household Labor: Modeling and Measuring the Social Embeddedness of Routine Family Work," *Journal of Marriage and the Family*, November 2000, page 1209.

251 *women doctors:* Rosalind Chait Barnett and Karen C. Gareis, "Full-time and Reduced-hours Work Schedules and Marital Quality," *Work and Occupations*, vol. 29, no. 3, 2002. "Switch to Part-time Work May Hurt Marriages, Study Finds," press release, Brandeis University, February 11, 2003.

251 *"stress hormones":* Linda Babcock and Sara Laschever, *Women Don't Ask: Negotiation and the Gender Divide* (New Jersey: Princeton University Press, 2003), page 181.

254 *peer marriages:* Scott Coltrane, "Research on Household Labor: Modeling and Measuring the Social Embeddedness of Routine Family Work," *Journal of Marriage and the Family*, November 2000, page 1220.

255 *"remarkable gender equality":* Robert Pear, "Married and Single Parents Spending More Time with Children, Study Finds," *The New York Times*, October 17, 2006.

256 *"Fathers born":* Celinda Lake and Kellyanne Conway, *What Women Really Want: How American Women Are Quietly Erasing Political, Racial, Class, and Religious Lines to Change the Way We Live* (New York: Free Press, 2005), page 81.

259 *traditional marriages:* W. Bradford Wilcox and Steven L. Nock, "What's Love Got to Do with It? Equality, Equity, Commitment and Women's Marital Quality," *Social Forces*, vol. 84, no. 3, March 2006. Charlotte Allen, "The Return of the Happy Housewife," *Los Angeles Times*, March 5, 2006.

259 *"twenty studies":* Caryl Rivers and Rosalind Chait Barnett, "Women Happier as Homemakers? Time to Recheck Data," Women's eNews, March 22, 2006.

261 *"When men perform":* Scott Coltrane, "Elite Careers and Family Commitment: It's (Still) About Gender," *Annals of the American Academy of Political and Social Science*, vol. 596, no. 1, 2004.

261 *"cause of the stress":* Linda Babcock and Sara Laschever, *Women Don't Ask: Negotiation and the Gender Divide* (New Jersey: Princeton University Press, 2003), page 182.

261   *breadwinner father:* Scott Coltrane, "Elite Careers and Family Commitment: It's (Still) About Gender,"*Annals of the American Academy of Political and Social Science*, vol. 596, no. 1, 2004.

262   *Coontz:* Claudia Dreifus, "Where Have You Gone, Norman Rockwell? A Fresh Look at the Family," *The New York Times*, June 14, 2005.


## Chapter Twelve

268   *"ambivalence":* Daphne de Marneffe, *Maternal Desire: On Children, Love, and the Inner Life* (New York: Little, Brown and Company, 2004). Laurie Abraham, "Balancing act," Salon.com, March 22, 2004. http://dir.salon.com/story/mwt/feature/2004/03/22/maternal_desire/index.html.

269   *maternal employment:* Jane Waldfogel, *What Children Need (The Family and Public Policy)* (Boston: Harvard University Press, 2006), page 45.

269   *"family's wealth":* Chrystia Freeland, "Women Are the Hidden Engine of World Growth," *The Financial Times*, August 28, 2006.

270   *"full-time mother":* Carol Sarler, "It's the Mother of All Myths," *The Times* (London), June 15, 2006.

271   *"time with their children":* Robert Pear, "Married and Single Parents Spending More Time with Children, Study Finds," *The New York Times*, October 17, 2006.

274   *"infant is with another caregiver":* Jane Waldfogel, *What Children Need (The Family and Public Policy)* (Boston: Harvard University Press, 2006), page 45.

274   *"day-care providers":* Carol Evans, *This Is How We Do It: The Working Mothers' Manifesto* (New York: Hudson Street Press, 2006), page 54.

275   *"Kids in accredited day care":* Ibid., page 55.

276   *patchwork of child-care providers:* Ibid., page 123.

278   *"The Travel Industry Association":* Melinda Ligos, "The Pacifier Isn't for the Child," *The New York Times*, May 3, 2005.


## Chapter Thirteen

287   *Fuller:* Deborah Solomon, "Too Much Isn't Enough," *The New York Times*, March 26, 2006.

287   *"jam-packed, maxed-out":* Bonnie Fuller, *The Joys of Much Too Much: Go for the Big Life—the Great Career, the Perfect Guy, and Everything Else You've Ever Wanted* (New York: Fireside, 2006).

291   *Princeton graduate:* Lisa Belkin, "The Opt-Out Revolution," *The New York Times,* October 26, 2003.

291   *American women become mothers:* Jane Lawler Dye, "Fertility of American Women: June 2004," U.S. Census Bureau Current Population Survey, December 2005. http://www.census.gov/population/www/socdemo/fertility .html.

292   *"Policies":* Jane Waldfogel, *What Children Need (The Family and Public Policy)* (Boston: Harvard University Press, 2006), pages 26–27.

293   *"elder-care crisis":* Sylvia Ann Hewlett, "The New Have-It-All Myth," *More* magazine, June 2005.

294   *Summers:* Rachel B. Tiven, "Candor and Anger at Harvard," Letter to the Editor, *The New York Times,* February 19, 2005.

294   *Yoder:* Anne D. Yoder, "People at Work: A Balancing Act," Letter to the Editor, *The New York Times,* May 27, 2005.

295   *"human problem":* Matt Miller, "Listen to My Wife," *The New York Times,* May 25, 2005.

300   *"fewer than 2 percent":* Claudia H. Deutsch, "Behind the Exodus of Executive Women: Boredom," *The New York Times,* May 1, 2005.

302   *"Women's progress":* Linda Babcock and Sara Laschever, *Women Don't Ask: Negotiation and the Gender Divide* (New Jersey: Princeton University Press, 2003), Preface, pages xii–xiii.

303   *sweeping social agenda:* Joan Blades and Kristin Rowe-Finkbeiner, *The Motherhood Manifesto: What America's Moms Want—and What to Do About It* (New York: Nation Books, 2006), page 16.

304   *"Parents' Action for Children":* Rob Reiner, "Letters" page, *Newsweek,* March 7, 2005.

### Chapter Fourteen

308   *woman's life span:* "Health, United States, 2005, with Chartbook on Trends in the Health of Americans," U.S. Department of Health and Human Services, Hyattsville, Maryland: 2005, page 64.

309   *"Society in general":* Simone de Beauvoir, *The Second Sex* (New York: Alfred A. Knopf, 1952), page 721.

311   *Mothers and More:* Jeanine Plant, "Anti-Unpaid-Work Polemicist Riles Full-Time Moms," Women's eNews, September 8, 2006. http://www.womensenews. org/article.cfm/dyn/aid/2881/context/archive.

312   *Hekker:* Terry Martin Hekker, "Paradise Lost (Domestic Division)," *The New York Times*, January 1, 2006. See also TerryMartinHekker.com.

312   *Women's eNews:* Jeanine Plant, "Anti-Unpaid-Work Polemicist Riles Full-Time Moms," Women's eNews, September 8, 2006. http://www.womensenews. org/article.cfm/dyn/aid/2881/context/archive.

314   *"Twenty-Five Things":* Nora Ephron, "Twenty-Five Things People Have a Shocking Capacity to Be Surprised By Over and Over Again," The Huffington Post, January 24, 2006. http://www.huffingtonpost.com/nora-ephron/twentyfive-things-people_b_14366.html.

315   *"womenomics":* Chrystia Freeland, "Women Are the Hidden Engine of World Growth," *The Financial Times*, August 28, 2006.

316   *careers in the sciences:* W. Michael Cox and Richard Alm, "Scientists Are Made, Not Born," *The New York Times*, February 28, 2005.

318   *motherhood in France:* Judith Warner, *Perfect Madness: Motherhood in the Age of Anxiety* (New York: Riverhead Books, 2005), page 9.

318   *Hirshman advises:* Linda Hirshman, *Get to Work: A Manifesto for Women of the World* (New York: Viking, 2006), pages 57, 62.

# INDEX